From the maelstrom of a sundered world, the Eight Realms were born. The formless and the divine exploded into life. Strange, new worlds appeared in the firmament, each one gilded with spirits, gods and men. Noblest of the gods was Sigmar. For years beyond reckoning he illuminated the realms, wreathed in light and majesty as he carved out his reign. His strength was the power of thunder. His wisdom was infinite. Mortal and immortal alike kneeled before his lofty throne. Great empires rose and, for a while, treachery was banished. Sigmar claimed the land and sky as his own and ruled over a glorious age of myth.

But cruelty is tenacious. As had been foreseen, the great alliance of gods and men tore itself apart. Myth and legend crumbled into Chaos. Darkness flooded the realms. Torture, slavery and fear replaced the glory that came before. Sigmar turned his back on the mortal kingdoms, disgusted by their fate. He fixed his gaze instead on the remains of the world he had lost long ago, brooding over its charred core, searching endlessly for a sign of hope. And then, in the dark heat of his rage, he caught a glimpse of something magnificent. He pictured a weapon born of the heavens. A beacon powerful enough to pierce the endless night. An army hewn from everything he had lost. Sigmar set his artisans to work and for long ages they toiled, striving to harness the power of the stars. As Sigmar's great work neared completion, he turned back to the realms and saw that the dominion of Chaos was almost complete. The hour for vengeance had come. Finally, with lightning blazing across his brow, he stepped forth to unleash his creation.

The Age of Sigmar had begun.

# CONTENTS

## DESIGNED BY GAMES WORKSHOP IN NOTTINGHAM

Games Workshop Ltd., Willow Road, Lenton, Nottingham, NG7 2WS, United Kingdom

Printed by Belmont, in the UK.

**games-workshop.com**

# HOW TO USE THIS BOOK

**Sigmar's Storm rolls out across the Mortal Realms, and beneath its boiling clouds the armies of Order gather for war. For too long the Dark Gods have ravaged the lands, and, at last, the vast celestial hosts of Azyr and their allies across the realms are ready to unleash their retribution.**

This book details the many factions that make up the noble, civilised and celestial armies of the Mortal Realms at the dawn of the Age of Sigmar. From the mighty Stormhosts and the armies of Azyrheim, to the Fyreslayer lodges, sylvaneth wargroves and seraphon constellations, the armies of Order fight to wrest their kingdoms and empires back from Chaos. This book explores the proud background and character of each faction, showing how they marshal for war, what motivates

their generals and where they stand in Sigmar's war to reclaim the Mortal Realms. You can use the information provided in this tome to provide you with an in-world context for your collection of Citadel Miniatures, and it will show you how to create an army to crush all who stand against them.

Within the pages of this book you will find an extensive range of warscrolls covering all of the individual units and characters available to collectors

of the armies of Order at the dawn of the Age of Sigmar. You will also find a number of example armies showing you how the various factions of Order gather for war, such as the Stonebreaker Battalions mustered to bring down enemy fortresses or the Wargrove of the Salish Woad that follows the Treelord Ancient Cuthrucu into battle. So sound the war horns of Azyrheim, rouse the children of Grimnir and call down the lightning upon which ride the legendary Stormcast Eternals!

# WARSCROLL BATTALIONS

**The warriors of the Mortal Realms often fight in battalions. Each of these deadly fighting formations consists of several units that are organised and trained to fight alongside each other. The units in warscroll battalions can employ special tactics on the battlefield, making them truly deadly foes.**

If you wish, you can organise the units in your army into a warscroll battalion. Doing so will give you access to additional abilities that can be used by the units in the battalion. The information needed to use these powerful formations can be found on the warscroll battalion sheets that we publish for *Warhammer Age of Sigmar*. Each warscroll battalion sheet lists the units that make it up, and the rules for any additional abilities that units from the warscroll battalion can use.

When you are setting up, you can set up all of the units in a warscroll battalion instead of setting up a single unit. Alternatively, you can set up some of the units from a warscroll battalion, and set up any remaining units individually later on, or you can set up all of the units individually. For example, in a battle where each player takes it in turns to set up one unit, you could set up one, some or all of the units belonging to a warscroll battalion in your army.

On the following pages you will find a selection of warscroll battalions. Usually, a unit can only belong to one battalion, and so can only benefit from a single set of battalion abilities. However, some very large battalions include other, smaller battalions, and in this case it is possible for a unit to benefit from the abilities of two different battalions at the same time.

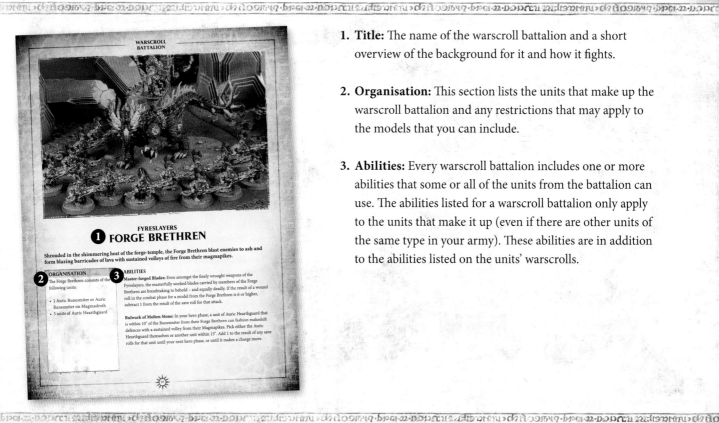

1. **Title:** The name of the warscroll battalion and a short overview of the background for it and how it fights.

2. **Organisation:** This section lists the units that make up the warscroll battalion and any restrictions that may apply to the models that you can include.

3. **Abilities:** Every warscroll battalion includes one or more abilities that some or all of the units from the battalion can use. The abilities listed for a warscroll battalion only apply to the units that make it up (even if there are other units of the same type in your army). These abilities are in addition to the abilities listed on the units' warscrolls.

# WARSCROLLS

**The warriors and creatures that battle in the Mortal Realms are incredibly diverse, each one fighting with their own unique weapons and combat abilities. To represent this, every model has a warscroll that lists the characteristics, weapons and abilities that apply to the model.**

Every Citadel Miniature in the Warhammer range has its own warscroll, which provides you with all of the information needed to use that model in a game of *Warhammer Age of Sigmar*. This means that you can use any Citadel Miniatures in your collection as part of an army as long as you have the right warscrolls.

When fighting a battle, simply refer to the warscrolls for the models you are using. Warscrolls for all of the other models in the *Warhammer Age of Sigmar* range are available from Games Workshop. Just visit our website at games-workshop.com for more information on how to obtain them.

The key below explains what you will find on a warscroll, and the *Warhammer Age of Sigmar* rules sheet explains how this information is used in a game. The warscroll also includes a picture of a unit of the models that the warscroll describes, and a short piece of text explaining the background for the models and how they fight.

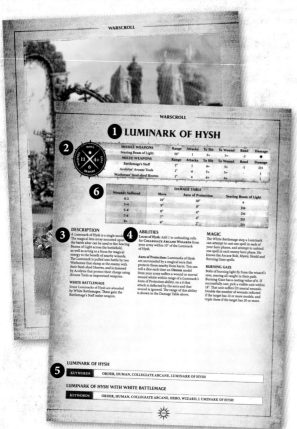

1. **Title:** The name of the model that the warscroll describes.

2. **Characteristics:** This set of characteristics tells you how fast, powerful and brave the model is, and how effective its weapons are.

3. **Description:** The description tells you what weapons the model can be armed with, and what upgrades (if any) it can be given. The description will also tell you if the model is fielded on its own as a single model, or as part of a unit. If the model is fielded as part of a unit, then the description will say how many models the unit should have (if you don't have enough models to field a unit, you can still field one unit with as many models as you have available).

4. **Abilities:** Abilities are things that the model can do during a game that are not covered by the standard game rules.

5. **Keywords:** All models have a list of keywords. Sometimes a rule will say that it only applies to models that have a specific keyword.

6. **Damage Table:** Some models have a damage table that is used to determine one or more of the model's characteristics. Look up the number of wounds the model has suffered to find the value of the characteristic in question.

# HINTS & TIPS

**Modifiers:** Many warscrolls include modifiers that can affect characteristics. For example, a rule might add 1 to the Move characteristic of a model, or subtract 1 from the result of a hit roll. Modifiers are cumulative.

**Random Values:** Sometimes, the Move or weapon characteristics on a warscroll will have random values. For example, the Move characteristic for a model might be 2D6 (two dice rolls added together), whereas the Attacks characteristic of a weapon might be D6.

When a unit with a random Move characteristic is selected to move in the movement phase, roll the indicated number of dice. The total of the dice rolled is the Move characteristic for all models in the unit for the duration of that movement phase.

Generate any random values for a weapon (except Damage) each time it is chosen as the weapon for an attack.

Roll once and apply the result to all such weapons being used in the attack. The result applies for the rest of that phase. For Damage, generate a value for each weapon that inflicts damage.

**When to Use Abilities:** Abilities that are used at the start of a phase must be carried out before any other actions. By the same token, abilities used at the end of the phase are carried out after all normal activities for the phase are complete.

If you can use several abilities at the same time, you can decide in which order they are used. If both players can carry out abilities at the same time, the player whose turn is taking place uses their abilities first.

**Save of '-':** Some models have a Save of '-'. This means that they automatically fail all save rolls (do not make the roll, even if modifiers apply).

**Keywords:** Keywords are sometimes linked to (or tagged) by a rule. For example, a rule might say that it applies to 'all STORMCAST ETERNALS'. This means that it would apply to models that have the Stormcast Eternal keyword on their warscroll.

Keywords can also be a useful way to decide which models to include in an army. For example, if you want to field a Stormcast Eternals army, just use models that have the Stormcast Eternal keyword.

**Minimum Range:** Some weapons have a minimum range. For example 6"-48". The weapon cannot shoot at an enemy unit that is within the minimum range.

**Weapons:** Some models can be armed with two identical weapons. When the model attacks with these weapons, do not double the number of attacks that the weapons make; usually, the model gets an additional ability instead.

# STORMCAST ETERNALS

**From the lightning-wreathed heart of Sigmar's Tempest emerge the Stormcast Eternals. Heroic warriors of the heavens, their shining Stormhosts sweep down into the Mortal Realms, reclaiming Realmgates, kingdoms and continents from the armies of the Dark Gods.**

The Stormcast Eternals are a brotherhood of heroes. Gathered up by the God-King Sigmar over aeons of war and carnage, they have been forged into soldiers of lightning and returned to the Mortal Realms to destroy the servants of Chaos. This Reforging is not a process to be taken lightly, as before a mortal can become a Stormcast Eternal they must be utterly shattered upon Sigmar's anvil, then remade with a measure of the God-King's power. The result is an immortal warrior of the heavens, for even should Stormcast Eternals fall in battle, they are called to Azyr, remade, and returned to the fray.

Organised into Stormhosts and their constituent chambers, the Stormcast Eternals are a martial force like nothing the races of the realms have ever seen. Under the command of Lord-Celestants, each chamber is an army in its own right, able to wage war bereft of its brothers and crush foes that outnumber it many times over.

The forces of Chaos first encountered the Stormcasts in the Igneous Delta of Aqshy. It was there, against the Bloodbound, and their cruel master Korghos Khul, that the initial blows of Sigmar's Realmgate Wars – the campaign to recapture the portals between worlds – were struck. Since that auspicious day of blood and flame, wrought by the Hammers of Sigmar, the Stormhosts of the Stormcast Eternals have made their presence felt in each of the Mortal Realms.

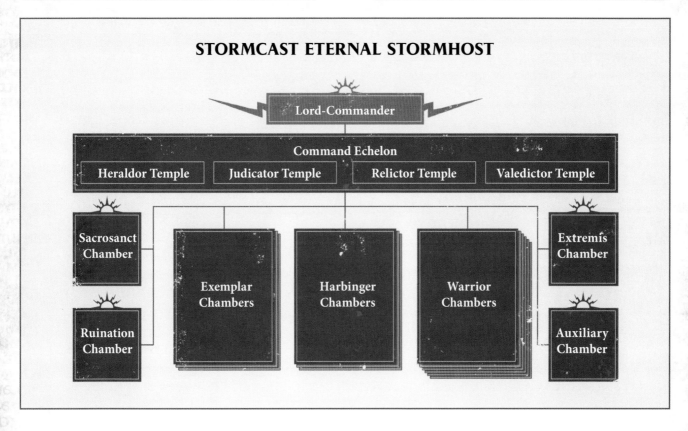

## STORMCAST ETERNAL STORMHOST

**Lord-Commander**

**Command Echelon**

| Heraldor Temple | Judicator Temple | Relictor Temple | Valedictor Temple |

Sacrosanct Chamber

Ruination Chamber

Exemplar Chambers

Harbinger Chambers

Warrior Chambers

Extremis Chamber

Auxiliary Chamber

---

Clad in gleaming armour and armed with weapons cast from the forges of Sigmaron, each Stormcast Eternal and the Stormhosts they serve have their role to play in the grand war for the Mortal Realms. The foundations of each host are its Warrior Chambers, formidable forces led by Lord-Celestants and filled with able warriors. Liberators, the foot soldiers of the Stormcast Eternals, fill out the ranks of these chambers, their sturdy shields, heavy hammers and keen-edged swords often the wall against which the enemies of Order break. Far from mundane rank and file soldiers, each Liberator towers over most mortal foes. Their armour makes them larger still, shining pauldrons, thick breastplates and expressionless war masks all adding to the effect of sigmarite statues come to life upon the battlefield.

Supporting the Liberators in each Warrior Chamber are a host of additional troops. Judicators scythe down enemies from afar with deadly weapons, each of their crackling lightning shafts and bolts punching warriors from their feet. Even as the deadly rain of missiles falls upon the Stormcasts' adversaries, Prosecutors are swooping down from the heavens to smash them apart. These flying heroes hurl down hammers or javelins of sparking light from their gauntleted fists. Each weapon whirls into the fray, crushing bones and smashing bodies; already another weapon is forming in the winged warrior's hand above, called from the storm. Where resistance remains, and the fire of Judicators or the hammers and swords of the Liberators have not broken the enemy, heavier troops move into the fray.

Decimators, Protectors and Retributors stride toward their victims, bringing great hammers, glaives and axes to bear. Able to weather the most determined of attacks and dish out punishing blows in return, they shatter shield walls and bring even great monsters crashing to their knees.

These warriors are forged together by the leadership of the Lord-Celestant, who is in turn guided by the chamber's Lord-Relictor, Knights-Azyros and Lord-Castellants. The result is a tight-knit fighting force without peer. Countless chambers in hundreds of Stormhosts have shattered the legions of Chaos, halted rampaging orruk armies, and sent skeletal hordes back to the grave. They are the will of the God-King loosed upon the realms, and the heralds of the Age of Sigmar.

## STORMCAST ETERNALS
# WARRIOR BROTHERHOOD

A potent measure of a full chamber, the Warrior Brotherhood enters battle to the sound of booming thunder and flashing lighting, its Stormcast Eternals made stronger by the presence of their brothers.

### ORGANISATION

A Warrior Brotherhood consists of the following units:

- 2 HEROES chosen in any combination from the following list: Lord-Celestant, Lord-Celestant on Dracoth, Lord-Castellant, Knight-Azyros, Knight-Venator, Knight-Vexillor, Knight-Heraldor
- 1 unit of Prosecutors
- 2 units of PALADINS
- 3 units of Liberators
- 2 units of Judicators

### ABILITIES

**Brothers in Arms:** Add 1 to the Bravery of any unit from this battalion that is within 6" of one or more other units from this battalion.

**Lightning Strike:** Instead of setting up a unit from this battalion on the battlefield, you can place it to one side and say that it is set up in the Celestial Realm. In any of your movement phases, you can transport the unit to the battlefield. When you do so, set it up on the battlefield more than 9" from any enemy models. This is its move for that movement phase.

**Warriors of Thunder:** You can re-roll wound rolls of 1 for units from the Warrior Brotherhood that are within 8" of at least two other units from the battalion when the wound rolls are made.

### STORMCAST ETERNALS
# THE SKYBORNE SLAYERS

Crashing from the sky in a meteoric blaze of force, the Skyborne Slayers strike at the enemy's heart, slaying their generals and leaving the leaderless masses of their foe ripe for destruction.

## ORGANISATION

The Skyborne Slayers consist of the following units:

- 1 Lord-Celestant
- 2 units of Liberators
- 2 units of Judicators
- 1 unit of Decimators
- 1 unit of Protectors

## ABILITIES

**Hurled by Sigmar's Hand:** Instead of setting up a unit from the Skyborne Slayers on the battlefield, you can place it to one side and say that it is set up in the Celestial Realm. In any of your movement phases, you can transport all of the units from the Skyborne Slayers that you have placed to one side onto the battlefield. When you do so, pick a point anywhere on the battlefield, then set up all of the units within 12" of that point and more than 5" from any enemy models. This is their move for that movement phase.

**Honour of the God-King:** Such is their dedication to the duty that Sigmar himself has given them, units from the Skyborne Slayers never need to take battleshock tests.

# CELESTANT-PRIME
## HAMMER OF SIGMAR

| MOVE 12" | WOUNDS 8 | SAVE 3+ | BRAVERY 10 |
| --- | --- | --- | --- |

| MISSILE WEAPONS | Range | Attacks | To Hit | To Wound | Rend | Damage |
| --- | --- | --- | --- | --- | --- | --- |
| The Cometstrike Sceptre | 24" | | | See below | | |

| MELEE WEAPONS | Range | Attacks | To Hit | To Wound | Rend | Damage |
| --- | --- | --- | --- | --- | --- | --- |
| Ghal Maraz, the Hammer of Sigmar | 2" | 2 | 3+ | 2+ | -3 | 3 |

## DESCRIPTION

The Celestant-Prime is a single model. He wields Ghal Maraz, the Hammer of Sigmar, and carries the Cometstrike Sceptre.

## FLY

The Celestant-Prime can fly.

## ABILITIES

**Cometstrike Sceptre:** In your shooting phase, the Celestant-Prime can hold the Cometstrike Sceptre aloft to seize a comet from the heavens, then send it crashing down amid the enemy. If he does, pick a point on the battlefield within range and roll a dice. Each unit within that many inches of that point suffers D3 mortal wounds.

**Retribution from On High:** Instead of setting up the Celestant-Prime on the battlefield, you must place him to one side and say that he is set up in the Celestial Realm. In each of your movement phases you must declare whether he will strike from the Heavens or remain in the Celestial Realm imbuing Ghal Maraz with additional energies. For each battle round that he remains in the Celestial Realm, add 2 to the Attacks characteristic of Ghal Maraz until the end of the battle.

When the Celestant-Prime strikes from the Heavens, set him up on the battlefield more than 9" from any enemy models. This is his move for that movement phase. Until your next hero phase, subtract 2 from the Bravery of all models in any enemy unit within 12" of him.

**Orrery of Celestial Fates:** A storm of celestial energy swirls around the Celestant-Prime's feet, granting him mystic insights that aid him in battle. Once per turn, you can change the roll of one dice for the Celestant-Prime to a roll of your choice, before applying any modifiers.

| KEYWORDS | ORDER, CELESTIAL, HUMAN, STORMCAST ETERNAL, HERO, CELESTANT-PRIME |
| --- | --- |

# LORD-CELESTANT ON DRACOTH

**MOVE** 10"
**WOUNDS** 7
**SAVE** 3+
**BRAVERY** 9

| MELEE WEAPONS | Range | Attacks | To Hit | To Wound | Rend | Damage |
|---|---|---|---|---|---|---|
| Stormstrike Glaive | 2" | 4 | 3+ | 4+ | -1 | 1 |
| Lightning Hammer | 1" | 3 | 3+ | 3+ | -1 | 2 |
| Thunderaxe | 2" | 3 | 3+ | 3+ | -1 | 2 |
| Tempestos Hammer | 2" | 3 | 3+ | 2+ | -1 | D3 |
| Dracoth's Claws and Fangs | 1" | 3 | 3+ | 3+ | -1 | 1 |

## DESCRIPTION

A Lord-Celestant on Dracoth is a single model. He wields either a Tempestos Hammer, a Thunderaxe, a Lightning Hammer or a Stormstrike Glaive. Some also carry a Sigmarite Thundershield. In any case, he rides a Dracoth which fights with its ferocious Claws and Fangs.

## ABILITIES

**Tempestos Hammer**: With the momentum of a charge behind it, few can stand against the impact of a Tempestos Hammer. If this model has made a charge move this turn, it can make D3 extra attacks with its Tempestos Hammer.

**Thunderaxe**: In the capable hands of a Lord-Celestant, a Thunderaxe draws on the celestial energies of those around him until it is crackling with barely contained power. Add 1 to the Attacks of this model's Thunderaxe for each other **STORMCAST ETERNAL** unit from your army within 5".

**Lightning Hammer**: If the result of a hit roll for this model's Lightning Hammer is 6 or more, the target unit immediately suffers two mortal wounds as warriors are blasted to ash, before the wound roll is made. If a unit suffers any mortal wounds in this way, it is stunned for the rest of the combat phase and cannot pile in before it attacks.

**Stormstrike Glaive:** Lowering his Stormstrike Glaive and wielding it as a lance, a Lord-Celestant can bring down the mightiest foes. If this model has made a charge move this turn, its Stormstrike Glaive causes 3 Damage rather than 1, and has a Rend of -2 rather than -1.

**Intolerable Damage:** If the wound roll for the Dracoth's Claws and Fangs attack is 6 or more, then that attack causes D6 Damage rather than 1.

**Storm Breath:** You can make a storm breath attack with this model in your shooting phase. To do so, pick a point on the battlefield that is within 12" of this model. Roll a dice for each unit (friend or foe) that is within 2" of the point that you picked. On a roll of 4 or more, the unit being rolled for suffers D3 mortal wounds.

## COMMAND ABILITY

**Lord of the Host:** If a Lord-Celestant uses this ability, until your next hero phase you do not have to take battleshock tests for this model or any friendly **STORMCAST ETERNALS** that are within 24" of this model at the start of the battleshock phase.

# LORD-CELESTANT

| | MOVE 5" | | | | | |
|---|---|---|---|---|---|---|
| WOUNDS 5 | | SAVE 3+ | | | | |
| | 9 BRAVERY | | | | | |

| MELEE WEAPONS | Range | Attacks | To Hit | To Wound | Rend | Damage |
|---|---|---|---|---|---|---|
| Sigmarite Runeblade | 1" | 4 | 3+ | 3+ | -1 | 1 |
| Warhammer | 1" | 2 | 4+ | 3+ | - | 1 |

## DESCRIPTION

A Lord-Celestant is a single model. He is armed with a fearsome Sigmarite Runeblade and a Warhammer, and wears a Sigmarite Warcloak.

## ABILITIES

**Inescapable Vengeance**: If this model has made a charge move this turn, it can make 1 extra attack with each of its melee weapons.

**Sigmarite Warcloak**: In your shooting phase, you can unleash D6 hammers from this model's Sigmarite Warcloak. Pick an enemy unit within 16" of this model for each hammer that is unleashed, then roll a dice for each unit you picked. On a roll of 4 or more the unit suffers a mortal wound. Note that you can pick the same unit more than once in a phase.

## COMMAND ABILITY

**Furious Retribution**: If this model is your general and uses this ability, then until your next hero phase you can add 1 to the result of any hit rolls in the combat phase for this model and friendly **STORMCAST ETERNAL** units within 9" of him.

| KEYWORDS | ORDER, CELESTIAL, HUMAN, STORMCAST ETERNAL, HERO, LORD-CELESTANT |
|---|---|

# LORD-CASTELLANT

| | | MOVE | | |
|---|---|---|---|---|
| WOUNDS 6 | | 5" | SAVE 3+ | |
| | | 9 | | |
| | | BRAVERY | | |

| MELEE WEAPONS | Range | Attacks | To Hit | To Wound | Rend | Damage |
|---|---|---|---|---|---|---|
| Castellant's Halberd | 2" | 3 | 3+ | 3+ | -1 | 2 |

## DESCRIPTION

A Lord-Castellant is a single model. He is armed with a Castellant's Halberd and carries a Warding Lantern.

## ABILITIES

**Warding Lantern:** In your hero phase the Lord-Castellant may unleash the magical energies of his Warding Lantern. If he does so, pick either a **Chaos** unit or a **Stormcast Eternal** unit that is within 12" of the Lord-Castellant.

If a **Chaos** unit is chosen it is struck by the searing light of the Celestial Realm and suffers a mortal wound. **Chaos Daemon** units cannot abide the touch of this light and suffer D3 mortal wounds instead.

If a **Stormcast Eternal** unit is chosen it is bathed in the healing energies of the lantern and you can add 1 to all save rolls it has to make until your next hero phase. In addition, until your next hero phase, each time you make a save roll of 7 or more for that unit, one model in the unit heals a wound.

| KEYWORDS | ORDER, CELESTIAL, HUMAN, STORMCAST ETERNAL, HERO, LORD-CASTELLANT |
|---|---|

# LORD-RELICTOR

**MOVE** 4"
**WOUNDS** 5
**SAVE** 3+
**BRAVERY** 9

| MELEE WEAPONS | Range | Attacks | To Hit | To Wound | Rend | Damage |
|---|---|---|---|---|---|---|
| Relic Hammer | 1" | 4 | 3+ | 3+ | -1 | 1 |

## DESCRIPTION

A Lord-Relictor is a single model. He is armed with a Relic Hammer.

## ABILITIES

**Lightning Storm:** In your hero phase, you can declare that the Lord-Relictor will pray for a lightning storm. If you do so, pick an enemy unit that is within 12" of this model and roll a dice. On a roll of 3 or more, the unit you picked suffers D3 mortal wounds, and your opponent must subtract 1 from all hit rolls for the unit until your next hero phase. A Lord-Relictor cannot pray for a lightning storm and a healing storm in the same turn.

**Healing Storm:** In your hero phase, you can declare that this model is praying for a healing storm. If you do so, pick a friendly model with the **STORMCAST ETERNAL** keyword that is within 12" of this model and roll a dice. On a roll of 3 or more you can heal up to D3 wounds that have been suffered by the model that you picked. A Lord-Relictor cannot pray for a healing storm and a lightning storm in the same turn.

| KEYWORDS | ORDER, CELESTIAL, HUMAN, STORMCAST ETERNAL, HERO, PRIEST, LORD-RELICTOR |
|---|---|

# KNIGHT-AZYROS

| | MOVE | | WOUNDS | SAVE | BRAVERY |
|---|---|---|---|---|---|
| | 12" | | 5 | 3+ | 9 |

| MELEE WEAPONS | Range | Attacks | To Hit | To Wound | Rend | Damage |
|---|---|---|---|---|---|---|
| Starblade | 1" | 4 | 3+ | 3+ | -1 | 1 |

## DESCRIPTION

A Knight-Azyros is a single model. He is armed with a Starblade and carries a Celestial Beacon.

**FLY**
A Knight-Azyros can fly.

## ABILITIES

**Leader of the Way:** STORMCAST ETERNAL units in your army that use the Lightning Strike ability to be transported to the battlefield can be set up within 5" of a Knight-Azyros, even if this would mean that they are within 9" of the enemy.

**Illuminator of the Lost:** In the shooting phase, you can re-roll hit rolls of 1 for attacks made against enemy units that are within 10" of a Knight-Azyros.

**The Light of Sigmar:** Once per battle, in your hero phase, you can declare that this model will unleash the searing light of its Celestial Beacon. If you do so, it cannot move, charge or pile in during your turn. However, each enemy unit within 8" of the Knight-Azyros when the searing light is unleashed suffers D3 mortal wounds as they are blinded and driven from the battlefield. The light is anathema to CHAOS units, so they suffer D6 mortal wounds instead.

| KEYWORDS | ORDER, CELESTIAL, HUMAN, STORMCAST ETERNAL, HERO, KNIGHT-AZYROS |
|---|---|

# KNIGHT-VENATOR

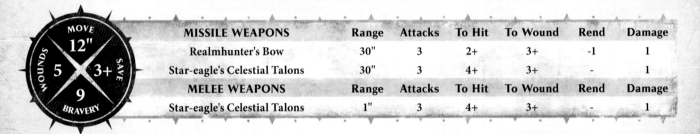

| | MOVE 12" | | WOUNDS 5 | SAVE 3+ | BRAVERY 9 |
|---|---|---|---|---|---|

| MISSILE WEAPONS | Range | Attacks | To Hit | To Wound | Rend | Damage |
|---|---|---|---|---|---|---|
| Realmhunter's Bow | 30" | 3 | 2+ | 3+ | -1 | 1 |
| Star-eagle's Celestial Talons | 30" | 3 | 4+ | 3+ | - | 1 |
| MELEE WEAPONS | Range | Attacks | To Hit | To Wound | Rend | Damage |
| Star-eagle's Celestial Talons | 1" | 3 | 4+ | 3+ | - | 1 |

## DESCRIPTION

A Knight-Venator is a single model. He is armed with a Realmhunter's Bow and is accompanied by a vicious Star-eagle that attacks with its Celestial Talons.

## FLY

A Knight-Venator can fly.

## ABILITIES

**Celestial Talons:** If the wound roll for the Star-eagle's Celestial Talons is 6 or more, that attack has a Rend of -3.

**Star-fated Arrow:** Once per battle, in your shooting phase, you can declare that this model will loose a Star-fated Arrow. When you do so, he makes 1 attack with his Realmhunter's Bow rather than 3, but it causes D3+3 Damage. If the target is a **HERO** or **MONSTER**, the Damage is D6+3 instead.

| KEYWORDS | ORDER, CELESTIAL, HUMAN, STORMCAST ETERNAL, HERO, KNIGHT-VENATOR |
|---|---|

# KNIGHT-VEXILLOR

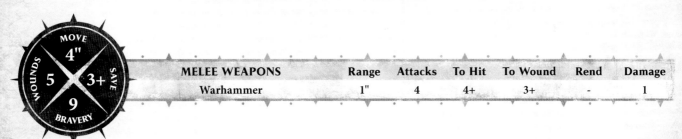

| | | | | |
|---|---|---|---|---|
| MOVE | 4" | | | |
| WOUNDS | 5 | SAVE | 3+ | |
| BRAVERY | 9 | | | |

| MELEE WEAPONS | Range | Attacks | To Hit | To Wound | Rend | Damage |
|---|---|---|---|---|---|---|
| Warhammer | 1" | 4 | 4+ | 3+ | - | 1 |

## DESCRIPTION

A Knight-Vexillor is a single model armed with a Warhammer. Some Knights-Vexillor carry a Meteoric Standard, while others carry a Pennant of the Stormbringer.

## ABILITIES

**Icon of War:** You can re-roll charge rolls for **Stormcast Eternal** units in your army that are within 12", as they are inspired to glorious acts of valour.

**Meteoric Standard:** Once per battle, a Knight-Vexillor carrying a Meteoric Standard can call down a comet in your hero phase. To do so, pick a point on the battlefield within 24" of this model and roll two dice, adding the results together. Each unit that is within that many inches of the point that you picked suffers D3 mortal wounds.

**Pennant of the Stormbringer:** Once per battle, a Knight-Vexillor carrying a Pennant of the Stormbringer can summon a mighty hurricane in your hero phase. To do so, pick a **Stormcast Eternal** unit in your army and remove it from play, then set it up anywhere more than 3" from the enemy. It cannot move in the following movement phase. After setting up the unit, roll a dice for each enemy unit within 6"; on a result of 4+, it is blasted by the gale and suffers D3 mortal wounds.

| KEYWORDS | ORDER, CELESTIAL, HUMAN, STORMCAST ETERNAL, HERO, TOTEM, KNIGHT-VEXILLOR |
|---|---|

# KNIGHT-HERALDOR

| | MOVE 5" | | | | | | | |
|---|---|---|---|---|---|---|---|---|
| WOUNDS 5 | | SAVE 4+ | | | | | | |
| | BRAVERY 8 | | | | | | | |

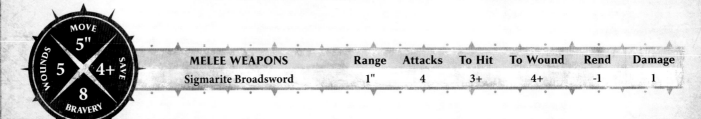

| MELEE WEAPONS | Range | Attacks | To Hit | To Wound | Rend | Damage |
|---|---|---|---|---|---|---|
| Sigmarite Broadsword | 1" | 4 | 3+ | 4+ | -1 | 1 |

## DESCRIPTION

A Knight-Heraldor is a single model. He is armed with a Sigmarite Broadsword, and carries a Battle-horn.

## ABILITIES

**Onwards to Glory:** In your hero phase, you can signal a call to arms with this model's Battle-horn. To do so, pick a STORMCAST ETERNAL unit that is within 10". That unit can charge this turn even if it retreats or runs in the movement phase.

**Thunderblast:** In your shooting phase a Knight-Heraldor can sound a thunderblast with his Battle-horn, shaking buildings to their foundations and causing trees to topple. If he does so, pick a terrain feature within 15" and roll a dice. Each unit within that many inches of the terrain feature suffers D3 mortal wounds.

| KEYWORDS | ORDER, CELESTIAL, HUMAN, STORMCAST ETERNAL, HERO, KNIGHT-HERALDOR |
|---|---|

# LIBERATORS

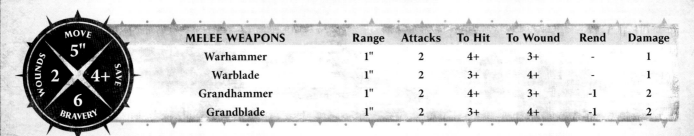

| MELEE WEAPONS | Range | Attacks | To Hit | To Wound | Rend | Damage |
|---|---|---|---|---|---|---|
| Warhammer | 1" | 2 | 4+ | 3+ | - | 1 |
| Warblade | 1" | 2 | 3+ | 4+ | - | 1 |
| Grandhammer | 1" | 2 | 4+ | 3+ | -1 | 2 |
| Grandblade | 1" | 2 | 3+ | 4+ | -1 | 2 |

**MOVE** 5"
**WOUNDS** 2
**SAVE** 4+
**BRAVERY** 6

## DESCRIPTION

A unit of Liberators has 5 or more models. Some units of Liberators are armed with a Warhammer in each hand, while others wield paired Warblades. Other units enter battle armed with a single Warhammer and carry Sigmarite Shields, and others still pair a Sigmarite Shield with a Warblade. In any case, 1 in every 5 models may instead be armed with either a Grandhammer, or a Grandblade.

### LIBERATOR-PRIME

The leader of this unit is the Liberator-Prime. A Liberator-Prime makes 3 attacks rather than 2.

## ABILITIES

**Paired Weapons:** An extra weapon allows a Liberator to feint and parry, creating openings in their opponent's guard. You can re-roll hit rolls of 1 for models armed with more than one Warhammer or Warblade.

**Lay Low the Tyrants:** If any model from this unit selects an enemy unit with a Wounds characteristic of 5 or more as the target for all of its attacks in a combat phase, add 1 to all of that model's hit rolls in that combat phase.

**Sigmarite Shields:** You can re-roll save rolls of 1 for this unit if any models from the unit are carrying Sigmarite Shields.

**KEYWORDS** | ORDER, CELESTIAL, HUMAN, STORMCAST ETERNAL, REDEEMER, LIBERATORS

# JUDICATORS

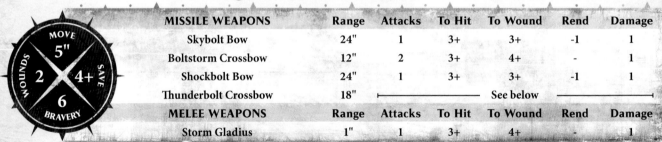

| MISSILE WEAPONS | Range | Attacks | To Hit | To Wound | Rend | Damage |
|---|---|---|---|---|---|---|
| Skybolt Bow | 24" | 1 | 3+ | 3+ | -1 | 1 |
| Boltstorm Crossbow | 12" | 2 | 3+ | 4+ | - | 1 |
| Shockbolt Bow | 24" | 1 | 3+ | 3+ | -1 | 1 |
| Thunderbolt Crossbow | 18" | | | See below | | |
| MELEE WEAPONS | Range | Attacks | To Hit | To Wound | Rend | Damage |
| Storm Gladius | 1" | 1 | 3+ | 4+ | - | 1 |

**MOVE** 5"
**WOUNDS** 2
**SAVE** 4+
**BRAVERY** 6

## DESCRIPTION

A unit of Judicators has 5 or more models. Units of Judicators are armed with either long-ranged Skybolt Bows or rapid-firing Boltstorm Crossbows. 1 in every 5 models may instead be armed with either a Shockbolt Bow or a Thunderbolt Crossbow. In addition, every model in the unit carries a sharp Storm Gladius.

## JUDICATOR-PRIME

A Judicator-Prime leads this unit. Add 1 to the hit rolls for a Judicator-Prime.

## ABILITIES

**Rapid Fire:** If a unit of Judicators does not move in the movement phase, then you can add 1 to the Attacks characteristic of any Boltstorm Crossbows the unit uses in the shooting phase of the same turn.

**Chained Lightning:** If a Judicator attacking with a Shockbolt Bow scores a hit then the bolt explodes into a storm of lightning. Instead of making a single wound roll, roll a dice and make a number of wound rolls equal to the number scored.

**Eternal Judgement:** You may re-roll any hit rolls of 1 when a Judicator attacks a CHAOS unit in the shooting phase.

**Thunderbolt Crossbow:** When a model attacks with a Thunderbolt Crossbow the target is struck by a mighty blast of Celestial energy; pick an enemy unit within 18" and roll a dice. Subtract 1 from the roll if the target is a MONSTER. If the result is equal to or less than the number of models in the unit, the unit suffers D3 mortal wounds.

---

**KEYWORDS** | ORDER, CELESTIAL, HUMAN, STORMCAST ETERNAL, JUSTICAR, JUDICATORS

# PROSECUTORS
## WITH CELESTIAL HAMMERS

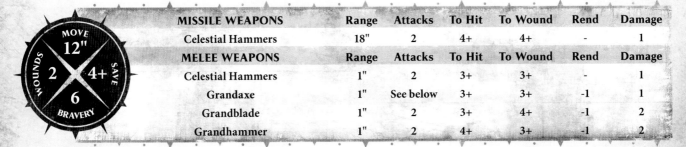

| MISSILE WEAPONS | Range | Attacks | To Hit | To Wound | Rend | Damage |
|---|---|---|---|---|---|---|
| Celestial Hammers | 18" | 2 | 4+ | 4+ | - | 1 |
| **MELEE WEAPONS** | **Range** | **Attacks** | **To Hit** | **To Wound** | **Rend** | **Damage** |
| Celestial Hammers | 1" | 2 | 3+ | 3+ | - | 1 |
| Grandaxe | 1" | See below | 3+ | 3+ | -1 | 1 |
| Grandblade | 1" | 2 | 3+ | 4+ | -1 | 2 |
| Grandhammer | 1" | 2 | 4+ | 3+ | -1 | 2 |

MOVE **12"**
WOUNDS **2**
SAVE **4+**
BRAVERY **6**

## DESCRIPTION
A unit of Prosecutors has 3 or more models. Some units are armed with a Celestial Hammer in each hand, while others go to battle armed with a single Celestial Hammer and carrying a Sigmarite Shield. 1 in every 3 models may instead be armed with a Grandaxe, Grandblade or Grandhammer.

## FLY
Prosecutors can fly.

## PROSECUTOR-PRIME
The leader of this unit is the Prosecutor-Prime. Trained for brutal melee, he makes 3 attacks rather than 2 in the combat phase.

## ABILITIES
**Heralds of Righteousness:** Roll 3 dice instead of 2 dice when determining the charge move for this unit. In addition, you can declare a charge with this unit if it is within 18" of the enemy rather than 12".

**Cleaving Blow:** When a model attacks with a Grandaxe, select a target unit and make one attack against it for each model it has within range.

**Paired Celestial Hammers:** You can re-roll hit rolls of 1 for models armed with more than one Celestial Hammer.

**Sigmarite Shields:** You can re-roll save rolls of 1 for this unit if any models from the unit are carrying Sigmarite Shields.

| KEYWORDS | ORDER, CELESTIAL, HUMAN, STORMCAST ETERNAL, ANGELOS, PROSECUTORS |
|---|---|

# PROSECUTORS
## WITH STORMCALL JAVELINS

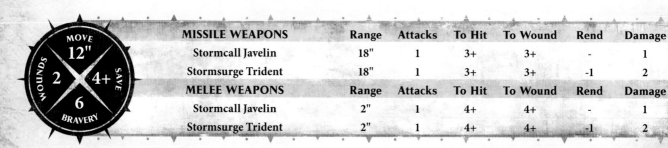

| MISSILE WEAPONS | Range | Attacks | To Hit | To Wound | Rend | Damage |
|---|---|---|---|---|---|---|
| Stormcall Javelin | 18" | 1 | 3+ | 3+ | - | 1 |
| Stormsurge Trident | 18" | 1 | 3+ | 3+ | -1 | 2 |
| MELEE WEAPONS | Range | Attacks | To Hit | To Wound | Rend | Damage |
| Stormcall Javelin | 2" | 1 | 4+ | 4+ | - | 1 |
| Stormsurge Trident | 2" | 1 | 4+ | 4+ | -1 | 2 |

**MOVE** 12"
**WOUNDS** 2
**SAVE** 4+
**BRAVERY** 6

## DESCRIPTION

A unit of Prosecutors has 3 or more models. They are armed with Stormcall Javelins and carry Sigmarite Shields. 1 in every 3 models may wield a Stormsurge Trident in place of their Stormcall Javelins.

## FLY

Prosecutors can fly.

## PROSECUTOR-PRIME

The leader of this unit is the Prosecutor-Prime. Raining death from afar, he makes 2 attacks rather than 1 in the shooting phase.

## ABILITIES

**Stormcall Javelin:** If a Prosecutor throws a Stormcall Javelin at a unit over 9" away, the javelin calls down a bolt of lightning; that attack has Damage 2 instead of 1.

**Heralds of Righteousness:** Roll 3 dice instead of 2 dice when determining the charge move for this unit. In addition, you can declare a charge with this unit if it is within 18" of the enemy rather than 12".

**Sigmarite Shields:** You can re-roll save rolls of 1 for this unit if any models from the unit are carrying Sigmarite Shields.

| KEYWORDS | ORDER, CELESTIAL, HUMAN, STORMCAST ETERNAL, ANGELOS, PROSECUTORS |
|---|---|

# RETRIBUTORS

| | MOVE 4" |
|---|---|
| WOUNDS 3 | SAVE 4+ |
| BRAVERY 7 | |

| MELEE WEAPONS | Range | Attacks | To Hit | To Wound | Rend | Damage |
|---|---|---|---|---|---|---|
| Lightning Hammer | 1" | 2 | 3+ | 3+ | -1 | 2 |
| Starsoul Mace | 1" | See below | | | | |

## DESCRIPTION

A unit of Retributors has 3 or more models. They are armed with Lightning Hammers. 2 in every 5 models may instead be armed with a Starsoul Mace.

### RETRIBUTOR-PRIME

The leader of this unit is the Retributor-Prime. A Retributor-Prime makes 3 attacks rather than 2 with a Lightning Hammer.

## ABILITIES

**Blast to Ashes:** If the hit roll for a model attacking with a Lightning Hammer is 6 or more, that blow strikes with a thunderous blast that inflicts 2 mortal wounds instead of its normal damage. Do not make a wound or save roll for the attack.

**Starsoul Mace:** A model armed with a Starsoul Mace can make a starblast attack in each combat phase. Pick an enemy unit that is within 1" of the model with the Starsoul Mace. That unit suffers D3 mortal wounds.

| KEYWORDS | ORDER, CELESTIAL, HUMAN, STORMCAST ETERNAL, PALADIN, RETRIBUTORS |
|---|---|

# DECIMATORS

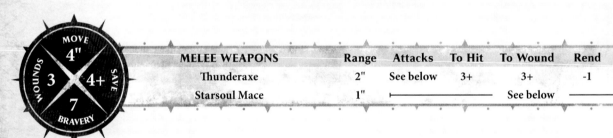

| | MOVE | | | | | |
|---|---|---|---|---|---|---|
| WOUNDS 3 | 4" | 4+ SAVE | | | | |
| | 7 | | | | | |
| | BRAVERY | | | | | |

| MELEE WEAPONS | Range | Attacks | To Hit | To Wound | Rend | Damage |
|---|---|---|---|---|---|---|
| Thunderaxe | 2" | See below | 3+ | 3+ | -1 | 1 |
| Starsoul Mace | 1" | See below | | | | |

## DESCRIPTION

A unit of Decimators has 5 or more models. They are armed with Thunderaxes. 2 in every 5 models may instead be armed with a Starsoul Mace.

## DECIMATOR-PRIME

The leader of this unit is the Decimator-Prime. Add 1 to the wound rolls for a Decimator-Prime.

## ABILITIES

**Cleaving Blow:** A single swing of a Thunderaxe can carve through several foes. When a model attacks with a Thunderaxe, select a target unit and make one attack against it for each model it has within range.

**Grim Harvesters:** Fear surrounds Decimators as they set about their gory work. Add 2 to the result of battleshock tests made for enemy units that are within 6" of any **DECIMATORS.**

**Starsoul Mace:** A model armed with a Starsoul Mace can make a starblast attack in each combat phase. Pick an enemy unit that is within 1" of the model with the Starsoul Mace. That unit suffers D3 mortal wounds.

| KEYWORDS | ORDER, CELESTIAL, HUMAN, STORMCAST ETERNAL, PALADIN, DECIMATORS |
|---|---|

# PROTECTORS

| MELEE WEAPONS | Range | Attacks | To Hit | To Wound | Rend | Damage |
|---|---|---|---|---|---|---|
| Stormstrike Glaive | 3" | 3 | 3+ | 3+ | -1 | 1 |
| Starsoul Mace | 1" | | | See below | | |

## DESCRIPTION

A unit of Protectors has 5 or more models. They are armed with Stormstrike Glaives. 2 in every 5 models may instead be armed with a Starsoul Mace.

## PROTECTOR-PRIME

The leader of this unit is the Protector-Prime. A Protector-Prime attacking with a Stormstrike Glaive makes 4 attacks rather than 3.

## ABILITIES

**Deathstrike:** A Stormstrike Glaive can slay monstrous foes with a single blow. If the wound roll for a Stormstrike Glaive is 6 or more and the target is a **MONSTER**, it does D6 Damage instead of 1.

**Storm-shield:** Arrows are deflected by the Protectors' weaving Glaives. Subtract 1 from the hit rolls of enemy shooting attacks that target a unit of Protectors, or which must cross a unit of Protectors to hit a model that lies beyond them.

**Starsoul Mace:** A model armed with a Starsoul Mace can make a starblast attack in each combat phase. Pick an enemy unit that is within 1" of the model with the Starsoul Mace. That unit suffers D3 mortal wounds.

**KEYWORDS** ORDER, CELESTIAL, HUMAN, STORMCAST ETERNAL, PALADIN, PROTECTORS

# GRYPH-HOUNDS

**MOVE** 9"
**WOUNDS** 3
**SAVE** -
**BRAVERY** 6

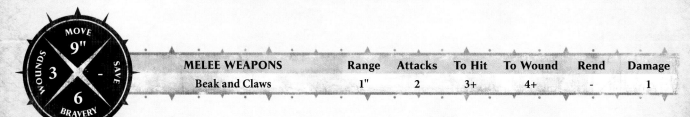

| MELEE WEAPONS | Range | Attacks | To Hit | To Wound | Rend | Damage |
|---|---|---|---|---|---|---|
| Beak and Claws | 1" | 2 | 3+ | 4+ | - | 1 |

## DESCRIPTION
A unit of Gryph-hounds can have any number of models. They savage their foe with their razor-sharp Beaks and Claws.

## ABILITIES
**Loyal Companion:** Once a Gryph-hound has bonded with a companion, it will defend it to the death. A Gryph-hound makes 4 attacks with its Beak and Claws rather than 2 if the target unit is within 3" of a **Lord-Castellant**.

**Darting Attacks:** Gryph-hounds attack in a series of darting strikes. Immediately after this unit attacks in the combat phase, roll a dice and move each model in the unit up to that many inches.

**Warning Cry:** It is said that it is impossible to sneak up on a Gryph-hound. If an enemy unit is set up within 10" of this unit, roll two dice. Any unit within that many inches of the Gryph-hounds is alerted to the enemy unit's presence, and can attack it with one of its weapons as though it were your shooting phase.

**KEYWORDS** | ORDER, CELESTIAL, STORMCAST ETERNAL, GRYPH-HOUNDS

# EXTREMIS CHAMBERS

**A roaring thunderhead of scale and storm, the Extremis Chambers are unleashed upon the Mortal Realms. Stardrakes darken the sky, lightning playing across their fangs as Drakesworn Templars gaze down from their backs, while beneath them the Dracothian Guard sweep across the battlefield.**

The Extremis Chambers are the hammer of the Heavens, hurled from Sigmar's mighty grip to crush the enemies of Order. Forged from the champions of the Stormhosts and the children of the Great Drake Dracothion, each Extremis Chamber is an elite company. Where the greatest beasts and the most vile hosts of Chaos gather, the Drakesworn Templars and Dracothian Guard ride to war. Beneath lightning-tortured skies they strike at the Mortal Realms to deliver a single earth-shattering blow to the enemy. Daemon armies scatter and great bastions are hurled down into ruin by their hand, for the Extremis Chambers are the most devastating weapon yet to be loosed from Sigmar's armouries.

Each Extremis Chamber is led by a Lord-Celestant, flanked by the Templars of the Drakesworn Temple. These champions and guardians ride Stardrakes, fearsome celestial creatures of storm and star. To even summon a Stardrake from the Heavens a Stormcast Eternal must seek out a rare and precious solargem. The Stormcast's reward is a bond with one of Dracothion's children, a celestial drake of prodigious power. From the back of such a creature the Templar becomes a demigod of war, laying enemies low with his lighting-wreathed weapon even as his mount devastates the battlefield. A single such warrior can turn the tide of battle, but an entire chamber can win wars.

Beneath the heroes of the Drakesworn Temple are the Dracothian Guard. No less fearsome in battle, they ride snarling, lightning-spitting Dracoths and wield the weapons of the Stormhost's Paladins. Each formation of the heavy cavalry has its role in battle: when the Lightning Echelon strikes, Fulminators wielding crackling stormstrike glaives hurtle toward the foe, their blades warding off missiles, while Tempestors return fire with volleystorm crossbows, causing chaos in their opponents' ranks. Behind them roar the Thunderwave Echelon – the Concussors' mighty lightning hammers can bring low even the greatest beasts, leaving them to be hewn apart by the thunderaxes of the Desolators.

## LORD-CELESTANT IMPERIUS

The first of the Stormhosts, the Hammers of Sigmar, was also the first to form an Extremis Chamber. Named the Hammers Draconis, their Reforging was completed just after the launch of Sigmar's war to reclaim the Mortal Realms. Lord-Celestant Imperius was placed in command of the Hammers Draconis, for he was born to lead in battle. The mortal Imperio was the last emperor of Hydonia, a continent-wide empire in Ghur. For years, Imperio fought valiantly against Chaos invaders, but his own brother turned to the Dark Gods, rising up to lead a great host of cultists in a civil war that engulfed his lands. Surrounded in his citadel, Imperio refused to be taken like a beast in a trap, and instead mounted his armoured ghurstryder and led his household knights on a final charge. Singing his deathsong, Imperio sallied out, driving deep into the encircling foes. Thus did Sigmar look down from the Heavens to see a leader undaunted. Although now reforged as Imperius, he still sees himself on that same last ride of vengeance.

With strikes of sky-splitting lightning, the Stormcast Eternals arrived in the Mortal Realms bringing bloody retribution to the minions of the Dark Gods. This was Sigmar's war – a crusade to free the realms, a campaign to exact vengeance for the wanton slaughter wrought in the Age of Chaos.

With the dawn of this new age, the armies at Sigmar's command had power enough to stand against the forces of Chaos. Yet as the shock of those initial strikes wore off, and the overwhelming numbers of the foe were brought to bear, the Stormhosts of the Heavens began to find themselves hard-pressed.

Had the God-King waited too long? Had his foes grown too powerful? Not even the divine are free of doubt.

As the Chaos Gods sent forth their seemingly endless counter-attacks, the Heavens too were emptied. In Sigmar's hour of need, Dracothion arrived once more. Roaring, the Great Drake released a bolt of celestial judgement, and across Sigmaron the doors of a hundred Temples opened.

It was time to unleash the might of the Extremis Chambers.

# LORD-CELESTANT ON STARDRAKE

| MELEE WEAPONS | Range | Attacks | To Hit | To Wound | Rend | Damage |
|---|---|---|---|---|---|---|
| Celestine Hammer | 2" | 3 | 3+ | 2+ | -1 | D3 |
| Stormbound Blade | 2" | 3 | 3+ | 4+ | -1 | 2 |
| Stardrake's Great Claws | 1" | 4 | ✹ | 3+ | -1 | D3 |

| DAMAGE TABLE | | | |
|---|---|---|---|
| Wounds Suffered | Move | Great Claws | Cavernous Jaws |
| 0-4 | 12" | 3+ | 3 |
| 5-8 | 11" | 3+ | 2 |
| 9-11 | 10" | 4+ | 2 |
| 12-13 | 8" | 4+ | 1 |
| 14+ | 6" | 5+ | 1 |

## DESCRIPTION

A Lord-Celestant on Stardrake is a single model. Whether the Lord-Celestant wields a Celestine Hammer or a Stormbound Blade, he will also bear an enchanted Sigmarite Thundershield. He rides a formidable Stardrake to battle, which rends its prey with its Great Claws.

## FLY

A Lord-Celestant on Stardrake can fly.

## ABILITIES

**Inescapable Vengeance:** If this model has made a charge move this turn, it can make D3 extra attacks with its Celestine Hammer or Stormbound Blade.

**Sigmarite Thundershield:** You can re-roll save rolls of 1 for this model. If the re-rolled save is successful, the shield unleashes a deafening peal and each enemy unit within 3" suffers a mortal wound.

**Stormbound Blade:** If the result of any hit roll for a Stormbound Blade is 6 or more, the target is wracked with the fury of the storm. Make three wound rolls against the target rather than one.

**Cavernous Jaws:** After this model piles in, but before it attacks, pick an enemy model within 3" and roll a dice. If the result is greater than that model's Wounds characteristic, it is swallowed whole and slain. You can do this as many times as shown on the damage table above.

**Sweeping Tail:** After this model has made all of its attacks in the combat phase, roll a dice for each enemy unit within 3". If the result is less than the number of models in the unit, it suffers D3 mortal wounds.

**Lord of the Heavens:** In your shooting phase, a Stardrake can either breathe a Roiling Thunderhead or call a Rain of Stars down from the heavens.

*Roiling Thunderhead:* Pick an enemy unit to be engulfed in a furious storm cloud, then roll a dice for each of its models that is within 18" of the Stardrake and which it can see. For each result of 6, a bolt of lightning streaks out and the unit suffers a mortal wound.

*Rain of Stars:* Roll a dice and choose that many enemy units on the battlefield, then roll a dice for each. On a result of 4 or more, the unit is struck by a fragment of a falling star and suffers D3 mortal wounds.

**Arcane Lineage:** Each time a casting roll is made for a **WIZARD** within 18" of any Stardrakes in your army, you can choose to increase or decrease the result by 1.

## COMMAND ABILITIES

**Lord of the Celestial Host:** The Stardrake ridden by a Lord-Celestant is more than a mere mount; it is an intelligent and cunning hunter in its own right, a radiating beacon of power for its star-spawned kin. If a Lord-Celestant uses this ability, all **STARDRAKES**, **DRACOTHIAN GUARD** and **STORMCAST ETERNAL HEROES** riding Dracoths in your army (including this one) are suffused with the power of Azyr. Until your next hero phase, you can re-roll failed wound rolls whenever those models attack with their Claws and Fangs or Great Claws.

| KEYWORDS | ORDER, CELESTIAL, HUMAN, STARDRAKE, STORMCAST ETERNAL, MONSTER, HERO, LORD-CELESTANT |
|---|---|

# DRAKESWORN TEMPLAR

| MISSILE WEAPONS | Range | Attacks | To Hit | To Wound | Rend | Damage |
|---|---|---|---|---|---|---|
| Skybolt Bow | 24" | 1 | 3+ | 3+ | -1 | 1 |
| MELEE WEAPONS | Range | Attacks | To Hit | To Wound | Rend | Damage |
| Tempest Axe | 2" | 6 | 3+ | 3+ | - | 1 |
| Arc Hammer | 1" | 2 | 3+ | 3+ | -1 | 3 |
| Stormlance | 3" | 3 | 3+ | 3+ | -1 | 2 |
| Stardrake's Great Claws | 1" | 4 | ☀ | 3+ | -1 | D3 |

**WOUNDS** 16
**SAVE** 3+
**BRAVERY** 9

| DAMAGE TABLE | | | |
|---|---|---|---|
| Wounds Suffered | Move | Great Claws | Cavernous Jaws |
| 0-4 | 12" | 3+ | 3 |
| 5-8 | 11" | 3+ | 2 |
| 9-11 | 10" | 4+ | 2 |
| 12-13 | 8" | 4+ | 1 |
| 14+ | 6" | 5+ | 1 |

## DESCRIPTION
A Drakesworn Templar is a single model. The Templar wields either a Tempest Axe, an Arc Hammer or a Stormlance, and some also bear a Skybolt Bow. He rides a fearsome Stardrake, which strikes down its prey with its Great Claws.

## FLY
A Drakesworn Templar can fly.

## ABILITIES
**Inspirational Lieutenant:** Although Drakesworn Templars do not often lead Sigmar's armies to war, they are held in awe by other Stormcasts for the bond they have forged with a Stardrake. Add 1 to the Bravery of **Stormcast Eternal** units in your army while they are within 10" of any Drakesworn Templars from your army.

**Tempest Axe:** A hurricane is unleashed each time a Tempest Axe strikes the foe. After this model attacks with its Tempest Axe, roll a dice for each unit that suffered any wounds from it. If the result is higher than the unit's Wounds characteristic, its models move 1" rather than 3" when they pile in until the end of the phase.

**Arc Hammer:** The static hum of an Arc Hammer rises to an almighty concussive crescendo as it strikes. If the hit roll for an Arc Hammer is 6 or more, make two wound rolls instead of one.

**Stormlance:** If the hit roll for a Stormlance is 6 or more and the target is a **Monster**, lightning surges forth and the attack inflicts D6 mortal wounds instead of its normal damage.

**Skybolt Bow:** Drakesworn Templars often direct attacks with well-placed skybolts. If this model scores a hit on an enemy unit with a Skybolt Bow, that unit is illuminated by a blazing bolt of lightning. In the next combat phase, you can add 1 to the result of any hit rolls for **Dracothian Guard** that attack that unit.

**Cavernous Jaws:** After this model piles in, but before it attacks, pick an enemy model within 3" and roll a dice. If the result is greater than that model's Wounds characteristic, it is swallowed whole and slain. You can do this as many times as shown on the damage table above.

**Sweeping Tail:** After this model has made all of its attacks in the combat phase, roll a dice for each enemy unit within 3". If the result is less than the number of models in the unit, it suffers D3 mortal wounds.

**Lord of the Heavens:** In your shooting phase, a Stardrake can either breathe a Roiling Thunderhead or call a Rain of Stars down from the heavens.

*Roiling Thunderhead:* Pick an enemy unit to be engulfed in a furious storm cloud, then roll a dice for each of its models that is within 18" of the Stardrake and which it can see. For each result of 6, a bolt of lightning streaks out and the unit suffers a mortal wound.

*Rain of Stars:* Roll a dice and choose that many enemy units on the battlefield, then roll a dice for each. On a result of 4 or more, the unit is struck by a fragment of a falling star and suffers D3 mortal wounds.

**Arcane Lineage:** Each time a casting roll is made for a **Wizard** within 18" of any Stardrakes in your army, you can choose to increase or decrease the result by 1.

| KEYWORDS | ORDER, CELESTIAL, HUMAN, STARDRAKE, STORMCAST ETERNAL, MONSTER, HERO, DRAKESWORN TEMPLAR |
|---|---|

# FULMINATORS

| MISSILE WEAPONS | Range | Attacks | To Hit | To Wound | Rend | Damage |
|---|---|---|---|---|---|---|
| Lightning Surge | 6" | D3 | 3+ | See below | | |
| **MELEE WEAPONS** | **Range** | **Attacks** | **To Hit** | **To Wound** | **Rend** | **Damage** |
| Stormstrike Glaive | 2" | 3 | 3+ | 3+ | -1 | 1 |
| Dracoth's Claws and Fangs | 1" | 3 | 3+ | 3+ | -1 | 1 |

**MOVE** 10"
**WOUNDS** 5
**SAVE** 3+
**BRAVERY** 7

## DESCRIPTION

A unit of Fulminators has any number of models. They bear gleaming Stormstrike Glaives and Sigmarite Shields, and ride ferocious Dracoths which unleash a Lightning Surge as they close in to attack with their enormous Claws and Fangs.

## ABILITIES

**Glaivewall:** Fulminators swing their glaives in great arcs as they advance, projecting a barrier of Azyrite force. Add 1 to the result of any save rolls you make for this unit during the shooting phase.

**Impaling Strikes:** This unit's Stormstrike Glaives cause 3 Damage rather than 1 if it charged in the same turn.

**Sigmarite Shields:** You can re-roll save rolls of 1 for this unit.

**Intolerable Damage:** If the wound roll for a Dracoth's Claws and Fangs is 6 or more, then that attack causes D6 Damage rather than 1.

**Lightning Surge:** Some Dracoths, trained for line breaking, spit a crackling torrent of energy at enemies that come too close. When a unit is hit by a Lightning Surge, do not make a wound roll; instead, the unit suffers a mortal wound, or two mortal wounds if it is within 3" of the attacking model.

**KEYWORDS** | ORDER, CELESTIAL, HUMAN, STORMCAST ETERNAL, DRACOTHIAN GUARD, FULMINATORS

# TEMPESTORS

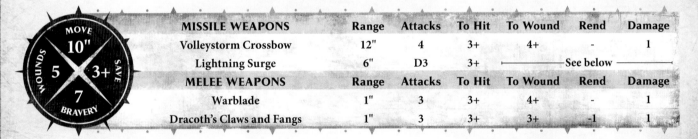

| MISSILE WEAPONS | Range | Attacks | To Hit | To Wound | Rend | Damage |
|---|---|---|---|---|---|---|
| Volleystorm Crossbow | 12" | 4 | 3+ | 4+ | - | 1 |
| Lightning Surge | 6" | D3 | 3+ | See below | | |
| MELEE WEAPONS | Range | Attacks | To Hit | To Wound | Rend | Damage |
| Warblade | 1" | 3 | 3+ | 4+ | - | 1 |
| Dracoth's Claws and Fangs | 1" | 3 | 3+ | 3+ | -1 | 1 |

**MOVE** 10"
**WOUNDS** 5
**SAVE** 3+
**BRAVERY** 7

## DESCRIPTION
A unit of Tempestors has any number of models. They are armed with rapid-firing Volleystorm Crossbows and bear lethal Warblades across their back, ready to face the foe at close quarters. They also carry Sigmarite Shields, and ride ferocious Dracoths which unleash a Lightning Surge as they close in to attack with their enormous Claws and Fangs.

## ABILITIES
**Disruptive Fire:** At the start of your shooting phase, you can declare that this unit will concentrate its fire on an enemy unit within 12". All models from this unit must attack that unit with their Volleystorm Crossbows. Until your next hero phase, your opponent must subtract 1 from the result of any hit rolls made for that unit.

**Sigmarite Shields:** You can re-roll save rolls of 1 for this unit.

**Intolerable Damage:** If the wound roll for a Dracoth's Claws and Fangs is 6 or more, then that attack causes D6 Damage rather than 1.

**Lightning Surge:** Some Dracoths, trained for line breaking, spit a crackling torrent at enemies that come too close. When a unit is hit by a Lightning Surge, do not make a wound roll; instead, the unit suffers a mortal wound, or two mortal wounds if it is within 3" of the attacking model.

| KEYWORDS | ORDER, CELESTIAL, HUMAN, STORMCAST ETERNAL, DRACOTHIAN GUARD, TEMPESTORS |
|---|---|

# CONCUSSORS

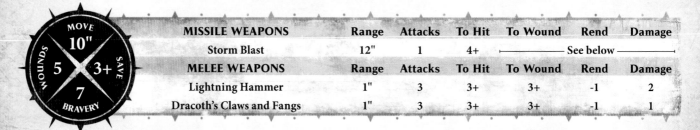

| MISSILE WEAPONS | Range | Attacks | To Hit | To Wound | Rend | Damage |
|---|---|---|---|---|---|---|
| Storm Blast | 12" | 1 | 4+ | See below | | |
| **MELEE WEAPONS** | **Range** | **Attacks** | **To Hit** | **To Wound** | **Rend** | **Damage** |
| Lightning Hammer | 1" | 3 | 3+ | 3+ | -1 | 2 |
| Dracoth's Claws and Fangs | 1" | 3 | 3+ | 3+ | -1 | 1 |

**MOVE** 10"
**WOUNDS** 5
**SAVE** 3+
**BRAVERY** 7

## DESCRIPTION

A unit of Concussors has any number of models. They wield sparking Lightning Hammers and carry Sigmarite Shields. They ride ferocious Dracoths which spit deadly Storm Blasts at their victims before attacking with their enormous Claws and Fangs.

## ABILITIES

**Thunderstrike:** If the result of a hit roll for this unit's Lightning Hammers is 6 or more, the attack inflicts a mortal wound in addition to any other damage it causes. If a unit suffers any mortal wounds in this way, it is stunned for the rest of the combat phase and cannot pile in before it attacks.

**Intolerable Damage:** If the wound roll for a Dracoth's Claws and Fangs is 6 or more, then that attack causes D6 Damage rather than 1.

**Sigmarite Shields:** You can re-roll save rolls of 1 for this unit.

**Storm Blast:** Dracoths can spit devastating bolts of lightning which blast open amid the enemy ranks, leaving warriors maimed and reeling. When a unit is hit by a Storm Blast, do not make a wound roll; instead, the unit suffers D3 mortal wounds.

**KEYWORDS** | ORDER, CELESTIAL, HUMAN, STORMCAST ETERNAL, DRACOTHIAN GUARD, CONCUSSORS

# DESOLATORS

| MOVE 10" | WOUNDS 5 | SAVE 3+ | BRAVERY 7 |
|---|---|---|---|

| MISSILE WEAPONS | Range | Attacks | To Hit | To Wound | Rend | Damage |
|---|---|---|---|---|---|---|
| Storm Blast | 12" | 1 | 4+ | See below | | |
| **MELEE WEAPONS** | **Range** | **Attacks** | **To Hit** | **To Wound** | **Rend** | **Damage** |
| Thunderaxe | 2" | 3 | 4+ | 3+ | -1 | 2 |
| Dracoth's Claws and Fangs | 1" | 3 | 3+ | 3+ | -1 | 1 |

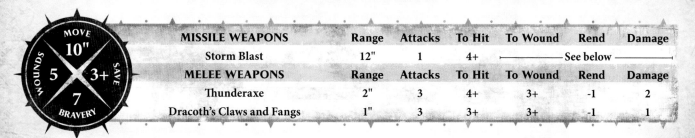

## DESCRIPTION

A unit of Desolators has any number of models. They bear keen-edged Thunderaxes for scything down entire ranks of the foe, and carry Sigmarite Shields. They ride ferocious Dracoths which spit deadly Storm Blasts at their victims before attacking with their enormous Claws and Fangs.

## ABILITIES

**Fury of the Storm:** Lightning crackles between the heads of the Desolators' axes when they attack as one. A Desolator makes 4 attacks with its Thunderaxe rather than 3 if there are at least 4 models in its unit, or 6 attacks if there are at least 6 models in its unit.

**Intolerable Damage:** If the wound roll for a Dracoth's Claws and Fangs is 6 or more, then that attack causes D6 Damage rather than 1.

**Sigmarite Shields:** You can re-roll save rolls of 1 for this unit.

**Storm Blast:** Dracoths can spit devastating bolts of lightning which blast open amid the enemy ranks, leaving warriors maimed and reeling. When a unit is hit by a Storm Blast, do not make a wound roll; instead, the unit suffers D3 mortal wounds.

**KEYWORDS** | ORDER, CELESTIAL, HUMAN, STORMCAST ETERNAL, DRACOTHIAN GUARD, DESOLATORS

# SERAPHON

**Ancient and ineffable, the Slann Starmasters wage their endless war against Chaos. From the blazing stars of Azyr, constellations of seraphon descend into the realms – ranks of snarling saurus, agile skink hunters and mighty reptilian monsters ready to sweep into battle against the enemies of Order.**

The Slann Starmasters traverse the realms at will, for time and space are theirs to command. Unimaginably powerful wizards, they can see the shifting strands of future days and work tirelessly to bring about the downfall of the Dark Gods, for the slann are children of Order and Chaos is anathema to them. To enact their will upon the world, the slann reach out with their minds into the distant stars of Azyr. From cords of glittering celestial energy they summon forth the seraphon, a long-lost race returned to reality by the power of the Starmasters.

Hosts of blazing heavenly power, the armies of the seraphon are filled with razor-toothed warriors both large and small. Savage saurus march to war behind drakescale shield walls, while diminutive skinks dart through the shadows raining celestial darts into the foe. Oldbloods and Scar-Veterans, the generals and champions of the seraphon starhosts, march and ride to war at the head of these great celestial armies. At their command, ranks of snarling cold one cavalry and skyborne Ripperdactyl and Terradon riders storm and swoop into the fray. But by far the most impressive weapons the Starmasters can call upon are the mighty Stegadons, Carnosaurs, Troglodons and Bastiladons. Huge saurian beasts, they thunder into battle, shrugging off all but the most terrible wounds and crushing all in their path.

The slann seers call down these star armies from the myriad constellations of Azyr, each glittering host representing one of the legendary seraphon gods or heroes, and led by unique champions and formations. Where the stars of Azyr shine, the claws of the seraphon are never far away, each constellation an army waiting to be ordered into battle. When they appear they step from the falling light of the heavens, their soldiers forged from celestial energy. These vast starhosts, their implacable warriors never faltering or breaking, march forth to lay waste to the works of the Dark Gods, and anything else that stands in the way of the slann's vision for a world dominated by perfect order.

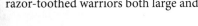

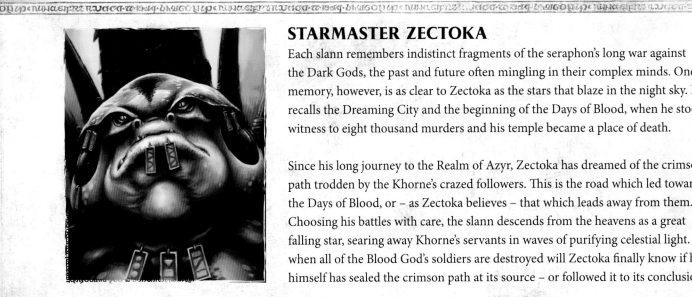

## STARMASTER ZECTOKA

Each slann remembers indistinct fragments of the seraphon's long war against the Dark Gods, the past and future often mingling in their complex minds. One memory, however, is as clear to Zectoka as the stars that blaze in the night sky. He recalls the Dreaming City and the beginning of the Days of Blood, when he stood witness to eight thousand murders and his temple became a place of death.

Since his long journey to the Realm of Azyr, Zectoka has dreamed of the crimson path trodden by the Khorne's crazed followers. This is the road which led towards the Days of Blood, or – as Zectoka believes – that which leads away from them. Choosing his battles with care, the slann descends from the heavens as a great falling star, searing away Khorne's servants in waves of purifying celestial light. Only when all of the Blood God's soldiers are destroyed will Zectoka finally know if he himself has sealed the crimson path at its source – or followed it to its conclusion.

# SERAPHON CONSTELLATIONS

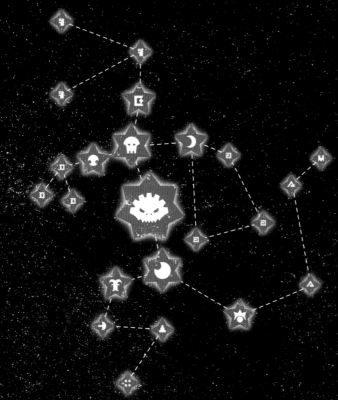

Seraphon constellations revolve around their core stars. Blazing brightest is the slann, to which all other stars are connected. Only slightly smaller are those of the Oldbloods and Starseers. Beyond them the cohorts of each starhost form a scattered carpet of jewels upon the sky. When linked together, these stars take a portentous shape; some seraphon constellations are great beasts of myth, while others are elements of a greater constellation, such as the Fangs of Sotek.

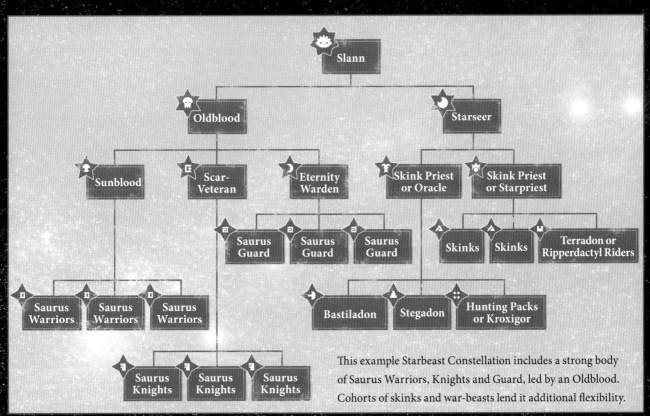

This example Starbeast Constellation includes a strong body of Saurus Warriors, Knights and Guard, led by an Oldblood. Cohorts of skinks and war-beasts lend it additional flexibility.

SERAPHON

# BLOODCLAW STARHOST

**With unflinching brutality the Saurus Oldblood leads its host into battle. A veteran of wars beyond count, the seraphon general focusses the savagery of its warriors into a series of murderous strike.**

## ORGANISATION

A Bloodclaw Starhost consists of the following units:

- 1 Saurus Oldblood or Saurus Oldblood on Carnosaur
- 3 HEROES chosen in any combination from the following list: Saurus Sunblood, Saurus Scar-Veteran, Saurus Scar-Veteran on Cold One, Saurus Scar-Veteran on Carnosaur, Saurus Eternity Warden
- 3-9 units chosen in any combination from the following list: Saurus Warriors, Saurus Knights, Saurus Guard

## ABILITIES

**Predatory Fighters:** Saurus Warriors, Knights or Guard from a Bloodclaw Starhost make one additional attack with their Powerful Jaws and Stardrake Shields in the combat phase.

**Strategic Mastery:** When an Oldblood is attended by capable lieutenants, it forms the warriors under its command into a lethal machine capable of incredible feats of strategy. The Saurus Oldblood, and any other HEROES from its starhost that are within 20" in the hero phase, can use the command abilities on their warscrolls even if they are not your general.

## SERAPHON
# HEAVENSWATCH STARHOST

The heavens move above the watchful eye of the Starseer. Prophecy entwines around its army like a living thing, the skink seer twisting it to aid the seraphon warriors or turn the fates against their foes.

## ORGANISATION

A Heavenswatch Starhost consists of the following units:

- 1 Skink Starseer
- 2 **Heroes** chosen in any combination from the following list: Skink Starpriest, Skink Priest, Troglodon
- 3-6 units chosen in any combination from the following list: Skinks, Terradon Riders, Ripperdactyl Riders, Bastiladon, Stegadon, Engine of the Gods, Kroxigor, Hunting Pack (each Hunting Pack consists of 1 unit of Skink Handlers and 1 unit of Razordons or Salamanders)

## ABILITIES

**The Trap is Sprung:** In your hero phase, pick an enemy unit that is visible to the Heavenswatch's Skink Starseer. Until your next hero phase, you can re-roll hit and wound rolls of 1 for units from this battalion that attack the unit you picked.

**Celestial Surge:** The great beasts of the seraphon are almost invincible when they march forth in a pack. In your hero phase, each **Monster** from this battalion heals a wound.

# SLANN STARMASTER

| MELEE WEAPONS | Range | Attacks | To Hit | To Wound | Rend | Damage |
|---|---|---|---|---|---|---|
| Azure Lightning | 3" | 6 | 4+ | 3+ | -1 | 1 |

**MOVE** 5"
**WOUNDS** 7
**SAVE** 4+
**BRAVERY** 10

## DESCRIPTION

A Slann Starmaster is a single model that sits atop a floating palanquin graven with strange symbols and humming with arcane power. Any enemies who come too close are immolated by crackling bolts of Azure Lightning that leap forth from the hovering throne.

## FLY

A Slann Starmaster can fly.

## ABILITIES

**Celestial Configuration:** If your army includes any Slann Starmasters, roll a dice after set-up is complete and consult the table below to see which constellation is in the ascendant, and how it affects your army. This effect lasts as long as you have a Slann Starmaster on the battlefield, or until a new constellation comes into effect.

| Roll | Ascendant Constellation |
|---|---|
| 1-2 | *The Hunter's Steed:* The image of a galloping war-beast blazes bright in the sky. Add 1 to run and charge rolls for **Seraphon** units in your army while this constellation is ascendant. |
| 3-4 | *The Sage's Staff:* This constellation is held as a mythical portent of wisdom and magic – while it is ascendant, add 1 to casting rolls when **Seraphon Wizards** in your army attempt to cast spells. |
| 5-6 | *The Great Drake:* The vast form of Dracothion himself writhes in the firmament. You can re-roll hit rolls of 1 for **Seraphon** units in your army while this constellation is ascendant. |

At the start of your hero phase, one Slann Starmaster in your army can attempt to turn the constellations to its advantage instead of casting one of its spells. If it does so, roll a dice. If the result is a 1, the Slann is distracted by its exertions and cannot cast any spells this phase. If the result is 4 or higher, you can pick a new ascendant constellation from the table. Otherwise, there is no effect.

**Arcane Vassal:** Before a Slann Starmaster attempts to cast a spell, you can pick a vassal to channel it; this can be a **Skink Hero** or Troglodon from your army that is within 15". If the spell is successfully cast, measure the range and visibility from the vassal rather than the Slann Starmaster.

## MAGIC

A Slann Starmaster is a wizard. It can attempt to cast three different spells in each of your own hero phases, and attempt to unbind three spells in each enemy hero phase. A Slann Starmaster knows the Arcane Bolt, Mystic Shield and Light of the Heavens spells.

## LIGHT OF THE HEAVENS

The Starmaster blinks slowly and raises its hands, bathing the battlefield in purest starlight. Light of the Heavens has a casting value of 6. If successfully cast, then until your next hero phase any battleshock tests for **Celestial Daemon** or **Chaos Daemon** units are made by rolling two dice rather than one. For **Celestial** units, discard the highest of the two dice; for **Chaos** units, discard the lowest.

## COMMAND ABILITY

**Gift from the Heavens:** If a Slann Starmaster uses this ability, **Seraphon** units from your army that are within 10" of him are wrapped in a mantle of Azyrite energy, allowing them to disregard the natural laws that govern the Mortal Realms. Until your next hero phase, those units can fly and you can re-roll failed save rolls for them in the shooting phase.

# LORD KROAK

**MOVE** 5"
**SAVE** 4+
**WOUNDS** 10
**BRAVERY** *

| MELEE WEAPONS | Range | Attacks | To Hit | To Wound | Rend | Damage |
|---|---|---|---|---|---|---|
| Ancient Spirits' Spectral Claws | 3" | 2D6 | 3+ | 3+ | -1 | 1 |

## DESCRIPTION

Lord Kroak is a single model, a long-dead and mummified slann seated upon a mystical stone palanquin. Any foes who dare approach are swarmed by the ancient spirits that surround him and torn asunder by their Spectral Claws.

## FLY

Lord Kroak can fly.

## ABILITIES

**Dead for Innumerable Ages:** Lord Kroak's physical form is ancient, withered and preserved only by his indomitable spirit. As such, he is immune to all but the most devastating attacks – those which can temporarily divorce his consciousness from his corpse.

In the battleshock phase of each turn, roll a dice and add the number of wounds that Lord Kroak suffered during the turn. If the result is higher than his Bravery, he is 'slain'. Otherwise, any wounds he has suffered are immediately healed. If an ability or rule would cause him to be slain outright, he is not; instead, he suffers D6 mortal wounds.

## MAGIC

Lord Kroak is a wizard. He can attempt to cast four spells in each of your own hero phases, and attempt to unbind four spells in each enemy hero phase. He knows the Arcane Bolt, Mystic Shield, Celestial Deliverance and Comet's Call spells.

## CELESTIAL DELIVERANCE

The spirits surrounding Kroak's palanquin quiver with unfettered force before exploding outwards to bring ruin to the enemies of the seraphon.

Lord Kroak can cast Celestial Deliverance up to three times in the hero phase. It has a casting value of 7 the first time it is cast, 8 the second time and 9 the third time. If it is successfully cast, roll three dice to determine the spirits' reach in inches. Each enemy unit within range suffers D3 mortal wounds. The vengeful spirits reserve a special hatred for **Chaos Daemons**, and tear into them with something akin to glee; as such, these units suffer D6 mortal wounds instead of D3.

## COMET'S CALL

His consciousness soaring up to the heavens, Lord Kroak summons a cluster of comets before sending them into the enemy's ranks. Comet's Call has a casting value of 7. If successfully cast, pick up to D3 enemy units, or D6 if the result of the casting roll was 10 or more. Each of these units is struck by a comet and suffers D3 mortal wounds.

## COMMAND ABILITY

**Impeccable Foresight:** Lord Kroak casts his consciousness ahead, reading the threads of destiny as easily as a mortal would read a map. If Lord Kroak uses this ability, roll three dice. For each one that scores 4 or more, Lord Kroak gains an insight into the future. Each insight can be used to re-roll any single dice before your next hero phase.

**KEYWORDS** | ORDER, CELESTIAL, SERAPHON, SLANN, HERO, WIZARD, LORD KROAK

# SAURUS OLDBLOOD

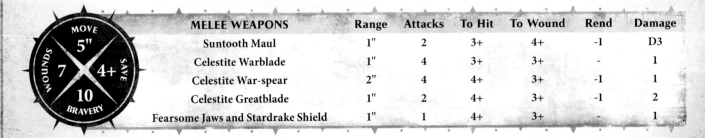

| MELEE WEAPONS | Range | Attacks | To Hit | To Wound | Rend | Damage |
|---|---|---|---|---|---|---|
| Suntooth Maul | 1" | 2 | 3+ | 4+ | -1 | D3 |
| Celestite Warblade | 1" | 4 | 3+ | 3+ | - | 1 |
| Celestite War-spear | 2" | 4 | 4+ | 3+ | -1 | 1 |
| Celestite Greatblade | 1" | 2 | 4+ | 3+ | -1 | 2 |
| Fearsome Jaws and Stardrake Shield | 1" | 1 | 4+ | 3+ | - | 1 |

**MOVE** 5"
**SAVE** 4+
**WOUNDS** 7
**BRAVERY** 10

## DESCRIPTION

A Saurus Oldblood is a single model. It takes to the field armed with a powerful Suntooth Maul or a swift Celestite weapon – either a Warblade, War-spear or Greatblade. A seasoned predator, an Oldblood also tears at its foes with its Fearsome Jaws and its Stardrake Shield, which is as deadly in offence as it is indomitable in defence.

## ABILITIES

**Stardrake Shield:** Saurus carry shields of celestial drakescale that are almost impervious to harm. When you make save rolls for this model, ignore the enemy's Rend characteristic unless it is -2 or better.

**Wrath of the Seraphon:** In the heat of battle, an Oldblood's cold fury radiates outward and drives its lesser kin into a rage of their own. You can re-roll wound rolls of 1 for **Saurus** models within 5" of an Oldblood.

## MAGIC

**Slann Wizards** know the Summon Oldblood spell, in addition to any others they know.

## SUMMON OLDBLOOD

Summon Oldblood has a casting value of 5. If successfully cast, you can set up a Saurus Oldblood within 15" of the caster and more than 9" from any enemy models. The model is added to your army but cannot move in the following movement phase.

## COMMAND ABILITY

**Paragon of Order:** The Saurus Oldblood gives an unspoken command, causing its warriors to snap into a new formation. If a Saurus Oldblood uses this ability, each **Seraphon** unit from your army within 10" can immediately reform around one of its models. That model must stay where it is, but each other model in the unit can move up to 3" so long as it does not end this move within 3" of the enemy.

| KEYWORDS | ORDER, DAEMON, CELESTIAL, SERAPHON, SAURUS, HERO, SAURUS OLDBLOOD |
|---|---|

# SAURUS SUNBLOOD

| | MOVE |
|---|---|
| WOUNDS | 5" | SAVE |
| 7 | | 4+ |
| | 10 | |
| | BRAVERY | |

| MELEE WEAPONS | Range | Attacks | To Hit | To Wound | Rend | Damage |
|---|---|---|---|---|---|---|
| Celestite War-mace | 1" | 5 | 3+ | 3+ | -1 | 1 |
| Fearsome Jaws and Aeon Shield | 1" | 2 | 4+ | 3+ | - | 1 |

## DESCRIPTION

A Saurus Sunblood is a single model. It is a ferocious exemplar of the saurus' martial might, crushing armour with its Celestite War-mace and tearing through flesh with its Fearsome Jaws and drakescale Aeon Shield. As well as being a deadly weapon, the Sunblood's massive Aeon Shield is almost impervious to damage.

## ABILITIES

**Aeon Shield:** When you make save rolls for this model, ignore the enemy's Rend characteristic unless it is -3 or better.

**Ferocious Rage:** A Sunblood in full battle-rage is the true embodiment of the seraphon's savage fury. If the hit roll for one of this model's attacks is 6 or higher, make D3 wound rolls rather than 1. If the wound roll for one of this model's attacks is 6 or higher, it causes D3 Damage rather than 1.

## MAGIC

**SLANN WIZARDS** know the Summon Sunblood spell, in addition to any others they know.

### SUMMON SUNBLOOD

Summon Sunblood has a casting value of 5. If successfully cast, you can set up a Saurus Sunblood within 15" of the caster and more than 9" from any enemy models. The model is added to your army but cannot move in the following movement phase.

## COMMAND ABILITY

**Scent of Weakness:** The Saurus Sunblood raises its war-mace, points it at an enemy and gives a predatory roar. If the Saurus Sunblood uses this ability, pick an enemy unit within 15" – until your next hero phase, re-roll failed hit rolls for attacks made in the combat phase against that unit by any of your **SAURUS** models.

| KEYWORDS | ORDER, DAEMON, CELESTIAL, SERAPHON, SAURUS, HERO, SAURUS SUNBLOOD |
|---|---|

# SAURUS OLDBLOOD ON CARNOSAUR

| MISSILE WEAPONS | Range | Attacks | To Hit | To Wound | Rend | Damage |
|---|---|---|---|---|---|---|
| Sunbolt Gauntlet | 18" | D6 | 3+ | 4+ | -1 | 1 |
| **MELEE WEAPONS** | **Range** | **Attacks** | **To Hit** | **To Wound** | **Rend** | **Damage** |
| Sunstone Spear | 2" | 3 | 3+ | 3+ | -1 | D3 |
| Carnosaur's Clawed Forelimbs | 2" | 2 | ✳ | 3+ | - | 2 |
| Carnosaur's Massive Jaws | 2" | ✳ | 4+ | 3+ | -1 | 3 |

**MOVE** ✳ | WOUNDS 12 | SAVE 4+ | BRAVERY 10

| DAMAGE TABLE | | | |
|---|---|---|---|
| Wounds Suffered | Move | Clawed Forelimbs | Massive Jaws |
| 0-2 | 10" | 3+ | 5 |
| 3-4 | 10" | 4+ | 4 |
| 5-7 | 8" | 4+ | 3 |
| 8-9 | 8" | 5+ | 2 |
| 10+ | 6" | 5+ | 1 |

## DESCRIPTION

A Saurus Oldblood on Carnosaur is a single model. Flashes of celestial fire leap forth from the Oldblood's Sunbolt Gauntlet while enemies are impaled on the shimmering blade of its Sunstone Spear. Its Carnosaur mount is a terrifying predator that grips enemies in its powerful Clawed Forelimbs before rending them with its Massive Jaws.

## ABILITIES

**Pinned Down:** Carnosaurs tackle large prey by pinning them in place before tearing into them with their massive jaws. If an enemy **Monster** is hit twice with the Carnosaur's Clawed Forelimbs, you can add 2 to the result when rolling to hit that target with the Carnosaur's Massive Jaws in the same turn.

**Blood Frenzy:** A Carnosaur that tastes the flesh of the enemy becomes a rampaging force of destruction. Once this model has slain an enemy with its Massive Jaws, it can run and charge in the same turn for the rest of the battle.

**Bloodroar:** The roar of a Carnosaur can cause even the most daring warrior to turn and flee. If your opponent takes a battleshock test for a unit within 8" of any Carnosaurs, roll a dice. If the result is higher than the result on your opponent's dice, D3 models flee from the unit (as well as any that flee because of the test).

**Blazing Sunbolts:** If the Saurus Oldblood atop the Carnosaur targets a **Chaos Daemon** unit with its Sunbolt Gauntlet, you can add 2 to the result of the wound rolls.

## MAGIC

**Slann Wizards** know the Summon Saurus Warlord spell, in addition to any others they know.

### SUMMON SAURUS WARLORD

Summon Saurus Warlord has a casting value of 10. If successfully cast, you can set up a Saurus Oldblood on Carnosaur within 15" of the caster and more than 9" from any enemy models. The model is added to your army but cannot move in the following movement phase.

## COMMAND ABILITY

**Ancient Warlord:** A Saurus Oldblood is a veteran of battles without number – an experienced leader who is as inspirational to its kin as it is terrifying to the enemy. If the Saurus Oldblood uses this ability, then until your next hero phase, whenever a **Saurus Hero** from your army within 20" attacks in the combat phase, pick one of its weapons and add 2 to its Attacks characteristic until the end of the phase.

**KEYWORDS** ORDER, DAEMON, CELESTIAL, SERAPHON, CARNOSAUR, SAURUS, MONSTER, HERO, SAURUS OLDBLOOD

# SAURUS ETERNITY WARDEN

| | MOVE |
|---|---|
| WOUNDS | 5" |
| 7 | SAVE 4+ |
| | 10 |
| | BRAVERY |

| MELEE WEAPONS | Range | Attacks | To Hit | To Wound | Rend | Damage |
|---|---|---|---|---|---|---|
| Star-stone Mace | 1" | 3 | 3+ | 3+ | -1 | 2 |
| Fearsome Jaws | 1" | 1 | 4+ | 4+ | - | 1 |

## DESCRIPTION
A Saurus Eternity Warden is a single model. It is armed with a Star-stone Mace and tears into enemies with its Fearsome Jaws.

## ABILITIES
**Selfless Protector:** Each time this model is within 2" of a SLANN that suffers a wound or mortal wound, it can attempt to intervene. If it does so, roll a dice. If the result is 2 or higher, the SLANN ignores that wound or mortal wound but this model suffers a mortal wound in its place.

**Alpha Warden:** Saurus Guard make an additional attack with their Celestite Polearms while their unit is within 5" of any Saurus Eternity Wardens from your army.

## MAGIC
**SLANN WIZARDS** know the Summon Eternity Warden spell, in addition to any others they know.

**SUMMON ETERNITY WARDEN**
Summon Eternity Warden has a casting value of 5. If successfully cast, you can set up an Eternity Warden within 15" of the caster and more than 9" from any enemy models. The model is added to your army but cannot move in the following movement phase.

**KEYWORDS**    ORDER, DAEMON, CELESTIAL, SERAPHON, SAURUS, HERO, SAURUS ETERNITY WARDEN

# SAURUS GUARD

| MELEE WEAPONS | Range | Attacks | To Hit | To Wound | Rend | Damage |
|---|---|---|---|---|---|---|
| Celestite Polearm | 1" | 2 | 3+ | 3+ | -1 | 1 |
| Powerful Jaws and Stardrake Shield | 1" | 1 | 5+ | 4+ | - | 1 |

**MOVE** 5"
**WOUNDS** 1
**SAVE** 4+
**BRAVERY** 10

## DESCRIPTION

A unit of Saurus Guard has 5 or more models. They wield heavy Celestite Polearms, and savage their foes with their Powerful Jaws and Stardrake Shields.

## ALPHA GUARDIAN

The leader of this unit is the Alpha Guardian. An Alpha Guardian makes 3 attacks rather than 2 with its Celestite Polearm.

## STARDRAKE ICON

Models in this unit may carry stardrake icons that pulse with the terrifying essence of a celestial predator. If a battleshock test is made for an enemy unit within 5" of any stardrake icons, add 1 to the result.

## WARDRUM

Models in this unit may carry wardrums. A unit that includes any wardrums can march in its movement phase. When it does so it doubles its Move characteristic, but cannot run or charge in the same turn.

## ABILITIES

**Stardrake Shields:** When you make save rolls for this unit, ignore the enemy's Rend characteristic unless it is -2 or better.

**Sworn Guardians:** Saurus Guard were created to protect their masters. If this unit is within 8" of any **Seraphon Heroes**, add 2 to its Bravery and 1 to the result of any save rolls for it.

## MAGIC

**Slann Wizards** know the Summon Saurus Guard spell, in addition to any others they know.

## SUMMON SAURUS GUARD

Summon Saurus Guard has a casting value of 6. If successfully cast, you can set up a unit of up to 5 Saurus Guard within 15" of the caster and more than 9" from any enemy models. The unit is added to your army but cannot move in the following movement phase. If the result of the casting roll was 11 or more, set up a unit of up to 10 Saurus Guard instead.

| KEYWORDS | ORDER, DAEMON, CELESTIAL, SERAPHON, SAURUS, SAURUS GUARD |
|---|---|

# SAURUS SCAR-VETERAN ON CARNOSAUR

| MELEE WEAPONS | Range | Attacks | To Hit | To Wound | Rend | Damage |
|---|---|---|---|---|---|---|
| Celestite Warblade | 1" | 6 | 3+ | 3+ | - | 1 |
| Celestite War-spear | 2" | 6 | 4+ | 3+ | -1 | 1 |
| Celestite Greatblade | 1" | 3 | 4+ | 3+ | -1 | 2 |
| Fearsome Jaws and Stardrake Shield | 1" | 1 | 4+ | 3+ | - | 1 |
| Carnosaur's Clawed Forelimbs | 2" | 2 | ✷ | 3+ | - | 2 |
| Carnosaur's Massive Jaws | 2" | ✷ | 3+ | 3+ | -1 | D3 |

**MOVE** ✷
**WOUNDS** 12
**SAVE** 4+
**BRAVERY** 10

| DAMAGE TABLE | | | |
|---|---|---|---|
| Wounds Suffered | Move | Clawed Forelimbs | Massive Jaws |
| 0-2 | 10" | 3+ | 5 |
| 3-4 | 10" | 4+ | 4 |
| 5-7 | 8" | 4+ | 3 |
| 8-9 | 8" | 5+ | 2 |
| 10+ | 6" | 5+ | 1 |

## DESCRIPTION

A Saurus Scar-Veteran on Carnosaur is a single model. It is a warrior as much as a leader, frighteningly adept with its Celestite Warblade, War-spear or Greatblade. It is almost as deadly with its Fearsome Jaws and toothed Stardrake Shield. Its Carnosaur mount is a terrifying predator that swipes at enemies with its powerful Clawed Forelimbs and tears at them with its Massive Jaws.

## ABILITIES

**Pinned Down:** Carnosaurs tackle large prey by pinning them in place before tearing into them with their massive jaws. If an enemy **MONSTER** is hit twice with the Carnosaur's Clawed Forelimbs, you can add 2 to the result when rolling to hit that target with the Carnosaur's Massive Jaws in the same turn.

**Blood Frenzy:** A Carnosaur that tastes the flesh of the enemy becomes a rampaging force of destruction. Once this model has slain an enemy with its Massive Jaws, it can run and charge in the same turn for the rest of the battle.

**Bloodroar:** The roar of a Carnosaur can cause even the most daring warrior to turn and flee. If your opponent takes a battleshock test for a unit within 8" of any Carnosaurs, roll a dice. If the result is higher than the result on your opponent's dice, D3 models flee from the unit (as well as any that flee because of the test).

**Stardrake Shield:** Saurus carry shields of celestial drakescale that are almost impervious to harm. When you make save rolls for this model, ignore the enemy's Rend characteristic unless it is -2 or better.

## MAGIC

**SLANN WIZARDS** know the Summon Carnosaur spell, in addition to any others they know.

## SUMMON CARNOSAUR

Summon Carnosaur has a casting value of 10. If successfully cast, you can set up a Scar-Veteran on Carnosaur within 15" of the caster and more than 9" from any enemy models. The model is added to your army but cannot move in the following movement phase.

## COMMAND ABILITY

**Saurian Savagery:** The Scar-Veteran looses an ear-splitting roar that drives nearby saurus into a frenzy. If the Saurus Scar-Veteran on Carnosaur uses this ability, pick a **SAURUS** unit within 15". Until your next hero phase, whenever you roll a hit roll of 6 or more for a model in that unit, that model can immediately make one additional attack using the same weapon.

| KEYWORDS | ORDER, DAEMON, CELESTIAL, SERAPHON, CARNOSAUR, SAURUS, MONSTER, HERO, SAURUS SCAR-VETERAN |
|---|---|

# SAURUS SCAR-VETERAN ON COLD ONE

| | MELEE WEAPONS | Range | Attacks | To Hit | To Wound | Rend | Damage |
|---|---|---|---|---|---|---|---|
| | Celestite War-pick | 1" | 3 | 3+ | 3+ | -1 | 1 |
| | Fearsome Jaws and Stardrake Shield | 1" | 1 | 4+ | 3+ | - | 1 |
| | Cold One's Vicious Bite | 1" | 2 | 3+ | 4+ | - | 1 |

**MOVE** 10"
**WOUNDS** 7
**SAVE** 4+
**BRAVERY** 10

## DESCRIPTION
A Saurus Scar-Veteran on Cold One is a single model. The Scar-Veteran fights with many weapons at once – a Celestite War-pick, its Fearsome Jaws and the serrated edge of its Stardrake Shield – while its Cold One mount is almost as deadly with its Vicious Bite.

## ABILITIES
**Fury of the Seraphon:** After this model has made all its Celestite War-pick attacks, roll a dice. If the result is 4 or higher, it can attack again with its Celestite War-pick. Roll again after those attacks; if the result is 6, it can attack for a third and final time.

**Stardrake Shield:** When you make save rolls for this model, ignore the enemy's Rend characteristic unless it is -2 or better.

## MAGIC
**Slann Wizards** know the Summon Knight Veteran spell, in addition to any others they know.

### SUMMON KNIGHT VETERAN
Summon Knight Veteran has a casting value of 5. If successfully cast, you can set up a Scar-Veteran on Cold One within 15" of the caster and more than 9" from any enemy models. The model is added to your army but cannot move in the following movement phase.

## COMMAND ABILITY
**Savage Charge:** The Scar-Veteran spurs its Cold One towards the enemy and urges its kin to follow. If a Scar-Veteran on Cold One uses this ability, then you can re-roll charge rolls and hit rolls of 1 for **Saurus** units within 8". In addition, until your next hero phase this model and any Saurus Knights within 8" make an additional attack with their Cold Ones' Vicious Bites.

| KEYWORDS | ORDER, DAEMON, CELESTIAL, SERAPHON, SAURUS, HERO, SAURUS SCAR-VETERAN ON COLD ONE |
|---|---|

# SAURUS WARRIORS

MOVE
5"
WOUNDS 1
SAVE 5+
10
BRAVERY

| MELEE WEAPONS | Range | Attacks | To Hit | To Wound | Rend | Damage |
|---|---|---|---|---|---|---|
| Celestite Club | 1" | 1 | 4+ | 3+ | - | 1 |
| Celestite Spear | 2" | 1 | 4+ | 4+ | - | 1 |
| Powerful Jaws and Stardrake Shield | 1" | 1 | 5+ | 4+ | - | 1 |

## DESCRIPTION
A unit of Saurus Warriors has 10 or more models. Some units of Saurus Warriors wield Celestite Clubs, while others are armed with Celestite Spears. In either case, they also maul the enemy with their Powerful Jaws and Stardrake Shields.

## ALPHA TALON
The leader of this unit is the Alpha Talon. An Alpha Talon makes 2 attacks rather than 1 with its Celestite Club or Spear.

## STARDRAKE ICON
Models in this unit may carry stardrake icons that pulse with the terrifying essence of a celestial predator. If a battleshock test is made for an enemy unit within 5" of any stardrake icons, add 1 to the result.

## WARDRUM
Models in this unit may carry wardrums. A unit that includes any wardrums can march in its movement phase. When it does so, it doubles its Move characteristic but cannot run or charge in the same turn.

## ABILITIES
**Stardrake Shields:** When you make save rolls for this unit, ignore the enemy's Rend characteristic unless it is -2 or better.

**Ordered Cohort:** Saurus are even deadlier when fighting in organised ranks. Add 1 to this unit's hit rolls if it has at least 20 models, and 1 to the number of attacks each model makes with its Celestite weapon if it has at least 30 models.

## MAGIC
**SLANN WIZARDS** know the Summon Saurus spell, in addition to any others they know.

## SUMMON SAURUS
Summon Saurus has a casting value of 6. If successfully cast, you can set up a unit of up to 10 Saurus Warriors within 15" of the caster and more than 9" from any enemy models. The unit is added to your army but cannot move in the following movement phase. If the result of the casting roll was 11 or more, set up a unit of up to 20 Saurus Warriors instead.

**KEYWORDS** ORDER, DAEMON, CELESTIAL, SERAPHON, SAURUS, SAURUS WARRIORS

# SAURUS ASTROLITH BEARER

| | MOVE |
|---|---|
| WOUNDS 6 | 5" |
| 10 | SAVE 4+ |
| BRAVERY | |

| MELEE WEAPONS | Range | Attacks | To Hit | To Wound | Rend | Damage |
|---|---|---|---|---|---|---|
| Celestite War-pick | 1" | 3 | 3+ | 3+ | -1 | 1 |
| Fearsome Jaws | 1" | 1 | 4+ | 4+ | - | 1 |

## DESCRIPTION

A Saurus Astrolith Bearer is a single model. It wields a Celestite War-pick and savages the enemy with its Fearsome Jaws. It carries an Astrolith, an ancient device that can increase the flow of celestial magic to the vicinity.

## ABILITIES

**Celestial Conduit:** In your hero phase, this model can plant its great Astrolith and activate its powers. Until your next hero phase, you may not move this model, but you may add 1 to the result of the casting roll when a **Seraphon Wizard** in your army attempts to cast any spells. If the spell is cast, add 8" to its range.

**Proud Defiance:** While the Astrolith is planted, you can re-roll any failed hit rolls made for this model and any **Seraphon** units from your army within 10".

## MAGIC

**Slann Wizards** know the Summon Astrolith Bearer spell, in addition to any others they know.

**SUMMON ASTROLITH BEARER**

Summon Astrolith Bearer has a casting value of 5. If successfully cast, you can set up an Astrolith Bearer within 15" of the caster and more than 9" from any enemy models. The model is added to your army but cannot move in the following movement phase.

| KEYWORDS | ORDER, DAEMON, CELESTIAL, SERAPHON, SAURUS, HERO, TOTEM, SAURUS ASTROLITH BEARER |
|---|---|

# SAURUS KNIGHTS

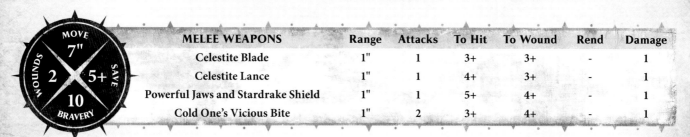

| | MELEE WEAPONS | Range | Attacks | To Hit | To Wound | Rend | Damage |
|---|---|---|---|---|---|---|---|
| **MOVE** 7" | Celestite Blade | 1" | 1 | 3+ | 3+ | - | 1 |
| **WOUNDS** 2 / **SAVE** 5+ | Celestite Lance | 1" | 1 | 4+ | 3+ | - | 1 |
| | Powerful Jaws and Stardrake Shield | 1" | 1 | 5+ | 4+ | - | 1 |
| **BRAVERY** 10 | Cold One's Vicious Bite | 1" | 2 | 3+ | 4+ | - | 1 |

## DESCRIPTION
A unit of Saurus Knights has 5 or more models. Some units wield Celestite Blades, while others prefer Celestite Lances. All attack with their heavy Stardrake Shields and Powerful Jaws, while their Cold One mounts give a Vicious Bite.

## ALPHA KNIGHT
The leader of this unit is the Alpha Knight. An Alpha Knight makes 2 attacks rather than 1 with its Celestite Blade or Lance.

## STARDRAKE ICON
Models in this unit may carry terrifying stardrake icons. If a battleshock test is made for an enemy unit within 5" of any stardrake icons, add 1 to the result.

## WARDRUM
Models in this unit may carry wardrums. A unit that includes any wardrums can march in its movement phase. When it does so it doubles its Move characteristic, but cannot run or charge in the same turn.

## ABILITIES
**Stardrake Shields:** When you make save rolls for this unit, ignore the enemy's Rend characteristic unless it is -2 or better.

**Blazing Lances:** As Saurus Knights charge, their lances burst into flame. If the wound roll for a Celestite Lance is 6 or higher and the model charged in the same turn, the attack inflicts an additional mortal wound.

## MAGIC
**SLANN WIZARDS** know the Summon Saurus Knights spell, in addition to any others they know.

## SUMMON SAURUS KNIGHTS
Summon Saurus Knights has a casting value of 6. If successfully cast, you can set up a unit of up to 5 Saurus Knights within 15" of the caster and more than 9" from any enemy models. The unit is added to your army but cannot move in the following movement phase. If the result of the casting roll was 11 or more, set up a unit of up to 10 Saurus Knights instead.

**KEYWORDS** | ORDER, DAEMON, CELESTIAL, SERAPHON, SAURUS, SAURUS KNIGHTS

# SKINK STARSEER

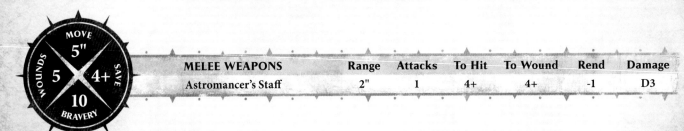

| | MOVE 5" | | SAVE 4+ | | BRAVERY 10 | WOUNDS 5 |
|---|---|---|---|---|---|---|

| MELEE WEAPONS | Range | Attacks | To Hit | To Wound | Rend | Damage |
|---|---|---|---|---|---|---|
| Astromancer's Staff | 2" | 1 | 4+ | 4+ | -1 | D3 |

## DESCRIPTION

A Skink Starseer is a single model carrying an Astromancer's Staff and seated upon a Palanquin of Constellations – a floating throne of carved stone that incorporates augurs and seeing-stones for discerning the future from the movement of the stars.

## FLY

A Skink Starseer can Fly.

## ABILITIES

**Cosmic Herald:** In your hero phase, a Skink Starseer can attempt to scry the future. Both you and your opponent secretly place a dice to show any number, then reveal them. You gain as many insights as the number on your dice –

however, if your opponent's dice shows the same number, the Starseer misreads the portents that are revealed and your opponent gains the insights instead! Each insight can be used to re-roll any single dice before your next hero phase.

## MAGIC

A Skink Starseer is a wizard. It can attempt to cast a spell in each of your hero phases, and unbind a spell in each enemy hero phase. It knows the Arcane Bolt, Curse of Fates and Mystic Shield spells.

## CURSE OF FATES

Curse of Fates has a casting value of 4. If successfully cast, pick a unit within 20".

Once per phase until your next hero phase, you can increase or decrease the result of a single dice roll for that unit by one.

**SLANN WIZARDS** know the Summon Starseer spell, in addition to any others they know.

## SUMMON STARSEER

Summon Starseer has a casting value of 5. If successfully cast, you can set up a Starseer within 15" of the caster and more than 9" from any enemy models. The model is added to your army but cannot move in the following movement phase.

| KEYWORDS | ORDER, DAEMON, CELESTIAL, SERAPHON, SKINK, HERO, WIZARD, SKINK STARSEER |
|---|---|

# SKINK STARPRIEST

| | MOVE 8" | | SAVE 5+ | WOUNDS 4 | BRAVERY 10 |
|---|---|---|---|---|---|

| MELEE WEAPONS | Range | Attacks | To Hit | To Wound | Rend | Damage |
|---|---|---|---|---|---|---|
| Star-stone Dagger | 1" | 3 | 3+ | 4+ | -1 | 1 |

## DESCRIPTION
A Skink Starpriest is a single model. It wields a Star-stone Dagger and carries a mystical Serpent Staff.

## ABILITIES
**Serpent Staff:** In your hero phase, a Skink Starpriest can level its staff at a **Seraphon** unit in your army that is within 8", granting them the venom of the two-headed celestial serpent. Until your next hero phase, whenever models from that unit attack with their bite or jaws, a wound roll of 6 or more causes twice the normal amount of Damage.

## MAGIC
A Skink Starpriest is a wizard. It can attempt to cast a spell in each of your own hero phases, and attempt to unbind a spell in each enemy hero phase. A Skink Starpriest knows the Arcane Bolt, Mystic Shield and Summon Starlight spells.

### SUMMON STARLIGHT
The Starpriest gestures with an open hand and calls the light of a distant star to the battlefield. Summon Starlight has a casting value of 6. If it is successfully cast, pick a unit within 20" to be bathed in starlight. If the unit is **Seraphon**, subtract 1 from the hit rolls of any attacks that target it until your next hero phase. Otherwise, subtract 1 from the hit rolls of any attacks that it makes until your next hero phase. If a unit of **Chaos Daemons** is bathed in starlight, it also suffers D3 mortal wounds.

**Slann Wizards** know the Summon Starpriest spell, in addition to any others they know.

### SUMMON STARPRIEST
Summon Starpriest has a casting value of 5. If successfully cast, you can set up a Starpriest within 15" of the caster and more than 9" from any enemy models. The model is added to your army but cannot move in the following movement phase.

| **KEYWORDS** | ORDER, DAEMON, CELESTIAL, SERAPHON, SKINK, HERO, PRIEST, WIZARD, SKINK STARPRIEST |
|---|---|

# TROGLODON

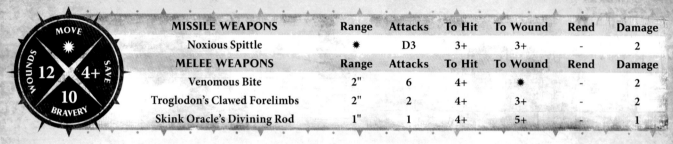

| MISSILE WEAPONS | Range | Attacks | To Hit | To Wound | Rend | Damage |
|---|---|---|---|---|---|---|
| Noxious Spittle | ✷ | D3 | 3+ | 3+ | - | 2 |
| **MELEE WEAPONS** | **Range** | **Attacks** | **To Hit** | **To Wound** | **Rend** | **Damage** |
| Venomous Bite | 2" | 6 | 4+ | ✷ | - | 2 |
| Troglodon's Clawed Forelimbs | 2" | 2 | 4+ | 3+ | - | 2 |
| Skink Oracle's Divining Rod | 1" | 1 | 4+ | 5+ | - | 1 |

**MOVE** ✷ **SAVE** 4+ **WOUNDS** 12 **BRAVERY** 10

| DAMAGE TABLE | | | |
|---|---|---|---|
| Wounds Suffered | Move | Noxious Spittle | Venomous Bite |
| 0-2 | 10" | 18" | 2+ |
| 3-4 | 9" | 15" | 3+ |
| 5-7 | 8" | 12" | 3+ |
| 8-9 | 7" | 9" | 4+ |
| 10+ | 6" | 6" | 5+ |

## DESCRIPTION

A Troglodon is a single model. It sprays Noxious Spittle at its enemies before pouncing on them with its Venomous Bite and Clawed Forelimbs. It is ridden by a Skink Oracle who wields a Divining Rod.

## ABILITIES

**Divining Rod:** The Skink Oracle can use its Divining Rod to attempt to unbind a spell in each enemy hero phase in the same manner as a wizard.

**Primeval Roar:** Enemy units within 8" of any Troglodons in the battleshock phase must subtract 1 from their Bravery.

**Drawn to the Screams:** If a unit suffers any wounds from this model's Noxious Spittle in the shooting phase, the sound of screams and the smell of sizzling flesh will help the Troglodon locate its prey. If the Troglodon charges in the subsequent charge phase, you can add 3" to its charge distance as long as it ends its charge within ½" of a screaming unit.

## MAGIC

**Slann Wizards** know the Summon Troglodon spell, in addition to any others they know.

## SUMMON TROGLODON

Summon Troglodon has a casting value of 10. If successfully cast, you can set up a Troglodon within 15" of the caster and more than 9" from any enemy models. The model is added to your army but cannot move in the following movement phase.

---

**KEYWORDS** | ORDER, DAEMON, CELESTIAL, SERAPHON, SKINK, MONSTER, TROGLODON

# SKINK PRIEST

MOVE **8"**
WOUNDS **4**
SAVE **5+**
BRAVERY **10**

| MISSILE WEAPONS | Range | Attacks | To Hit | To Wound | Rend | Damage |
|---|---|---|---|---|---|---|
| Starbolt | 18" | D3 | 3+ | 3+ | -1 | 1 |
| MELEE WEAPONS | Range | Attacks | To Hit | To Wound | Rend | Damage |
| Star-stone Staff | 1" | 3 | 4+ | 3+ | -1 | 1 |

## DESCRIPTION

A Skink Priest is a single model wielding a Star-stone Staff. Each has its own methods of performing celestial rites; some garb for war in a colourful Cloak of Feathers and cap their staff with an Azyrite gem that looses searing Starbolts, while others prefer to carry a variety of Priestly Trappings, from small glyph-stones to the bleached skulls of their foes.

## ABILITIES

**Priestly Trappings:** A Skink Priest wearing Priestly Trappings affects all **SERAPHON** units from your army within 8" when it performs a celestial rite, rather than a single unit.

**Celestial Rites:** In your hero phase, a Skink Priest can perform a rite to harness the power of the cosmos. If it does so, roll a dice. If the result is 4 or more, pick a **SERAPHON** unit within 8". You can re-roll run rolls, charge rolls and save rolls for that unit until your next hero phase.

**Cloak of Feathers:** The colourful cloaks worn by some Skink Priests are woven from the feathers of star-eagles. A Skink Priest wearing a Cloak of Feathers has a Save of 4+ rather than 5+, a Move of 14" rather than 8", and can fly.

## MAGIC

**SLANN WIZARDS** know the Summon Skink Priest spell, in addition to any others they know.

**SUMMON SKINK PRIEST**
Summon Skink Priest has a casting value of 5. If successfully cast, you can set up a Skink Priest within 15" of the caster and more than 9" from any enemy models. The model is added to your army but cannot move in the following movement phase.

**KEYWORDS** | ORDER, DAEMON, CELESTIAL, SERAPHON, SKINK, HERO, PRIEST, SKINK PRIEST

# SKINKS

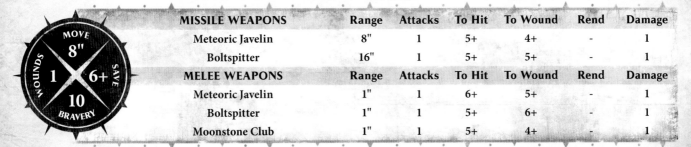

| MISSILE WEAPONS | Range | Attacks | To Hit | To Wound | Rend | Damage |
|---|---|---|---|---|---|---|
| Meteoric Javelin | 8" | 1 | 5+ | 4+ | - | 1 |
| Boltspitter | 16" | 1 | 5+ | 5+ | - | 1 |
| MELEE WEAPONS | Range | Attacks | To Hit | To Wound | Rend | Damage |
| Meteoric Javelin | 1" | 1 | 6+ | 5+ | - | 1 |
| Boltspitter | 1" | 1 | 5+ | 6+ | - | 1 |
| Moonstone Club | 1" | 1 | 5+ | 4+ | - | 1 |

MOVE 8"
WOUNDS 1
SAVE 6+
BRAVERY 10

## DESCRIPTION
A unit of Skinks has 10 or more models. Some units wield Meteoric Javelins and carry Star-bucklers. Others loose crackling projectiles from Boltspitters and either wield Moonstone Clubs or carry Star-bucklers, while some fight up close with Moonstone Clubs and Star-bucklers.

## ALPHA
The leader of this unit is the Alpha. An Alpha makes 2 attacks rather than 1 in the combat phase.

## ABILITIES
**Celestial Cohort:** A large group of skinks fighting in unison is a terrifying foe, becoming deadlier as celestial energy coruscates between them. Add 1 to hit rolls for this unit in the shooting phase if it has at least 20 models, or add 2 if it has at least 30 models.

**Star-buckler:** Some Skinks carry bucklers as resilient as the scales of stardrakes. When you make save rolls for a unit carrying Star-bucklers, ignore the enemy's Rend characteristic unless it is -2 or better.

**Wary Fighters:** When it is this unit's turn to pile in and attack, it can withdraw instead. Move each model in the unit up to 8", so that each one ends up at least 3" from the enemy.

## MAGIC
**Slann Wizards** know the Summon Skinks spell, in addition to any others they know.

## SUMMON SKINKS
Summon Skinks has a casting value of 5. If successfully cast, you can set up a unit of up to 10 Skinks within 15" of the caster and more than 9" from any enemy models. The unit is added to your army but cannot move in the following movement phase. If the result of the casting roll was 10 or more, set up a unit of up to 20 Skinks instead.

KEYWORDS | ORDER, DAEMON, CELESTIAL, SERAPHON, SKINKS

# CHAMELEON SKINKS

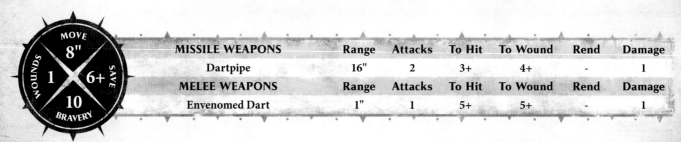

| MOVE 8" |
|---|
| WOUNDS 1 |
| SAVE 6+ |
| BRAVERY 10 |

| MISSILE WEAPONS | Range | Attacks | To Hit | To Wound | Rend | Damage |
|---|---|---|---|---|---|---|
| Dartpipe | 16" | 2 | 3+ | 4+ | - | 1 |
| MELEE WEAPONS | Range | Attacks | To Hit | To Wound | Rend | Damage |
| Envenomed Dart | 1" | 1 | 5+ | 5+ | - | 1 |

## DESCRIPTION

A unit of Chameleon Skinks has 5 or more models armed with Dartpipes that loose lethal projectiles sparkling with deadly star-venom. They prefer to keep the enemy at range, but are able to defend themselves by wielding their darts in close quarters.

## ABILITIES

**Chameleon Ambush:** Instead of setting up this unit on the battlefield, you can place it to one side and say that it is in hiding. In any of your movement phases, you can reveal a unit that is in hiding by setting it up anywhere on the battlefield.

**Disappear from Sight:** In your hero phase, this unit can blend with its surroundings and go into hiding. If it does so, remove it from the battlefield. You can reveal it as described above in any subsequent turn.

**Perfect Mimicry:** If all models in this unit are within or on a terrain feature, their Save characteristic is 3+ rather than 6+. This includes the bonus for being in cover.

**Star-venom:** If the hit roll is 6 or higher when a model attacks with a Dartpipe, the attack's Damage characteristic is 2 rather than 1, or 3 rather than 1 if the target is a **CHAOS DAEMON**.

## MAGIC

**SLANN WIZARDS** know the Summon Chameleon Skinks spell, in addition to any others they know.

### SUMMON CHAMELEON SKINKS

Summon Chameleon Skinks has a casting value of 6. If successfully cast, you can set up a unit of up to 5 Chameleon Skinks within 15" of the caster and more than 9" from any enemy models. The unit is added to your army but cannot move in the following movement phase. If the result of the casting roll was 11 or more, set up a unit of up to 10 Chameleon Skinks instead.

| KEYWORDS | ORDER, DAEMON, CELESTIAL, SERAPHON, SKINK, CHAMELEON SKINKS |
|---|---|

# SALAMANDERS

MOVE
8"
WOUNDS 3
SAVE 5+
10
BRAVERY

| MISSILE WEAPONS | Range | Attacks | To Hit | To Wound | Rend | Damage |
|---|---|---|---|---|---|---|
| Stream of Fire | 8" | 1 | 3+ | 3+ | -2 | D6 |
| MELEE WEAPONS | Range | Attacks | To Hit | To Wound | Rend | Damage |
| Corrosive Bite | 1" | 3 | 3+ | 3+ | -1 | 1 |

## DESCRIPTION

A unit of Salamanders has any number of models. The Salamander spits a caustic Stream of Fire at its prey and attacks with a Corrosive Bite.

## ABILITIES

**Goaded to Fury:** The range of a Salamander's Stream of Fire attack is increased to 12" while its unit is within 3" of any Skink Handlers from your army.

**It Burns!:** Roll a dice at the end of the shooting phase for each unit that suffered any wounds from a Salamander's Stream of Fire in that phase. If the result is 4 or higher, the unit suffers D3 mortal wounds as the corrosive liquid eats through armour, flesh and bone.

## MAGIC

**Slann Wizards** know the Summon Salamanders spell, in addition to any others they know.

### SUMMON SALAMANDERS

Summon Salamanders has a casting value of 6. If successfully cast, you can set up a unit of up to 3 Salamanders within 15" of the caster and more than 9" from any enemy models. The unit is added to your army but cannot move in the following movement phase.

| KEYWORDS | ORDER, DAEMON, CELESTIAL, SERAPHON, SALAMANDERS |
|---|---|

# RAZORDONS

| MISSILE WEAPONS | Range | Attacks | To Hit | To Wound | Rend | Damage |
|---|---|---|---|---|---|---|
| Volley of Spikes | 12" | 2D6 | 3+ | 4+ | - | 1 |
| MELEE WEAPONS | Range | Attacks | To Hit | To Wound | Rend | Damage |
| Fierce Bite and Spiked Tail | 1" | 3 | 4+ | 3+ | - | 1 |

MOVE 8"
WOUNDS 3
SAVE 4+
BRAVERY 10

## DESCRIPTION
A unit of Razordons has any number of models. A Razordon can unleash a deadly Volley of Spikes and attack with its Fierce Bite and Spiked Tail.

## ABILITIES
**Piercing Barbs:** If a Razordon shoots a Volley of Spikes at a target within 6", it has a Rend characteristic of -1 rather than '-'.

**Instinctive Defence:** Once per turn, if an enemy unit ends a charge move within 3" of this unit, roll a dice. If the result is 4 or higher, the Razordons immediately attack the charging unit with their Volleys of Spikes.

**Goaded to Anger:** You can re-roll all hit rolls of 1 for a Razordon in the shooting phase while its unit is within 3" of any Skink Handlers from your army.

## MAGIC
**Slann Wizards** know the Summon Razordons spell, in addition to any others they know.

## SUMMON RAZORDONS
Summon Razordons has a casting value of 6. If successfully cast, you can set up a unit of up to 3 Razordons within 15" of the caster and more than 9" from any enemy models. The unit is added to your army but cannot move in the following movement phase.

**KEYWORDS**    ORDER, DAEMON, CELESTIAL, SERAPHON, RAZORDONS

# SKINK HANDLERS

| | MELEE WEAPONS | Range | Attacks | To Hit | To Wound | Rend | Damage |
|---|---|---|---|---|---|---|---|
| | Goad-spears | 2" | 1 | 5+ | 5+ | - | 1 |

MOVE 8"
WOUNDS 1
SAVE 6+
BRAVERY 10

## DESCRIPTION

A unit of Skink Handlers can have any number of models. Each Skink Handler is equipped with a Goad-spear, which they use to encourage seraphon war beasts to advance on the foe, or to jab at enemies who get too close.

## ABILITIES

**Aim for their Eyes:** If you roll a hit roll of 6 or more for a Goad-spear, that attack has struck the target in the eyes and wounds automatically – there is no need to make a wound roll for that attack.

## MAGIC

**SLANN WIZARDS** know the Summon Skink Handlers spell, in addition to any others they know.

### SUMMON SKINK HANDLERS

Summon Skink Handlers has a casting value of 4. If successfully cast, you can set up a unit of up to 3 Skink Handlers within 15" of the caster and more than 9" from any enemy models. The unit is added to your army but cannot move in the following movement phase.

| KEYWORDS | ORDER, DAEMON, CELESTIAL, SERAPHON, SKINK, SKINK HANDLERS |
|---|---|

# KROXIGOR

| MELEE WEAPONS | Range | Attacks | To Hit | To Wound | Rend | Damage |
|---|---|---|---|---|---|---|
| Drakebite Maul | 2" | 4 | 4+ | 3+ | - | 2 |
| Moon Hammer | 2" | See below | 4+ | 3+ | -1 | 2 |
| Vice-like Jaws | 1" | 1 | 4+ | 3+ | -1 | 1 |

**MOVE** 8"
**WOUNDS** 4
**SAVE** 4+
**BRAVERY** 10

## DESCRIPTION
A unit of Kroxigor has 3 or more models. They are armed with mighty Drakebite Mauls. 1 in every 3 models may instead be armed with a Moon Hammer. Even unarmed, Kroxigor are feared for the terrifying bite of their Vice-like Jaws.

## ABILITIES
**Energy Transference:** When skinks are nearby, Kroxigor are energised by the nimbus of light that plays around the diminutive creatures. You can re-roll wound rolls of 1 for Kroxigor that are within 3" of any **SKINKS**.

**Sweeping Blows:** When a Kroxigor attacks with a Moon Hammer, it swings it in a wide arc that hits a number of foes. Select a target unit and make one attack against it for each of its models within range.

**Jaws like a Steel Trap:** If the wound roll for an attack made with a model's Vice-like Jaws is 6 or higher, the Kroxigor clamps its massive teeth around its victim and shakes it back and forth. Both you and your opponent roll a dice. If you score higher, your opponent does not make a save roll – instead, the target suffers a number of mortal wounds equal to the difference between the two dice rolls. Otherwise, the victim slips free and the attack causes no damage.

## MAGIC
**SLANN WIZARDS** know the Summon Kroxigor spell, in addition to any others they know.

**SUMMON KROXIGOR**
Summon Kroxigor has a casting value of 6. If successfully cast, you can set up a unit of up to 3 Kroxigor within 15" of the caster and more than 9" from any enemy models. The unit is added to your army but cannot move in the following movement phase. If the result of the casting roll was 11 or more, set up a unit of up to 6 Kroxigor instead.

| KEYWORDS | ORDER, DAEMON, CELESTIAL, SERAPHON, KROXIGOR |
|---|---|

# BASTILADON

| | MOVE | |
|---|---|---|
| WOUNDS | 5" | SAVE |
| 8 | ⊗ | 3+ |
| 10 | | |
| | BRAVERY | |

| MISSILE WEAPONS | Range | Attacks | To Hit | To Wound | Rend | Damage |
|---|---|---|---|---|---|---|
| Searing Beam | 20" | 2D6 | 4+ | 3+ | -1 | 2 |
| Meteoric Javelins | 8" | 4 | 5+ | 4+ | - | 1 |
| MELEE WEAPONS | Range | Attacks | To Hit | To Wound | Rend | Damage |
| Bludgeoning Tail | 2" | 3 | 3+ | 3+ | -1 | D3 |

## DESCRIPTION

A Bastiladon is a single model. It attacks with its Bludgeoning Tail, while the skinks riding atop it hurl Meteoric Javelins. Some Bastiladons carry a mysterious Ark of Sotek on their backs, which unleashes a tide of snakes to overwhelm the foe – others bear a devastating Solar Engine, capable of emitting a Searing Beam of celestial energy.

## ABILITIES

**Impervious Defence:** When you make save rolls for a Bastiladon, ignore the attacker's Rend characteristic. In addition, roll a dice whenever it suffers a mortal wound. On a result of 4 or higher, the wound is ignored.

**Light of the Heavens:** The light of a Solar Engine is utterly lethal to the minions of Chaos. If this model's Searing Beam targets a unit of **CHAOS DAEMONS**, its Damage characteristic is 3 rather than 2.

**Tide of Snakes:** At the start of each combat phase, a Bastiladon carrying an Ark of Sotek can unleash a tide of venomous serpents. Pick up to six enemy units within 8" and mark each one with a dice showing a different number. Then roll twelve dice to see where the snakes go. Each enemy unit suffers one mortal wound for each roll that matches the number on its dice. Any dice that do not roll a matching number have no effect as the snakes slither away.

## MAGIC

**SLANN WIZARDS** know the Summon Bastiladon spell, in addition to any others they know.

## SUMMON BASTILADON

Summon Bastiladon has a casting value of 8. If successfully cast, you can set up a Bastiladon within 15" of the caster and more than 9" from any enemy models. The model is added to your army but cannot move in the following movement phase.

| KEYWORDS | ORDER, DAEMON, CELESTIAL, SERAPHON, SKINK, MONSTER, BASTILADON |
|---|---|

# TERRADON RIDERS

**MOVE** 14"
**WOUNDS** 3
**SAVE** 5+
**BRAVERY** 10

| MISSILE WEAPONS | Range | Attacks | To Hit | To Wound | Rend | Damage |
|---|---|---|---|---|---|---|
| Starstrike Javelin | 10" | 2 | 4+ | 3+ | - | 1 |
| Sunleech Bolas | 5" | 1 | 4+ | 4+ | - | 1 |
| MELEE WEAPONS | Range | Attacks | To Hit | To Wound | Rend | Damage |
| Terradon's Razor-sharp Beak | 1" | 4 | 4+ | 4+ | - | 1 |
| Skyblade | 1" | 3 | 3+ | 4+ | - | 1 |

## DESCRIPTION

A unit of Terradon Riders has 3 or more models. Some units of Terradon Riders throw Starstrike Javelins, while others wield Sunleech Bolas. Their Terradon mounts make low dives to attack with their Razor-sharp Beaks.

## UNIT LEADER

The leader of this unit is either an Alpha or a Master of the Skies. An Alpha's missile weapon has a To Hit characteristic of 3+ rather than 4+, while a Master of the Skies is armed with a Skyblade instead of its missile weapon.

## FLY

Terradon Riders can fly.

## ABILITIES

**Deadly Cargo:** Terradons carry heavy boulders hewn from meteoric rock and carved with sigils of destruction, ready to be dropped at a command from their riders. Once per game, the unit can drop its boulders onto an enemy unit it moves over during the movement phase. Roll a dice for each Terradon in this unit; for each result of 4 or more, the enemy unit is struck by an exploding boulder and suffers D3 mortal wounds.

**Sunleech Bolas:** If an attack made with a Sunleech Bolas scores a hit, the projectile bursts and spreads flames among the foe. Roll a dice and make that many wound rolls.

**Swooping Dive:** At the end of your movement phase, you can declare that this unit will swoop down to attack the foe at close quarters. If you do so, then in the following combat phase you can re-roll failed hit and wound rolls for this unit as the enemy reels from the sudden assault. Until your next hero phase, measure range and visibility for models in this unit as though they were on the ground.

**Skyblade:** If the target of an attack made with a Skyblade can fly, you can re-roll failed hit rolls.

## MAGIC

**SLANN WIZARDS** know the Summon Terradons spell, in addition to any others they know.

## SUMMON TERRADONS

Summon Terradons has a casting value of 6. If successfully cast, you can set up a unit of up to 3 Terradon Riders within 15" of the caster and more than 9" from any enemy models. The unit is added to your army but cannot move in the following movement phase. If the result of the casting roll was 11 or more, set up a unit of up to 6 Terradon Riders instead.

**KEYWORDS** | ORDER, DAEMON, CELESTIAL, SERAPHON, SKINK, TERRADON RIDERS

# RIPPERDACTYL RIDERS

| MELEE WEAPONS | Range | Attacks | To Hit | To Wound | Rend | Damage |
|---|---|---|---|---|---|---|
| Moonstone War-spear | 2" | 1 | 4+ | 4+ | - | 1 |
| Ripperdactyl's Slashing Claws | 1" | 3 | 3+ | 3+ | - | 1 |
| Ripperdactyl's Vicious Beak | 1" | 1 | 4+ | 3+ | - | 1 |

## DESCRIPTION
A unit of Ripperdactyl Riders has 3 or more models. The skink riders are armed with Moonstone War-spears and carry Star-bucklers, while their mounts attack with Slashing Claws and Vicious Beaks.

## ALPHA
The leader of this unit is the Alpha. An Alpha makes 2 attacks rather than 1 with its Moonstone War-spear.

## FLY
Ripperdactyl Riders can fly.

## ABILITIES
**Swooping Dive:** At the end of your movement phase, you can declare that this unit will swoop down to attack the foe at close quarters. If you do so, then in the following combat phase you can re-roll failed hit and wound rolls for this unit as the enemy reels from the sudden assault. Until your next hero phase, measure range and visibility for models in this unit as though they were on the ground.

**Star-bucklers:** Ripperdactyl Riders carry bucklers as resilient as the scales of stardrakes. When you make save rolls for this unit, ignore the enemy's Rend characteristic unless it is -2 or better.

**Voracious Appetite:** Each time a model from this unit attacks with its Vicious Beak and scores a hit, immediately make another hit roll against the same target. Carry on until a hit roll does not score a hit, then make any wound rolls.

**Toad Rage:** Ripperdactyls become utterly frenzied whenever they catch the scent of a Blot Toad, and it is no coincidence that these diminutive creatures seem to materialise amid the enemy whenever the winged beasts are near. In your first hero phase, place a Blot Toad anywhere on the battlefield for each of your units of Ripperdactyl Riders. In each of your movement phases, roll a dice and move the Blot Toad up to that many inches. Blot Toads do not count as enemy models to either side. If a Ripperdactyl attacks an enemy unit that is within 2" of any Blot Toad, it makes 3 attacks with its Vicious Beak instead of 1.

## MAGIC
**SLANN WIZARDS** know the Summon Ripperdactyls spell, in addition to any others they know.

**SUMMON RIPPERDACTYLS**
Summon Ripperdactyls has a casting value of 6. If successfully cast, you can set up a unit of up to 3 Ripperdactyl Riders within 15" of the caster and more than 9" from any enemy models. The unit is added to your army but cannot move in the following movement phase. If the result of the casting roll was 11 or more, set up a unit of up to 6 Ripperdactyl Riders instead.

| KEYWORDS | ORDER, DAEMON, CELESTIAL, SERAPHON, SKINK, RIPPERDACTYL RIDERS |
|---|---|

# STEGADON

| MISSILE WEAPONS | Range | Attacks | To Hit | To Wound | Rend | Damage |
|---|---|---|---|---|---|---|
| Meteoric Javelins | 8" | 4 | 5+ | 4+ | - | 1 |
| Skystreak Bow | 25" | 3 | 4+ | 3+ | -1 | D3 |
| Sunfire Throwers | 8" | See below | 3+ | 3+ | - | 1 |
| MELEE WEAPONS | Range | Attacks | To Hit | To Wound | Rend | Damage |
| Massive Horns | 2" | 3 | 3+ | 3+ | ✱ | 2 |
| Crushing Stomps | 1" | ✱ | 4+ | 3+ | - | 1 |

| DAMAGE TABLE | | | |
|---|---|---|---|
| Wounds Suffered | Move | Massive Horns | Crushing Stomps |
| 0-2 | 8" | -3 | 3D6 |
| 3-4 | 7" | -2 | 2D6 |
| 5-6 | 6" | -2 | 2D6 |
| 7-8 | 5" | -1 | D6 |
| 9+ | 4" | -1 | D6 |

## DESCRIPTION

A Stegadon is a single model. It impales enemies upon its Massive Horns and pounds them with its Crushing Stomps. From its howdah, the Stegadon's skink crew hurl Meteoric Javelins that streak outwards in the form of shooting stars. The howdah also supports either a mighty Skystreak Bow or a set of Sunfire Throwers, and some Stegadons bear a Skink Alpha to battle, who directs nearby units from his lofty perch.

## ABILITIES

**Unstoppable Stampede:** When a Stegadon attacks with its Crushing Stomps, add 1 to any wound rolls if it charged in the same turn.

**Steadfast Majesty:** Stegadons are fearless beasts, and their stubborn refusal to back down when faced by even the most fearsome foes inspires great courage in the lesser seraphon that swarm around them. You can re-roll battleshock tests for units of **Skinks** within 5" of any **Stegadons**.

**Gout of Sunfire:** The Sunfire Throwers mounted on some howdahs unleash a great roiling cloud of cosmic flame. When a Stegadon attacks with its Sunfire Throwers, select a target unit and make one attack against it for each of its models within range.

**Skink Alpha:** If a Stegadon is ridden by a Skink Alpha, then in your hero phase the Alpha can give orders to a **Skink** unit within 8". If that unit is not within 3" of an enemy unit, you can immediately roll a dice and move each of its models up to that many inches. In addition, until your next hero phase, you can re-roll hit rolls of 1 for that unit.

## MAGIC

**Slann Wizards** know the Summon Stegadon spell, in addition to any others they know.

### SUMMON STEGADON

Summon Stegadon has a casting value of 10. If successfully cast, you can set up a Stegadon within 15" of the caster and more than 9" from any enemy models. The model is added to your army but cannot move in the following movement phase.

---

**KEYWORDS** | ORDER, DAEMON, CELESTIAL, SERAPHON, SKINK, MONSTER, STEGADON

# ENGINE OF THE GODS

| MISSILE WEAPONS | Range | Attacks | To Hit | To Wound | Rend | Damage |
|---|---|---|---|---|---|---|
| Meteoric Javelins | 8" | 4 | 5+ | 4+ | - | 1 |
| MELEE WEAPONS | Range | Attacks | To Hit | To Wound | Rend | Damage |
| Sharpened Horns | 2" | 4 | 3+ | 3+ | -1 | 2 |
| Crushing Stomps | 1" | ✳ | 4+ | 4+ | - | 1 |

| DAMAGE TABLE | | | |
|---|---|---|---|
| Wounds Suffered | Move | Crushing Stomps | Cosmic Engine |
| 0-2 | 8" | 3D6 | 3 dice |
| 3-4 | 7" | 2D6 | 3 dice |
| 5-6 | 6" | 2D6 | 2 dice |
| 7-8 | 5" | D6 | 2 dice |
| 9+ | 4" | D6 | 1 dice |

## DESCRIPTION

An Engine of the Gods is a single model crewed by a Skink Priest and a number of skinks. The Stegadon bearing the engine attacks with its Sharpened Horns and flattens the foe with its Crushing Stomps, while the skinks riding in its howdah hurl Meteoric Javelins – enchanted projectiles that transmute into meteors as they soar towards the enemy.

## ABILITIES

**Unstoppable Stampede:** When an Engine of the Gods attacks with its Crushing Stomps, add 1 to any wound rolls if it charged in the same turn.

**Cosmic Engine:** The Engine of the Gods is an ancient device, so powerful that it is capable of disrupting the natural laws of the universe. In your hero phase, roll a number of dice as shown on the Cosmic Engine column of the damage table above and consult the following table. If there is a SLANN within 10", it can flex its will to better control the engine; roll one additional dice, then discard one of your choice before adding them together.

| Total | Effect |
|---|---|
| 1-2 | The Engine of the Gods shakes violently as the universe resists its pull. This model suffers D3 mortal wounds. |
| 3-5 | The great dial thrums furiously and a brilliant white light shines forth. The Engine of the Gods and any SERAPHON units within 3" each heal D3 wounds. |
| 6-9 | An enemy unit within 25" is hit with a bolt of azure energy that shoots from the engine, suffering D6 mortal wounds. |
| 10-13 | A whirlpool of starfire engulfs the enemy. Roll a dice for each enemy unit within 10". If the result is 4 or higher, the unit suffers D3 mortal wounds. |
| 14-17 | A SERAPHON unit is called forth from Azyr to join your army. Set up all of its models within 8" of this model, at least 9" away from the enemy. |
| 18+ | Time crawls to a halt around your army. After this turn, you can immediately take another. If you roll this result a second time in the same turn, you count as having rolled 14-17 instead. |

**Steadfast Majesty:** Stegadons are fearless beasts, and their stubborn refusal to back down when faced by even the most fearsome foes inspires great courage in the lesser seraphon that swarm around them. You can re-roll battleshock tests for units of SKINKS within 5" of any STEGADONS.

## MAGIC

SLANN WIZARDS know the Summon Engine of the Gods spell, in addition to any others they know.

**SUMMON ENGINE OF THE GODS**

Summon Engine of the Gods has a casting value of 10. If successfully cast, you can set up an Engine of the Gods within 15" of the caster and more than 9" from any enemy models. The model is added to your army but cannot move in the following movement phase.

| KEYWORDS | ORDER, DAEMON, CELESTIAL, SERAPHON, STEGADON, SKINK, MONSTER, HERO, PRIEST, SKINK PRIEST, ENGINE OF THE GODS |
|---|---|

# SYLVANETH

**The magical woodlands of the realms burgeon with forest spirits and ancient creatures of bough and branch. Fickle and deadly, their armies fall upon any that would trespass upon their domains, bark-skinned warriors ripping, tearing and crushing invaders under root and claw.**

The children of the goddess Alarielle have suffered greatly under the yoke of the Dark Gods. Their emerald kingdoms and woodland refuges in the Realm of Life have been infected and ravaged by the vile servants of Nurgle, until little but rot and decay remains. As Sigmar's Tempest rolls out across the realms, however, a new age of hope is dawning, and the treefolk stir within their devastated forests and glades, taking up arms once more against those who have invaded their lands.

As the great queen Alarielle passes through her varied seasons, her servants rally to protect her. From the hidden vales, where the goddess' kindred rest and ready themselves for battle, arboreal generals and vengeful forest spirits march forth. Mighty Treelords crash across the land, their huge legs driving enemy warriors into the ground under tons of stone-hard wood and snaking roots. From their long arms reach out living blades and branch-like talons, impaling enemies on their oaken points in sprays of crimson gore. Around the lumbering stride of the Treelords scuttle stealthy throngs of Dryads, seldom seen until their gnarled talons are around the necks of their foes. As they fight they sing the fey songs of their queen, their haunting melody cutting through weak minds and making their prey easier to drag down, until the enemies of Order vanish completely under a moving thicket of writhing thorns.

Among these teeming armies stand the Branchwraiths, sorcerers who can rouse the woods themselves to fight alongside the sylvaneth. Enchanted oaks burst from the ground and vines move among the enemy like venomous snakes. To face the sylvaneth is to feel the wrath of nature set loose.

In recent times the sylvaneth have joined the legions of Order in their war against the Dark Gods. Though the forest queen and her minions have fought for centuries beyond count, during the Age of Chaos theirs was always a losing battle. So it has come to pass that they have entered into alliances with Stormcast Eternals and mortal heroes, lending their eternal strength to the rising star of Azyrheim and Sigmar's legions of conquest. Creaking Treelords and rustling Branchwraiths stride to war alongside gleaming plate-clad Liberators, stout Dispossessed and noble Freeguild warriors alike.

Such alliances are far from unshakeable pacts, however. Despite their common foe, the sylvaneth remain distrustful of any not of their kind. Men and duardin are seen as destroyers and easily corrupted by Chaos, while aelves are seen as estranged cousins at best, in the case of the Wanderers, and as treacherous and bloodthirsty at worst. Even Stormcast Eternals are regarded with unease by the sylvaneth, for they are not of the natural cycle, their endless Reforging breaking the seasonal balance of the Mortal Realms. Only the commands of Alarielle compel the sylvaneth to stand beside such warriors in battle, but even then they rustle with discontent like a steady breeze moving through a forest canopy. It is not unheard of for a slight misunderstanding to cause the sylvaneth to depart from their erstwhile allies, or even to attack them should they appear to threaten lands the sylvaneth hold sacred.

Tarik backed away from the Bloodbound assault, stumbling and falling to the forest floor. Throughout the wood his brother Freeguilders were likewise breaking before the Chaos assault, men falling back between the trees as armoured shapes chased them down. Suddenly, a Chaos Warrior loomed over him, a crimson shape blotting out the sky. He raised his shield, but his foe smashed it aside before raising an impossibly large axe to cut Tarik down. Then the trees moved.

Roots and vines shot out of the shadows like thorny serpents, enveloping his attacker. Elsewhere in the gloom Tarik heard the screams and curses of the Chaos horde as new adversaries joined the fray. The Bloodbound lashed out at the branches as they struck, but it was as if the whole world had turned against them. Tarik watched, transfixed, as the vines tightened around the killer that moments ago had been poised to end his life. Appearing as if out of nowhere, the Dryad embraced her victim, his bones snapping at her touch. As the broken Chaos Warrior fell to the ground, Tarik looked into the Dryad's eyes and felt a cold chill run down his spine.

## THE LADY OF VINES

Gnarled and weathered by centuries of war, the Lady of Vines is Alarielle's seneschal, and one of her greatest generals. The Branchwraith is quite literally the right hand of her queen, cut from Alarielle's wrist and nurtured into a courageous and skilled lieutenant. The Queen of the Radiant Wood sprouted a new hand soon enough, for her veins sing with the magic of life, and the sacrifice was worth making – in creating her favoured daughter from the stuff of her own body she ensured unquestioning loyalty. However, the Branchwraith was born while Alarielle remained in her summer aspect, full of wrath and energy. Thus, as Ghyran's queen faded into torpor over the course of the War of Life, the Lady of Vines remained as aggressive and certain of victory as ever. Just as summer waited for its time to come again, she felt convinced that her mother would one day rejoin the fight. Those doubts that Nurgle sent to worm their way into her heartwood were swiftly burned away by the radiant vigour and certainty that permeated her being.

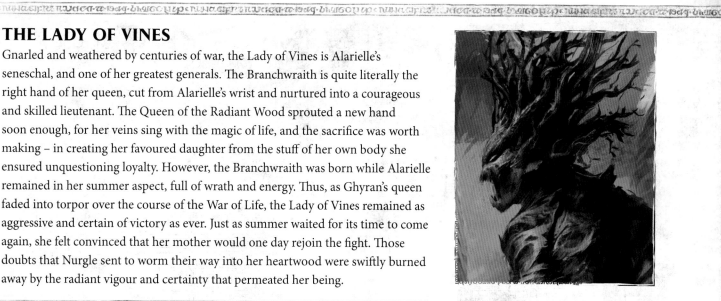

# WARGROVE OF THE SALISH WOAD

**For many centuries the pestilence of Nurgle has beset the Salish Woad. Once the woodland sea was one of Ghyran's lush Jade Kingdoms, but now it has been almost completely reduced to a wasteland of rot and decay. However, it still beats with life, defended to the last by the sylvaneth.**

In the heart of the Salish Woad there lives the great oaken Treelord Ancient Cuthrucu. Though the long Age of Chaos he slumbered, even as invaders ravaged his wood. Now at last the Storm of Sigmar has roused him to action, and with a deafening bellow he has called forth the Wargrove of the Salish Woad. From the remaining forests of the Woad, Dryads and their kin spill forth, falling upon the servants of the Dark Gods with claw and talon, making the invaders pay for the destruction they have wrought. Even the Salish Woad itself is hearkening to Cuthrucu's call, wyldwoods rising up from the wasteland to wreak their own vengeance upon the forces of Chaos.

## SYLVANETH
# FOREST SPIRIT WARGROVE

**With a creaking crash the woods come alive. Treelords reach down from the canopy to scoop up screaming victims, while Dryads rise out of the undergrowth to tear apart their startled prey.**

## ORGANISATION

A Forest Spirit Wargrove consists of the following units:

- 1 Treelord Ancient
- 2 Treelords
- 1 Branchwraith
- 3 units of Dryads

## ABILITIES

**Hidden Sanctuaries:** Instead of setting up a unit from this battalion on the battlefield, you can place it to one side and say that it is set up in the hidden sanctuaries. In any of your movement phases, you can transport the unit to the battlefield. When you do so, set it up so that all models are within 3" of a table edge or a SYLVANETH WYLDWOOD, and more than 9" from any enemy models. This is its move for that movement phase.

**Alarielle's Blessing:** WIZARDS in this battalion know the Alarielle's Blessing spell in addition to any other spells they know. Alarielle's Blessing has a casting value of 5. If successfully cast, pick a model from the battalion that is within 18" of the caster. The model you pick heals D3 wounds.

# TREELORD ANCIENT

| | MOVE | |
|---|---|---|
| WOUNDS 12 | 5" | SAVE 3+ |
| | 9 | |
| | BRAVERY | |

| MISSILE WEAPONS | Range | Attacks | To Hit | To Wound | Rend | Damage |
|---|---|---|---|---|---|---|
| Doom Tendril Staff | 18" | 1 | ✹ | 3+ | -1 | D6 |
| **MELEE WEAPONS** | **Range** | **Attacks** | **To Hit** | **To Wound** | **Rend** | **Damage** |
| Sweeping Blows | 3" | ✹ | 3+ | 3+ | -1 | D6 |
| Massive Impaling Talons | 1" | 1 | 3+ | ✹ | -2 | 1 |

| | DAMAGE TABLE | | |
|---|---|---|---|
| Wounds Suffered | Doom Tendril Staff | Sweeping Blows | Massive Impaling Talons |
| 0-2 | 2+ | 3 | 2+ |
| 3-4 | 3+ | 2 | 2+ |
| 5-7 | 4+ | 2 | 3+ |
| 8-9 | 5+ | 1 | 3+ |
| 10+ | 6+ | 1 | 4+ |

## DESCRIPTION

A Treelord Ancient is a single model. A Treelord Ancient is armed with Massive Impaling Talons, and can also attack with huge Sweeping Blows, or from afar with its Doom Tendril Staff.

## ABILITIES

**Groundshaking Stomp:** At the start of the combat phase the Treelord Ancient stomps the ground; roll a dice for each enemy unit within 3" of this model. On a roll of 4 or more that unit is knocked off their feet by the impact and must subtract 1 from all hit rolls in that combat phase as they regain their footing.

**Impale:** If a Treelord Ancient's Massive Impaling Talons inflict a wound on an enemy model, roll a dice and subtract 1 from the roll. If the result equals or exceeds the number of wounds the enemy model has remaining, it is slain.

**Spirit Paths:** If a Treelord Ancient is within 3" of a SYLVANETH WYLDWOOD at the start of your movement phase it can travel along the spirit paths. If it does so, remove the Treelord Ancient from the battlefield, and then set it up within 3" of a different SYLVANETH WYLDWOOD, more than 9" from any enemy models. This is its move for the movement phase.

## MAGIC

A Treelord Ancient is a wizard. It can attempt to cast one spell in each of your own hero phases, and attempt to unbind one spell in each enemy hero phase. It knows the Arcane Bolt, Mystic Shield and Awakening The Wood spells.

### AWAKENING THE WOOD

Awakening the Wood has a casting value of 6. If successfully cast, pick a SYLVANETH WYLDWOOD that is within 24" of the caster. Each enemy unit within 3" of this SYLVANETH WYLDWOOD suffers D3 mortal wounds as the trees come to life and attack with twisted branches and thorny boughs.

| KEYWORDS | ORDER, SYLVANETH, MONSTER, HERO, WIZARD, TREELORD ANCIENT |
|---|---|

# TREELORD

| MISSILE WEAPONS | Range | Attacks | To Hit | To Wound | Rend | Damage |
|---|---|---|---|---|---|---|
| Strangleroots | 12" | 5 | ✹ | 3+ | -1 | 1 |
| MELEE WEAPONS | Range | Attacks | To Hit | To Wound | Rend | Damage |
| Sweeping Blows | 3" | ✹ | 3+ | 3+ | -1 | D6 |
| Massive Impaling Talons | 1" | 1 | 3+ | ✹ | -2 | 1 |

**MOVE** 6"
**WOUNDS** 12
**SAVE** 3+
**BRAVERY** 6

| DAMAGE TABLE | | | |
|---|---|---|---|
| Wounds Suffered | Strangleroots | Sweeping Blows | Massive Impaling Talons |
| 0-2 | 2+ | 4 | 2+ |
| 3-4 | 3+ | 3 | 2+ |
| 5-7 | 4+ | 2 | 3+ |
| 8-9 | 5+ | 2 | 3+ |
| 10+ | 6+ | 1 | 4+ |

## DESCRIPTION

A Treelord is a single model. Treelords are armed with Massive Impaling Talons, and can also attack with huge Sweeping Blows, or from afar with writhing Strangleroots.

## ABILITIES

**Groundshaking Stomp:** At the start of the combat phase the Treelord stomps the ground; roll a dice for each enemy unit within 3" of this model. On a roll of 4 or more that unit is knocked off their feet by the impact and must subtract 1 from all hit rolls in that combat phase as they regain their footing.

**Impale:** If a Treelord's Massive Impaling Talons inflict a wound on an enemy model, roll a dice and subtract 1 from the roll. If the result equals or exceeds the number of wounds the enemy model has remaining, it is slain.

**Spirit Paths:** If a Treelord is within 3" of a SYLVANETH WYLDWOOD at the start of your movement phase it can travel along the spirit paths. If it does so, remove the Treelord from the battlefield, and then set it up within 3" of a different SYLVANETH WYLDWOOD, more than 9" from any enemy models. This is its move for the movement phase.

# BRANCHWRAITH

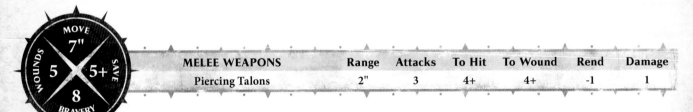

| | MOVE 7" | | MELEE WEAPONS | Range | Attacks | To Hit | To Wound | Rend | Damage |
|---|---|---|---|---|---|---|---|---|---|
| WOUNDS 5 | | SAVE 5+ | Piercing Talons | 2" | 3 | 4+ | 4+ | -1 | 1 |
| | 8 BRAVERY | | | | | | | | |

## DESCRIPTION

A Branchwraith is a single model. It is armed with vicious Piercing Talons.

## ABILITIES

**Blessings of the Forest:** Subtract 1 from all hit rolls made against this unit if it is within 3" of a SYLVANETH WYLDWOOD.

## MAGIC

A Branchwraith is a wizard. It can attempt to cast one spell in each of your own hero phases, and attempt to unbind one spell in each enemy hero phase. It knows the Arcane Bolt, Mystic Shield and Roused To Wrath spells.

## ROUSED TO WRATH

Roused to Wrath has a casting value of 7. If successfully cast, set up a unit of 2D6 Dryads more than 3" from the enemy, and fully within a SYLVANETH WYLDWOOD that is within 12" of the caster.

| KEYWORDS | ORDER, SYLVANETH, HERO, WIZARD, BRANCHWRAITH |
|---|---|

# DRYADS

| | MELEE WEAPONS | Range | Attacks | To Hit | To Wound | Rend | Damage |
|---|---|---|---|---|---|---|---|
| | Wracking Talons | 2" | 2 | 4+ | 4+ | - | 1 |

## DESCRIPTION
A unit of Dryads has 5 or more models. They are armed with vicious Wracking Talons.

### BRANCH NYMPH
The leader of this unit is a Branch Nymph. A Branch Nymph makes 3 attacks rather than 2.

## ABILITIES
**Blessings of the Forest:** Subtract 1 from all hit rolls made against this unit if it is within 3" of a SYLVANETH WYLDWOOD.

**Enrapturing Song:** In your own combat phase, you can enrapture one enemy unit that is within 3" of this unit. Add 1 to the hit rolls for attacks made by this unit against the enraptured unit in that combat phase.

**Impenetrable Thicket:** When Dryads gather in great numbers their many twisting limbs and branches form an interlocking shield of thorns that protects them against the enemy's blows. You can add 1 to the result of save rolls for this unit if it includes at least 12 models.

| KEYWORDS | ORDER, SYLVANETH, DRYADS |
|---|---|

# FYRESLAYERS

**Possessed by the furious power of Grimnir, the Fyreslayers are fearsome duardin warriors and master smiths. Oath-makers and skull-breakers, they sell their skills at war across the Mortal Realms, trading the blood of their foes for a price in gold in their continuing quest to restore their fallen god.**

The Fyreslayer lodges are scattered across the Mortal Realms. Worshippers of the dead duardin god Grimnir, they have a well-deserved reputation as mercenaries and berserkers. Under the leadership of their Runefathers and Runesons the Fyreslayers charge into battle armed with axe and pick, bladed shield and burning flail. The true power of the Fyreslayers, though, comes from the shimmering golden runes hammered into their scorched flesh. Crafted by the lodge's Runemaster,

these are made from ur-gold, which contain the scattered spirit of Grimnir. In battle the Fyreslayers' runes glow with a blazing light, infusing a measure of divine might into those duardin who bear them.

The Fyreslayers believe that it is their sacred duty to gather up all these pieces of Grimnir, and so they hunt for ur-gold across the Mortal Realms. Mined from the depths of the earth, taken from the lairs of legendary beasts or

stolen from the ruins of broken cities, this gold is gathered in great measure, even when it is defended by vast armies or watched over by great beasts. By far though the greatest amount is won in battle, in payment for fighting along the races of the realms in their endless wars. Such is the reputation of the Fyreslayers that they need not look far for work – for what king would not want a great horde of flame-wreathed berserkers and their magmadroth-riding lords on his side?

# FYRESLAYER LODGE

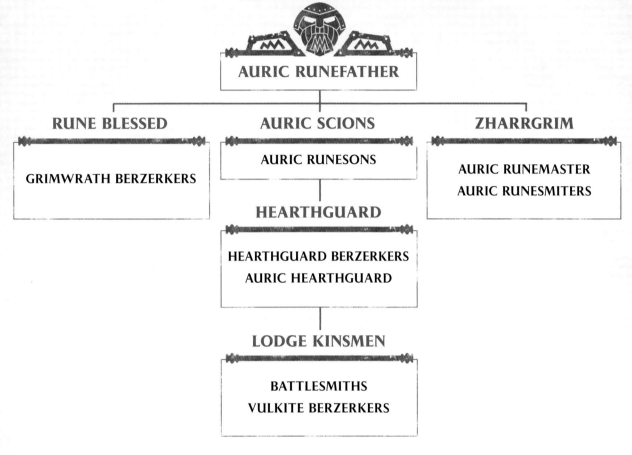

**AURIC RUNEFATHER**

### RUNE BLESSED

GRIMWRATH BERZERKERS

### AURIC SCIONS

AURIC RUNESONS

#### HEARTHGUARD

HEARTHGUARD BERZERKERS
AURIC HEARTHGUARD

#### LODGE KINSMEN

BATTLESMITHS
VULKITE BERZERKERS

### ZHARRGRIM

AURIC RUNEMASTER
AURIC RUNESMITERS

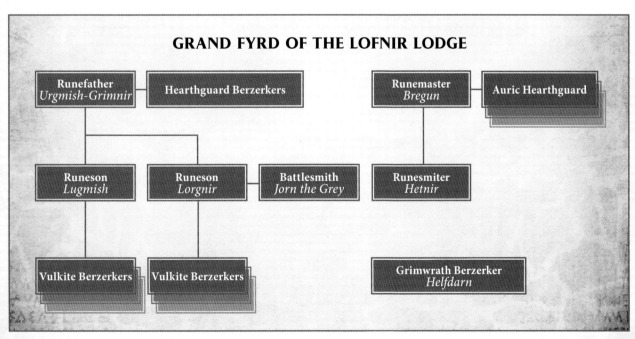

## GRAND FYRD OF THE LOFNIR LODGE

| Runefather *Urgmish-Grimnir* | Hearthguard Berzerkers |
| Runeson *Lugmish* | Runeson *Lorgnir* | Battlesmith *Jorn the Grey* |
| Vulkite Berzerkers | Vulkite Berzerkers |

| Runemaster *Bregun* | Auric Hearthguard |
| Runesmiter *Hetnir* |
| Grimwrath Berzerker *Helfdarn* |

## FYRESLAYERS
# LORDS OF THE LODGE

Led by the will of the Runefather and guided by the wisdom of the Runemaster, the Lords of the Lodge are the white-hot core of a Fyreslayer army, their burning rage tempered by sacred oaths of war.

### ORGANISATION

The Lords of the Lodge consists of the following units:

- 1 Auric Runefather or Auric Runefather on Magmadroth
- 1 Auric Runemaster
- 1 Battlesmith
- 1 unit of Hearthguard Berzerkers

### ABILITIES

**Hot-blooded Fury:** The Fyreslayers' impetuosity makes them unpredictable foes – something that their leaders can turn to their advantage. Once per battle, before rolling the dice to see who takes the first turn in a battle round, you can declare that you will seize the initiative. Add 1 to the result of your dice roll for each **Hero** from the Lords of the Lodge that is on the battlefield.

**Oathbound Guardians:** It is the duty of Hearthguard Berzerkers to defend their lords on the field of battle, and they would rather die than be found wanting. The Hearthguard Berzerkers in the Lords of the Lodge can be selected to pile in and attack twice in the combat phase, but only if they are within 6" of a **Hero** that is also part of the battalion the second time they are selected.

## FYRESLAYERS
# FORGE BRETHREN

**Shrouded in the shimmering heat of the forge-temple, the Forge Brethren blast enemies to ash and form blazing barricades of lava with sustained volleys of fire from their magmapikes.**

## ORGANISATION

The Forge Brethren consists of the following units:

- 1 Auric Runesmiter or Auric Runesmiter on Magmadroth
- 3 units of Auric Hearthguard

## ABILITIES

**Master-forged Blades:** Even amongst the finely wrought weapons of the Fyreslayers, the masterfully worked blades carried by members of the Forge Brethren are breathtaking to behold – and equally deadly. If the result of a wound roll in the combat phase for a model from the Forge Brethren is 6 or higher, subtract 1 from the result of the save roll for that attack.

**Bulwark of Molten Stone:** In your hero phase, a unit of Auric Hearthguard that is within 10" of the Runesmiter from their Forge Brethren can fashion makeshift defences with a sustained volley from their Magmapikes. Pick either the Auric Hearthguard themselves or another unit within 15". Add 1 to the result of any save rolls for that unit until your next hero phase, or until it makes a charge move.

# AURIC RUNEFATHER ON MAGMADROTH

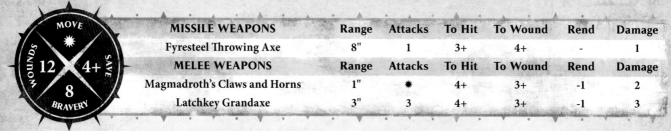

| MISSILE WEAPONS | Range | Attacks | To Hit | To Wound | Rend | Damage |
|---|---|---|---|---|---|---|
| Fyresteel Throwing Axe | 8" | 1 | 3+ | 4+ | - | 1 |
| **MELEE WEAPONS** | **Range** | **Attacks** | **To Hit** | **To Wound** | **Rend** | **Damage** |
| Magmadroth's Claws and Horns | 1" | ✱ | 4+ | 3+ | -1 | 2 |
| Latchkey Grandaxe | 3" | 3 | 4+ | 3+ | -1 | 3 |

MOVE 12" · SAVE 4+ · WOUNDS 8 · BRAVERY

| DAMAGE TABLE | | | |
|---|---|---|---|
| **Wounds Suffered** | **Move** | **Roaring Fyrestream** | **Claws and Horns** |
| 0-2 | 12" | 1 dice | 6 |
| 3-5 | 10" | 1 dice | 5 |
| 6-7 | 8" | 2 dice | 4 |
| 8-9 | 7" | 2 dice | 3 |
| 10+ | 6" | 3 dice | 2 |

## DESCRIPTION

An Auric Runefather on Magmadroth is a single model. He wields a mighty Latchkey Grandaxe, a symbol of office that unlocks the great vaults within his lodge's forge-temple, and he carries a brace of Fyresteel Throwing Axes. He takes to battle seated atop a terrifying Magmadroth, a volcanic creature with fire in its veins. It swipes at the foe with its Lashing Tail or tears them apart with its Claws and Horns.

## ABILITIES

**Roaring Fyrestream:** Throwing back its head, a Magmadroth can spew a wave of flaming bile that sears through armour as though it were wax. In your shooting phase, pick an enemy unit within 15" and roll a number of dice as shown on the damage table above. If the result is the same as or less than the number of models in the unit, the unit suffers D3 mortal wounds. If it is within 5" of the Magmadroth it suffers D6 mortal wounds instead.

**Lashing Tail:** Magmadroths use their tails to communicate with their kin, but also to slaughter scores of lesser prey with a single swipe. At the end of the combat phase, roll a dice for each enemy unit within 3" of the Magmadroth. If the result is less than the number of models in the unit, it suffers D3 mortal wounds.

**Volcanic Blood:** Magmadroths pulse with the heat of the volcanic caverns where they make their homes. At the end of each phase in which a Magmadroth suffered any wounds, roll a dice for each unit within 3". If the result is lower than the number of wounds the Magmadroth suffered during the phase, the unit is hit by a jet of fiery blood and suffers D3 mortal wounds. **FYRESLAYER** units, experienced at fighting alongside these beasts, only suffer wounds if the result of the roll is 1.

**Stare Down:** In your hero phase, the Runefather can fix an enemy unit within 3" with a level stare, the sort that can bring doubt to the mind of even the mightiest warrior. Subtract D3 from that unit's Bravery until your next hero phase.

**Weapon-breaker:** A Latchkey Grandaxe's unique design allows a Runefather to catch an enemy's weapon between the teeth and give a sharp twist. If the Runefather is attacked in the combat phase by a **HERO** or **MONSTER**, and the result of a save roll is 6 or higher, roll another dice. If the result is 4 or more, the attacking weapon is damaged for the rest of the battle. Your opponent must re-roll successful hit rolls for damaged weapons.

## COMMAND ABILITY

**Steadfast Advance:** Gazing sternly down from his throne atop a mighty Magmadroth, a Runefather can compel his kin to march into battle against a thousand times their number in search of ur-gold. If you use this ability, then until your next hero phase you can re-roll save rolls of 1 and battleshock tests for **FYRESLAYER** units from your army whilst they are within 20".

# AURIC RUNESMITER ON MAGMADROTH

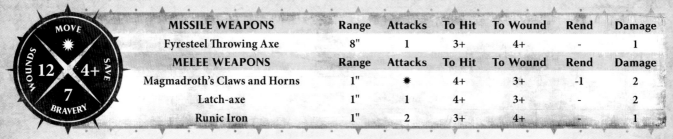

| MISSILE WEAPONS | Range | Attacks | To Hit | To Wound | Rend | Damage |
|---|---|---|---|---|---|---|
| Fyresteel Throwing Axe | 8" | 1 | 3+ | 4+ | - | 1 |
| **MELEE WEAPONS** | **Range** | **Attacks** | **To Hit** | **To Wound** | **Rend** | **Damage** |
| Magmadroth's Claws and Horns | 1" | ✷ | 4+ | 3+ | -1 | 2 |
| Latch-axe | 1" | 1 | 4+ | 3+ | - | 2 |
| Runic Iron | 1" | 2 | 3+ | 4+ | - | 1 |

| | DAMAGE TABLE | | |
|---|---|---|---|
| **Wounds Suffered** | **Move** | **Roaring Fyrestream** | **Claws and Horns** |
| 0-2 | 12" | 1 dice | 6 |
| 3-5 | 10" | 1 dice | 5 |
| 6-7 | 8" | 2 dice | 4 |
| 8-9 | 7" | 2 dice | 3 |
| 10+ | 6" | 3 dice | 2 |

## DESCRIPTION

An Auric Runesmiter on Magmadroth is a single model. The Runesmiter is armed with a Latch-axe, and many also carry Fyresteel Throwing Axes. Some Runesmiters also fight with a Runic Iron, while others bear a Forge Key – an ur-gold artefact with both symbolic and mystical power. He rides a great Magmadroth, which swipes at prey with a Lashing Tail and gouges them with its many Claws and Horns.

## ABILITIES

**Roaring Fyrestream:** Throwing back its head, a Magmadroth can spew a wave of flaming bile that sears through armour as though it were wax. In your shooting phase, pick an enemy unit within 15" and roll a number of dice as shown on the damage table above. If the result is the same as or less than the number of models in the unit, the unit suffers D3 mortal wounds. If it is within 5" of the Magmadroth it suffers D6 mortal wounds instead.

**Lashing Tail:** Magmadroths use their tails to communicate with their kin, but also to slaughter scores of lesser prey with a single swipe. At the end of the combat phase, roll a dice for each enemy unit within 3" of the Magmadroth. If the result is less than the number of models in the unit, it suffers D3 mortal wounds.

**Volcanic Blood:** Magmadroths pulse with the heat of the volcanic caverns where they make their homes. At the end of each phase in which a Magmadroth suffered any wounds, roll a dice for each unit within 3". If the result is lower than the number of wounds the Magmadroth suffered during the phase, the unit is hit by a jet of fiery blood and suffers D3 mortal wounds. **FYRESLAYER** units, experienced at fighting alongside these beasts, only suffer wounds if the result of the roll is 1.

**Runic Empowerment:** In your hero phase, a Runesmiter can raise his weapons and intone a sonorous chant, infusing the ur-gold runes set into the flesh of his Fyreslayer kin with power. Pick a unit of **FYRESLAYERS** within 10", or 20" if the Runesmiter bears a Forge Key. Until your next hero phase, you can re-roll failed wound rolls for that unit.

**Grand Ritual of Awakening:** Once per battle, the Runesmiter can consecrate a small nugget of ur-gold over the runic altar, then consume it to unleash a wave of energy. Until your next hero phase, re-roll failed wound rolls for **FYRESLAYER** units from your army whilst they are within 10" of the Runesmiter.

| KEYWORDS | ORDER, DUARDIN, MAGMADROTH, FYRESLAYERS, MONSTER, HERO, PRIEST, AURIC RUNESMITER |
|---|---|

# AURIC RUNESON ON MAGMADROTH

| MISSILE WEAPONS | Range | Attacks | To Hit | To Wound | Rend | Damage |
|---|---|---|---|---|---|---|
| Wyrmslayer Javelin | 12" | 1 | 3+ | 3+ | -1 | D3 |
| Fyresteel Throwing Axe | 8" | 1 | 3+ | 4+ | - | 1 |
| MELEE WEAPONS | Range | Attacks | To Hit | To Wound | Rend | Damage |
| Magmadroth's Claws and Horns | 1" | ☀ | 4+ | 3+ | -1 | 2 |
| Ancestral War-axe | 1" | 3 | 3+ | 4+ | - | D3 |
| Wyrmslayer Javelin | 3" | 1 | 4+ | 3+ | -1 | 1 |

**MOVE** ☀ **SAVE** 12 ⨯ 4+ 7 **WOUNDS** **BRAVERY**

| DAMAGE TABLE | | | |
|---|---|---|---|
| Wounds Suffered | Move | Roaring Fyrestream | Claws and Horns |
| 0-2 | 12" | 1 dice | 6 |
| 3-5 | 10" | 1 dice | 5 |
| 6-7 | 8" | 2 dice | 4 |
| 8-9 | 7" | 2 dice | 3 |
| 10+ | 6" | 3 dice | 2 |

## DESCRIPTION

An Auric Runeson on Magmadroth is a single model. Some Runesons wield an Ancestral War-axe, while others prefer a clutch of Wyrmslayer Javelins, but in either case they are armed with fine Fyresteel Throwing Axes. A Magmadroth is a great predator, attacking both with its Lashing Tail and its many Claws and Horns.

## ABILITIES

**Roaring Fyrestream:** Throwing back its head, a Magmadroth can spew a wave of flaming bile that sears through armour as though it were wax. In your shooting phase, pick an enemy unit within 15" and roll a number of dice as shown on the damage table above. If the result is the same as or less than the number of models in the unit, the unit suffers D3 mortal wounds. If it is within 5" of the Magmadroth it suffers D6 mortal wounds instead.

**Lashing Tail:** Magmadroths use their tails to communicate with their kin, but also to slaughter scores of lesser prey with a single swipe. At the end of the combat phase, roll a dice for each enemy unit within 3" of the Magmadroth. If the result is less than the number of models in the unit, it suffers D3 mortal wounds.

**Volcanic Blood:** Magmadroths pulse with the heat of the volcanic caverns where they make their homes. At the end of each phase in which a Magmadroth suffered any wounds, roll a dice for each unit within 3". If the result is lower than the number of wounds the Magmadroth suffered during the phase, the unit is hit by a jet of fiery blood and suffers D3 mortal wounds. **Fyreslayer** units, experienced at fighting alongside these beasts, only suffer wounds if the result of the roll is 1.

**Explosive Rage:** It takes very little to draw the ire of a Runeson, and they can go from smouldering contemplation to blazing anger in a heartbeat. In the hero phase, pick an enemy unit that is visible to the Runeson to be the subject of his latest outburst of wrath and rage. Until your next hero phase, you can re-roll hit rolls of 1 when the Runeson attacks that unit. In addition, if a battleshock test is made for the unit before your next hero phase, add 1 to the result of the dice roll if you can deliver a suitably characterful insult or furious put-down (aimed at the unit in question, of course – not your opponent!).

**Wyrmslayer Javelins:** These brutal missiles are best suited against large creatures, where their cruel hooks will catch onto thick hide before gouging deep. Add 2 to the Damage of a Wyrmslayer Javelin in the shooting phase if the target is a **Monster**.

## COMMAND ABILITY

**Furious Onslaught:** A Runeson is a master of utilising his indignant fury, not to mention his extensive vocabulary, to drive his kin deep into the enemy's ranks. If you use this ability, then until your next hero phase you can roll three dice (instead of two) and discard the lowest for any **Fyreslayer** units from your army that are within 10" of the Runeson when they charge.

| KEYWORDS | ORDER, DUARDIN, MAGMADROTH, FYRESLAYERS, HERO, MONSTER, AURIC RUNESON |
|---|---|

# AURIC RUNEFATHER

| | MOVE | | | |
|---|---|---|---|---|
| WOUNDS 6 | 4" | SAVE 4+ | | |
| | 8 | | | |
| | BRAVERY | | | |

| MISSILE WEAPONS | Range | Attacks | To Hit | To Wound | Rend | Damage |
|---|---|---|---|---|---|---|
| Fyresteel Throwing Axe | 8" | 1 | 3+ | 4+ | - | 1 |
| MELEE WEAPONS | Range | Attacks | To Hit | To Wound | Rend | Damage |
| Latchkey Grandaxe | 3" | 3 | 4+ | 3+ | -1 | 3 |

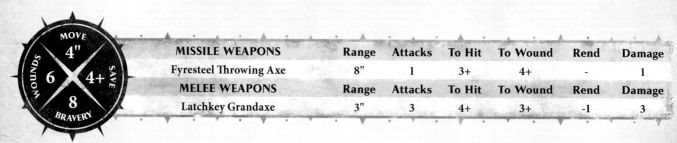

## DESCRIPTION

An Auric Runefather is a single model. He wields a Latchkey Grandaxe and carries a set of Fyresteel Throwing Axes.

## ABILITIES

**Stare Down:** In your hero phase, the Runefather can fix an enemy unit within 3" with a level stare, the sort that can bring doubt to the mind of even the mightiest warrior. Subtract D3 from that unit's Bravery until your next hero phase.

**Weapon-breaker:** A Latchkey Grandaxe's unique design allows a Runefather to catch an enemy's weapon between the teeth and give a sharp twist. If the Runefather is attacked in the combat phase by a **HERO** or **MONSTER**, and the result of a save roll is 6 or higher, roll another dice. If the result is 4 or more, the attacking weapon is damaged for the rest of the battle. Your opponent must re-roll successful hit rolls for damaged weapons.

## COMMAND ABILITY

**Lodge Leader:** Marching at the head of his army, a Runefather inspires fierce pride in the loyal warriors under his command. If you use this ability, then until your next hero phase, **FYRESLAYERS** within 8" of the Runefather can move up to 5" when they pile in. In addition, each time the Runefather suffers a wound or mortal wound, pick a **FYRESLAYER** unit from your army within 3" and roll a dice. If the result is 4 or more, the Fyreslayer unit suffers the wound instead of the Runefather.

| KEYWORDS | ORDER, DUARDIN, FYRESLAYERS, HERO, AURIC RUNEFATHER |
|---|---|

# AURIC RUNESMITER

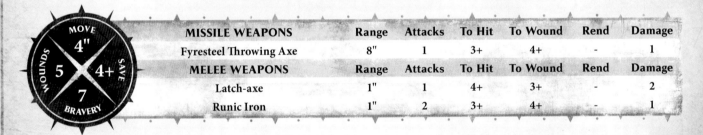

| MISSILE WEAPONS | Range | Attacks | To Hit | To Wound | Rend | Damage |
|---|---|---|---|---|---|---|
| Fyresteel Throwing Axe | 8" | 1 | 3+ | 4+ | - | 1 |
| MELEE WEAPONS | Range | Attacks | To Hit | To Wound | Rend | Damage |
| Latch-axe | 1" | 1 | 4+ | 3+ | - | 2 |
| Runic Iron | 1" | 2 | 3+ | 4+ | - | 1 |

**MOVE** 4"
**WOUNDS** 5
**SAVE** 4+
**BRAVERY** 7

## DESCRIPTION

An Auric Runesmiter is a single model. All Runesmiters carry a Latch-axe, and many also keep Fyresteel Throwing Axes close at hand. Some also bear a Runic Iron, as much a weapon as it is a tool of office. If a Runesmiter has proven himself worthy he might instead carry a Forge Key, an artefact of pure ur-gold forged from the remains of a deceased Runefather, which has both symbolic and mystical power.

## ABILITIES

**Runic Empowerment:** In your hero phase, a Runesmiter can raise his weapons and intone a sonorous chant, infusing the ur-gold runes set into the flesh of his Fyreslayer kin with power. Pick a unit of **Fyreslayers** within 10", or 20" if the Runesmiter bears a Forge Key. Until your next hero phase, you can re-roll failed wound rolls for that unit.

**Magmic Tunnelling:** When a Runesmiter sets his feet upon stone he can command it to flow aside and allow him passage. Instead of setting up an Auric Runesmiter and up to one other **Fyreslayer** unit, you can set them to one side and declare that they are underground. They can emerge in any of your movement phases; set up both units anywhere on the battlefield, within 3" of each other and more than 9" from the enemy. This counts as their move for that movement phase.

| KEYWORDS | ORDER, DUARDIN, FYRESLAYERS, HERO, PRIEST, AURIC RUNESMITER |
|---|---|

# AURIC RUNESON

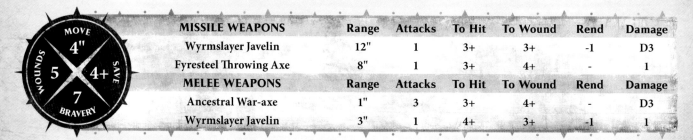

| | MOVE | | | |
|---|---|---|---|---|
| WOUNDS | **4"** | SAVE | | |
| **5** | | **4+** | | |
| **7** | | | | |
| BRAVERY | | | | |

| MISSILE WEAPONS | Range | Attacks | To Hit | To Wound | Rend | Damage |
|---|---|---|---|---|---|---|
| Wyrmslayer Javelin | 12" | 1 | 3+ | 3+ | -1 | D3 |
| Fyresteel Throwing Axe | 8" | 1 | 3+ | 4+ | - | 1 |
| MELEE WEAPONS | Range | Attacks | To Hit | To Wound | Rend | Damage |
| Ancestral War-axe | 1" | 3 | 3+ | 4+ | - | D3 |
| Wyrmslayer Javelin | 3" | 1 | 4+ | 3+ | -1 | 1 |

## DESCRIPTION

An Auric Runeson is a single model. Some Runesons wield an Ancestral War-axe, while others prefer Wyrmslayer Javelins. They also carry Fyresteel Throwing Axes.

## ABILITIES

**Wyrmslayer Javelins:** A Runeson armed with these javelins can bring down even the fiercest creatures. Add 2 to the Damage of a Wyrmslayer Javelin in the shooting phase if the target is a **MONSTER**.

**Explosive Rage:** In the hero phase, pick an enemy unit that is visible to the Runeson to be the subject of his latest outburst of wrath and rage. Until your next hero phase, you can re-roll hit rolls of 1 when the Runeson attacks that unit. In addition, if a battleshock test is made for the unit before your next hero phase, add 1 to the result of the dice roll if you can deliver a suitably characterful insult or furious put-down (aimed at the unit in question, of course – not your opponent!).

## COMMAND ABILITY

**Dauntless Assault:** Runesons are intrepid to the last; to them, even the most fearsome enemy is simply a worthy challenge for the Fyreslayers. If you use this ability, then until your next hero phase you can re-roll failed wound rolls for the Runeson and any **FYRESLAYER** units from your army within 15" if the unit they are attacking has a Wounds characteristic of 3 or more.

| KEYWORDS | ORDER, DUARDIN, FYRESLAYERS, HERO, AURIC RUNESON |
|---|---|

# GRIMWRATH BERZERKER

| MOVE 4" | | | | | | |
|---|---|---|---|---|---|---|

| MISSILE WEAPONS | Range | Attacks | To Hit | To Wound | Rend | Damage |
|---|---|---|---|---|---|---|
| Fyresteel Throwing Axe | 8" | 1 | 3+ | 4+ | - | 1 |
| MELEE WEAPONS | Range | Attacks | To Hit | To Wound | Rend | Damage |
| Fyrestorm Greataxe | 1" | 4 | 3+ | 3+ | -1 | D3 |

Stat wheel: MOVE 4", WOUNDS 6, SAVE 4+, BRAVERY 9

## DESCRIPTION
A Grimwrath Berzerker is a single model armed with a Fyrestorm Greataxe. Some also carry Fyresteel Throwing Axes.

## ABILITIES
**Unstoppable Berzerker:** Each time a Grimwrath Berzerker suffers a wound or mortal wound, roll a dice, adding 1 to the result for each enemy unit within 3". If the result is 6 or more, he is too enraged to notice the wound and it has no effect.

**Dead, But Not Defeated:** Tales abound of mortally wounded Grimwrath Berzerkers still fighting on, determined to wreak destruction upon whichever fools had the temerity to kill them. If a Grimwrath Berzerker is slain in the combat phase, roll a dice. If the result is 2 or more, he is not removed as a casualty until the end of the phase, and in the meantime can still pile in and attack as normal.

**Battle Fury:** As a Grimwrath Berzerker hews left and right with his Greataxe, felling scores of foes, he enters a state of single-minded frenzy. Once per turn, after this model has made its attacks, you can roll a dice. If the result is less than the number of wounds that the Grimwrath Berzerker has inflicted this phase and there are still enemy models within 3", he can immediately pile in and attack again.

| KEYWORDS | ORDER, DUARDIN, FYRESLAYERS, HERO, GRIMWRATH BERZERKER |
|---|---|

# AURIC RUNEMASTER

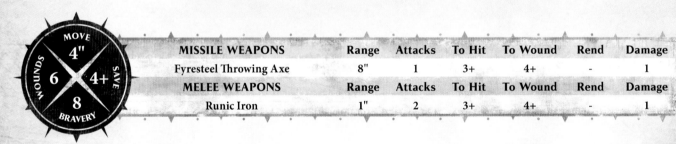

| MISSILE WEAPONS | Range | Attacks | To Hit | To Wound | Rend | Damage |
|---|---|---|---|---|---|---|
| Fyresteel Throwing Axe | 8" | 1 | 3+ | 4+ | - | 1 |
| MELEE WEAPONS | Range | Attacks | To Hit | To Wound | Rend | Damage |
| Runic Iron | 1" | 2 | 3+ | 4+ | - | 1 |

**MOVE** 4"
**WOUNDS** 6
**SAVE** 4+
**BRAVERY** 8

## DESCRIPTION

An Auric Runemaster is a single model. He is armed with a Runic Iron and Fyresteel Throwing Axes.

## ABILITIES

**Holy Seeker:** After set-up is complete, your opponent must pick a unit from their army to be the unwitting bearers of a small amount of ur-gold. Your opponent can re-roll wound rolls of 1 for that unit, but if the Runemaster is within 10" of it at the end of any of your movement phases, he spots a tell-tale glint and gives a triumphant cry. For the rest of the battle, add 1 to the Attacks characteristic of any weapons used by FYRESLAYERS to attack that unit.

**Volcano's Call:** In your hero phase, this model can hold aloft his staff and speak words of power, coaxing a stream of magma to bubble up from the ground. Pick a terrain feature within 20" and roll a dice for each model within 1" of it. For each roll of a 6, that model's unit suffers a mortal wound. In addition, until your next hero phase, roll a dice for any model that makes a run or charge move across, or finishing on, this terrain feature. On a roll of 1, the model is slain.

**KEYWORDS** | ORDER, DUARDIN, FYRESLAYERS, HERO, PRIEST, AURIC RUNEMASTER

# BATTLESMITH

| MOVE | 4" |
|---|---|
| WOUNDS | 5 |
| SAVE | 4+ |
| BRAVERY | 7 |

| MISSILE WEAPONS | Range | Attacks | To Hit | To Wound | Rend | Damage |
|---|---|---|---|---|---|---|
| Fyresteel Throwing Axe | 8" | 1 | 3+ | 4+ | - | 1 |
| MELEE WEAPONS | Range | Attacks | To Hit | To Wound | Rend | Damage |
| Ancestral Battle-axe | 1" | 3 | 3+ | 3+ | -1 | 1 |

## DESCRIPTION

A Battlesmith is a single model. He is armed with an Ancestral Battle-axe and carries an Icon of Grimnir. Some Battlesmiths also carry a brace of Fyresteel Throwing Axes.

## ABILITIES

**Icon of Grimnir:** In your hero phase, you can declare that a Battlesmith will raise his icon of Grimnir and recount tales of past glories, inspiring all **FYRESLAYER** units from your army within 8" to fight to the bitter end. Until your next hero phase, those units (including the Battlesmith) cannot retreat, but you can re-roll failed save rolls for them.

**None Shall Defile the Icon:** The holy icon of Grimnir is one of the strongest connections the Fyreslayers have to their absent god, and they will not see it lost. If this model is slain, any **FYRESLAYER** units from your army within 5" can swear to protect the fallen icon. These units cannot move for the rest of the battle other than to pile in, but you can re-roll any failed hit and wound rolls for their attacks.

| KEYWORDS | ORDER, DUARDIN, FYRESLAYERS, HERO, TOTEM, BATTLESMITH |
|---|---|

# VULKITE BERZERKERS

| MISSILE WEAPONS | Range | Attacks | To Hit | To Wound | Rend | Damage |
|---|---|---|---|---|---|---|
| Fyresteel Throwing Axe | 8" | 1 | 4+ | 4+ | - | 1 |
| **MELEE WEAPONS** | **Range** | **Attacks** | **To Hit** | **To Wound** | **Rend** | **Damage** |
| Fyresteel Handaxe | 1" | 2 | 4+ | 3+ | - | 1 |
| Fyresteel War-pick | 1" | 2 | 4+ | 4+ | -1 | 1 |

**MOVE** 4"
**WOUNDS** 1
**SAVE** 5+
**BRAVERY** 7

## DESCRIPTION

A unit of Vulkite Berzerkers has 5 or more models. Some units of Vulkite Berzerkers are armed with Fyresteel Handaxes or War-picks and carry Bladed Slingshields, while other units fight with a Fyresteel Handaxe in each hand. Some also carry well-balanced Fyresteel Throwing Axes at their belts.

## KARL

The leader of this unit is the Karl. A Karl's Fyresteel Handaxe or Fyresteel War-pick causes 2 Damage rather than 1.

## HORN OF GRIMNIR

Models in this unit may carry a horn of Grimnir. After making a charge roll for a unit that contains any horns of Grimnir, you can sound the advance and re-roll one of the dice.

## ABILITIES

**Berserk Fury:** Vulkite Berzerkers are as stubborn as they are resilient – even the deadliest blows fail to slow their advance. Each time this unit suffers a wound or mortal wound, roll a dice. If the result is 6 or higher, the wound is ignored. Add 1 to the result if the unit had 10 or more models at the start of the phase, or 2 if it had 20 or more; after all, no Vulkite Berzerker will easily accept death's embrace while his kin are still fighting.

**Fyresteel Handaxes:** When attacking with two Fyresteel Handaxes, a Vulkite Berzerker can easily turn aside an enemy's defence before landing a flurry of furious blows. Re-roll failed hit rolls for models armed with two Fyresteel Handaxes.

**Bladed Slingshield:** Some Vulkite Berzerkers carry razor-sharp shields which they hurl at the enemy as they charge. After a unit with Bladed Slingshields makes a charge move, pick an enemy unit within ½" and roll a dice for each model carrying a Bladed Slingshield. For each result of 6, the unit you picked suffers a mortal wound. Vulkite Berzerkers carrying Bladed Slingshields have a Save of 4+ in the combat phase of turns in which they did not charge.

**KEYWORDS** | ORDER, DUARDIN, FYRESLAYERS, VULKITE BERZERKERS

# AURIC HEARTHGUARD

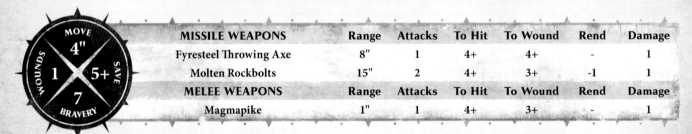

| MISSILE WEAPONS | Range | Attacks | To Hit | To Wound | Rend | Damage |
|---|---|---|---|---|---|---|
| Fyresteel Throwing Axe | 8" | 1 | 4+ | 4+ | - | 1 |
| Molten Rockbolts | 15" | 2 | 4+ | 3+ | -1 | 1 |
| MELEE WEAPONS | Range | Attacks | To Hit | To Wound | Rend | Damage |
| Magmapike | 1" | 1 | 4+ | 3+ | - | 1 |

Move 4"
Wounds 1
Save 5+
Bravery 7

## DESCRIPTION

A unit of Auric Hearthguard has 5 or more models. They are each armed with a Magmapike, a bladed polearm that can loose Molten Rockbolts at the enemy. Some units also carry Fyresteel Throwing Axes as a backup weapon.

## KARL

The leader of this unit is the Karl. A Karl's Magmapike causes 2 Damage rather than 1.

## ABILITIES

**Molten Rockbolts:** Magmapikes spit gobbets of molten rock that solidify around large targets, and Hearthguard often use them to ensnare wild Magmadroths. Roll a dice at the end of the shooting phase for each **Monster** that was wounded by a Molten Rockbolt but was not slain. On a result of 5 or more, it is encased in rapidly cooling stone. Until the end of its next turn, halve its Move and subtract 1 from any hit rolls for its attacks.

**Sworn Protectors:** Auric Hearthguard are fiercely protective of those who rule the lodges that they guard. Add 1 to the result of any hit rolls for Auric Hearthguard if their target unit is within 5" of a **Fyreslayer Hero** from your army.

| KEYWORDS | ORDER, DUARDIN, FYRESLAYERS, AURIC HEARTHGUARD |
|---|---|

# HEARTHGUARD BERZERKERS

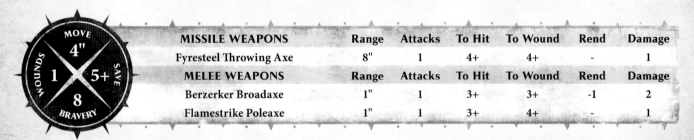

| MISSILE WEAPONS | Range | Attacks | To Hit | To Wound | Rend | Damage |
|---|---|---|---|---|---|---|
| Fyresteel Throwing Axe | 8" | 1 | 4+ | 4+ | - | 1 |
| MELEE WEAPONS | Range | Attacks | To Hit | To Wound | Rend | Damage |
| Berzerker Broadaxe | 1" | 1 | 3+ | 3+ | -1 | 2 |
| Flamestrike Poleaxe | 1" | 1 | 3+ | 4+ | - | 1 |

**MOVE** 4"
**WOUNDS** 1
**SAVE** 5+
**BRAVERY** 8

## DESCRIPTION

A unit of Hearthguard Berzerkers has 5 or more models. Some units wield mighty Berzerker Broadaxes, while others carry Flamestrike Poleaxes, trailing smouldering braziers on lengths of chain. Some units also carry Fyresteel Throwing Axes.

## KARL

The leader of this unit is the Karl. A Karl's Berzerker Broadaxe inflicts 3 Damage rather than 2, and a Karl's Flamestrike Poleaxe inflicts 2 Damage rather than 1.

## ABILITIES

**Duty Unto Death:** Hearthguard Berzerkers are sworn to protect their lodge and its masters to their dying breath. Each time this unit suffers a wound or mortal wound, roll a dice. If the result is 6 or higher, the wound is ignored. Add 2 to the result if there is a **Fyreslayer Hero** from your army within 10" of this unit.

**Smouldering Braziers:** With each swing of a Flamestrike Poleaxe, the brazier chained to it arcs toward the foe, sparks and fire trailing in its wake. Each time a model attacking with a Flamestrike Poleaxe scores a hit, roll a dice. If the result is 3 or more the target suffers a mortal wound after the attacks have been resolved.

| KEYWORDS | ORDER, DUARDIN, FYRESLAYERS, HEARTHGUARD BERZERKERS |
|---|---|

# THE GLORY OF AZYRHEIM

**A city like no other, Azyrheim is the last of its kind. Behind its high alabaster walls dwell men, aelves, duardin and more: the resolute survivors of the Age of Chaos. Far from a simple relic of a lost past, Azyrheim is a bastion of Order, a validation of the power of unity and a symbol of hope unwaning.**

The city of Azyrheim was founded long ago, early in the time now known as the Age of Myth. It was the God-King Sigmar who chose the glorious tract of land, a location at the very heart of the sprawling realm of Azyr, and directly below Sigendil, the High Star. He himself laid the city's first stones, and the walls grew quickly, for there the divine and mortal kind laboured alongside one another – man and god working as one. All the members of Sigmar's pantheon lent their matchless powers and craft, so that out of nothing rose high-pillared halls and domed buildings. Spinning orreries captured the light of the heavens, and many of Azyrheim's fountains splashed not with water, but with streams of celestial energy. Below ground the duardin carved out many kingdoms' worth of holds and mines, grand passages that led to vast quarries and forgeworks.

In Azyrheim, as in the other great cities rising across the Mortal Realms, Order was made manifest. There grew a place of culture, learning and wonder. It was a city of harmony, as many races worked together, sharing their expertise so that within a few generations Azyrheim had doubled in size, then doubled again. The varied tribes forsook their feral existences, making their homes instead in this new nation-city. Trade from distant lands poured into Azyrheim, even materials

from the other realms, for the city stood near the Three Brethren – a trio of Realmgates, each leading to different lands. Soon, the city walls encompassed the Three Brethren, stretching past the horizon. Each new day brought greater prosperity and still greater possibilities.

And then Chaos came.

From out of the Realm of Chaos, the daemons brought hellfire and contamination, bloodshed and disease. Foul forces and horrific monsters marched to war, swift and terrible. Multiple incursions burst across the realms of Ghyran, Ghur, Aqshy, Hysh, Ulgu, Shyish, and Chamon. Azyr alone was spared the worst of the invasions, or so it seemed. Many believed the favoured lands of Sigmar would remain safe from the corruptions of the Dark Gods, but they were wrong.

Aware of only a few beasts that stalked his realm, Sigmar worried more about the daemon legions assailing the other realms. In haste, the God-King gathered the citizen warhosts of Azyrheim. Out marched duardin from their underground districts – the Dispossessed, the bitter remnants of the Khazalid empires, and the Ironweld Arsenal alliances they formed with mankind. Aelves from the Phoenix Temple formed silent phalanxes while great horns called the Lion Rangers

out of the wilds. The nations of mankind united beneath proud city banners, marching out with their allies to do battle. Alongside them came armies of older, stranger heritage. As Azyrheim had been built to last forever, some called it the Eternal City. However, there was another reason for the moniker. In several quarters of Azyrheim time travelled slowly, or perhaps not at all. There, the folk spoke the common tongue with accents that came not from the vastness of the Mortal Realms, but from a time older still. Few recognized such elder signs and only Sigmar and the Eldritch Council knew the truth, but there could be no doubt those armies were eager to sate long-held vendettas against the Dark Gods.

Even as Sigmar and the armies of Azyrheim fought great battles in the other realms, corrupting forces wormed their way into Azyr. The valiant Freeguild Guard of Azyrheim rallied to keep their grand city safe, a refuge open to those kingdoms elsewhere that were overwhelmed. In the other realms, Sigmar and his pantheon initially drove off the invaders. Yet such victories grew more difficult and more costly, and before long the fighting bogged down into arduous campaigns that struggled to stave off disasters across the Mortal Realms. The Chaos threat only grew, increasing across thousands of different

fronts. One by one the alliances of Order were splintered by the pressure, and many defeats followed. For the first time, the call of betrayal was heard, as former brothers in arms turned upon one another in anger. After the great loss at the Battle of the Burning Skies and the ensuing Nexus Wars, Sigmar had seen enough. The God-King retreated with his remaining armies, returning to Azyr. He ordered all Realmgates leading to that realm locked behind him.

The Three Brethren were the last of the Gates of Azyr to be locked, and thus the last of the refuges flooded directly into Azyrheim. No further foes could enter Azyr, and Sigmar decreed that the Cleansing begin – a systematic search to root out and destroy all influences of Chaos throughout his realm. Yet even as the God-King did so, trouble erupted

in Azyrheim itself. The varied races of the city had always coexisted, if not in complete agreement, then at least peaceably. This swiftly came to an end in a terrible civil war. Armies marched and one-time allies turned upon each other in a flurry of bloodshed. In the midst of battle, Sigmar himself appeared in the heart of the city, his first return to Azyrheim since he stormed back to Sigmaron and ordered the gates closed behind him. Lightnings blazing in the God-King's eyes and he was terrible in his wrath. The Chaos Sorcerers and daemons at the root of the uprisings were destroyed, and those beguiled by Chaos were swiftly slain. Furthermore, such was his fury that any who could not let go of their need for vengeance were turned to cinders by Sigmar's gaze. These were hard times and the God-King would brook no lingering hatred. Never again have

the forces of Chaos entered Azyrheim, and since that great battle the first Grand Conclave was formed, chosen by Sigmar himself. Upon his command, the armies combined under the Lords of the Heavenhall.

The Grand Conclave was ceaseless in its vigilance, sending army after army out across Azyr to scour the lands. It took centuries of battle to eradicate the last vestiges of Chaos from the realm. Since Gorkamorka had led the Great Waaagh! and turned upon the pantheon of Sigmar, the orruks too were sought out, the armies of Azyrheim hunting down greenskins to the ends of Azyr. The monsters that stalked the inhabited kingdoms were likewise slain, although to this day the hinterlands and the stars themselves remain breeding grounds for countless more creatures.

The armies of Azyrheim have remained active and regularly send patrols to confront the beasts native to Azyr, even though they no longer bear even the slightest taint of Chaos. However, though Azyr seemed free of corruption, the same could not be said of the other realms…

As the Age of Chaos blazed across the Mortal Realms, it was not long before the last of the great cities fell to ruin, their populaces scattered or slain. Azyrheim stood alone. Everywhere else, the legions of Chaos reigned, subjecting the lands and peoples of the Mortal Realms to the cruellest of whims. Meanwhile, Azyrheim grew stronger, but they had not forgotten the lands from which they were cast, nor

had they ever lost sight of the ultimate goal that united each of their many factions: revenge.

At last, with great thunder from Sigmar's floating palace in the Heavens, a new age was begun. The God-King unleashed his Stormcast Eternals and once more the gates of Azyr were opened. Long had the peoples of Azyrheim awaited such an hour and they rejoiced at the sight of the winged Knights-Azyros that heralded this new era. Fanfares swept over the city, a clarion call of battle. Always on a war footing, the Grand Conclave called for crusades, and armies gathered to march on campaigns of their own, or to fight alongside the Stormcast Eternals as Sigmar launched the

growing Realmgate Wars. Still others prepared to retake their ancestral lands, or visit revenge against the most reviled warlords of Chaos. In the heavens above, the star of Sigmar shone brighter than ever, the God-King's palace flashing with lightning. Already Scourge Privateer fleets had set sail from the vast Azyrheim docks, their eager aelf crews plying the watery realmgates to travel afar. Dragonlords had taken to the skies, ancient princes returning to the hunting grounds of their forefathers to recover lost heirlooms or rescue fresh dragon eggs. All knew that this new age of battle would herald a return to greatness, or mark the last charge of those doomed to fall before the onslaught of Chaos.

# CHAOS

Beyond the boundaries of reality lies the ever-changing Realm of Chaos. There, the Dark Gods rule supreme. However, it is their nature to hunger after all they espy, and they covet the Mortal Realms, forever warring and scheming to conquer them. These vile deities are Khorne, the god of battle, Nurgle, the lord of disease, and Tzeentch, the god of sorcery and deceit. Slaanesh, the fourth Dark God and lord of excess, is lost, and his followers seek him throughout the realms. Vying for a place in the pantheon is the Great Horned Rat, the god of blight and pestilence. Each of the gods seeks dominance over his rivals, but they unite in common cause when doing so best serves their rapacious needs. The daemon legions are theirs to command, as are the creatures of Chaos – twisted monsters, corrupted mortals, and the ratmen known as skaven.

# THE GRAND CONCLAVE

A senate representing the city's largest factions originally governed Azyrheim. It was this body, in part, that enabled the infiltration of Sigmar's city by the agents of Chaos and caused the ensuing civil war. In the aftermath of that war, it was Sigmar himself who appointed the first of the new leaders, standing in the largest of the remaining temples built to his glory. The God-King called forth two hundred and forty-four of the city's finest leaders, bestowing upon each of them a title and command. They were chosen not by race, or for their political prowess, but for individual strengths. Their new authority crossed city district, race, and religion. Thus four of the six High Artisans were duardin, one an aelf, the other a human, yet they controlled the building and engineering work across all of Azyrheim. So it was with titles for civic duties or command of armies and navies. Each of Sigmar's appointees understood their primary duty: to unify and protect. It was decreed that they would meet regularly in that very temple, so Sigmar created a massive hammer-shaped table and set it before his own starmetal statue. Rarely would he attend, he said, but beneath the gaze of his statue they might still draw on his wisdom, or, failing that, at least remember his wrath. This ruling body was known as the Grand Conclave, and the individual members became known as the Lords of the Heavenhall, after the building in which they met. Always they have numbered two hundred and forty-four, and always they have served Azyrheim in the name of Order and the God-King himself, setting aside their own agendas to work for the betterment of all.

# THE WINGS OF AZYR

**When the citizens of the foundling cities cry out for aid it is the Wings of Azyr that they hope will descend from the heavens. Forged from the greatest heroes of Order, the formation fills the sky with mythic beasts, celestial dragons and winged warriors alight with the might of Azyr.**

The Drakesworn Templars are legendary champions of the Stormcast Eternals. These Stardrake riders are among the greatest of Sigmar's warriors in the realms, and like the High Star that shines down upon Azyrheim, are an example to all that set eyes upon them. In times of direst need it is the Drakesworn Templars around which the heroes of the Eternal City gather. These heavenly lords swoop down from Sigmaron, often with Prosecutor escorts, to come to the aid of Sigmar's people. They are joined by dragon- and griffon-riders to form the Wings of Azyr – often the only force able to reach beleaguered cities in time and strong enough to make a difference.

Where the ravening minions of the Dark Gods try to tear down what the Free Peoples have built up, or reclaim lands conquered by the Stormhosts, the Wings of Azyr darken the skies. Through twisting pillars of smoke and embers, aelf dragon-riders swoop down into the fray. Screaming servants of Chaos are snatched up and torn apart or hurled back into their kin to break and burst upon the ground. Griffon-riding generals rip into the foe, creating a crimson storm with flashing talons and brilliant steel. Aelf and human sorcerers lend their powers to the Wings of Azyr, and from the backs of their noble beasts unleash earth-shattering spells. Men and beasts are turned into clouds of flaming meat or explode from within, their bones erupting into crimson shards. The most formidable warriors amongst the Wings of Azyr, though, are the Drakesworn Templars and Prosecutors. Fuelled by celestial lightning, they lay waste to vast swathes of the battlefield.

Many battles have been turned by the timely arrival of the Wings of Azyr, and many citizens of the Mortal Realms live only because of their valour. Cities that counted their future in but a few savage blood-filled hours have seen the enemy turned back from their gates. Emerging into a smouldering battlefield, the citizens behold fields of the dead, torn, twisted and blackened by fire. Looking up into the sky, they might catch a glimpse of draconic silhouettes swooping off into the Heavens.

# STONEBREAKER BATTALION

**Great fortresses dedicated to the Dark Gods cover the lands like a collar of bloody iron. To bring down these edifices of evil the Stormhosts often call upon the Stonebreaker Battalions of Azyrheim, each one adept at reducing even the most impressive keep to naught but dust and rubble.**

Centuries of tyranny and torment have seen the minions of Chaos cement their control of the realms. Skull-covered fortresses and great brass bastions rise above kingdoms littered with bones, their foundations digging into the ground like meat hooks driven through a carcass. To shatter the hold these places have upon the lands, the Lords of the Heavenhall muster their Stonebreaker Battalions. They call upon the skills of the Ironweld Arsenal, and gun lines and cunning engineer lords gather, eager to bring their weapons to bear against the ancient foe. Cannons roar, sending solid shot crashing into ensorcelled stone, while Gyrocopters sweep overhead, clearing

the ramparts and towers of defenders. Once a breach has been wrought by the thundering war machines, the allies of the Ironweld pour into the gap to take the fort. Here the grim determination of the Dispossessed comes into its own, and the duardin often take the lead in such attacks. Ironbreakers clad in thick plate bull their way forward, while Hammerers and Longbeards reap a hefty toll upon any enemies that stand in their way. With systematic precision the Dispossessed destroy the fortress, killing every defender and then setting about reducing the walls to rubble. As they go about their work, the guns and war machines of the Ironweld Arsenal continue to hammer the defences. Stormcast Eternal troops may also lend their might to the Stonebreakers, especially against the most formidable of enemy defences. Should a Lord-Celestant decree it, his warriors will march alongside the Ironweld engineers and Dispossessed. The firepower of Judicators blasts the servants of Chaos from the walls or scythes down enemy counter-attacks, while Retributors form the face of the hammer, smashing an entrance for the duardin and human troops to exploit. In this way, many of the greatest bastions of the Ruinous Powers have fallen to the Stonebreaker Battalions. The Wyrdflame Shard of Firegulf and its Arcanite hosts, the Bloodbrass Bridgeforts and the Rotfanes of Gurgli have all been marked as victories on the standards of the Stonebreakers.

# AZYRHEIM LANCEHOST

**A glittering forest of spear tips and blades greets the light of the High Star as an Azyrheim Lancehost rides forth from the gates of the Eternal City. A keen sword wielded by an arm of martial pride and skill, it punches through the opposing ranks leaving a trail of shattered defenders behind.**

When the armies of Order have need of not just speed and skill but also a hammer strong enough to shatter any defence, they turn to the Lancehosts. Born of the informal councils between the martial orders and Freeguilds,

and augmented with the cream of the Dracothian Guard, it is a rolling storm of hooves, claws and wheels that scythes apart everything it meets. Enemies have been known to turn tail and flee at the very sight of such

a formation, their breath and courage stolen by its terrible majesty. It is said that even before a Lancehost has crested the horizon its presence can already be felt. The ground shakes to the rumbling beat of countless steeds,

while a glow suffuses the sky as the light of the heavens is reflected from polished helms and shields. When at last the knights gallop into view, it is as if a tide of steel is rising to consume their enemies. Proud aelf nobles upon purebred steeds stand shoulder to shoulder with drakespawn riders and Demigryph Knights, their snarling mounts and wicked weapons promising swift death. To stand before such a force is to know the remainder of your life can be measured in seconds.

In the first battles after the opening of the gates of Azyr, the Lancehosts were made of but aelves and men. Sigmar watched their early battles with interest, and as the hosts thundered out into the Igneous Delta in the wake of Korghos Khul's defeat, they reaped a hefty toll from the Chaos tribes still plaguing the burning plains.

So pleased was the God-King with the bravery of these mortal warriors that he despatched some of his Dracothian

Guard to aid their campaigns. So it was that the Lancehosts grew in size and strength, and wherever the storms of war raged, their banners snapped in the wind and their warriors bore down upon the servants of the Dark Gods.

Since those first campaigns the Azyrheim Lancehosts have grown in size and scale. Though each of the city's knightly orders maintains its own traditions and agendas, when Sigmar requests their aid they will fight as one.

# LEGIONS OF RECONQUEST

**The lords of the Stormhosts lead the armies of the Azyrheim in wars of reconquest. The soldiers of the Eternal City are eager for their long-awaited retribution now the gates of Azyr yawn wide, and Stormcast Eternals and mortal warriors fight side by side, restoring the rule of Order to the realms.**

Beyond the gates of Azyrheim rage wars of vengeance and reclamation. Where the Stormhosts have scoured the lands, the Legions of Reconquest follow. Many Lord-Celestants have been charged by Sigmar to lead the free armies of Azyr and cement the Stormcasts' hold in the war-ravaged realms. So vast are the battlefields and so numerous the enemy's strongholds that Sigmar must use every loyal warrior he can muster. These legions serve to supplement the Stormcast Eternals, but perhaps more importantly they restore the pride and hope of men, aelves and duardin, who see the enemy is not invincible and that the armies of the Dark Gods can be beaten.

Ranks of soldiers and noble sons of Azyrheim have sworn their allegiance to the lords of the Stormhosts. The towering Stormcast Eternals move among the mortals like gods of war, their gleaming armour a beacon of the God-King's strength. When battle is joined the Stormcasts are the vanguard, wading into the fray with crackling hammers and ready blades. Inspired by the example of Sigmar's champions, their allies hurl themselves against their opponents. Drawing their soldiery from the free races of the realms, the Legions of Reconquest can take many forms. Proud Dragonlords ride beside lightning-winged Prosecutors, stout Dispossessed duardin form shield walls next to sigmarite-clad Liberators, while the fervent prayers of Lord-Relictors and the Devoted rouse a mighty chorus to the glory of Sigmar.

Fighting with the Freeguilds, the Stormhosts secure fortresses to garrison and push back raiding tribes and marauding beasts; the Devoted fight bitterly to secure sites of divine power, often with the aid of the Stormcast Eternals. In addition to those armies that march forth from the gates of Azyrheim, some legions also set out from the foundling cities now taking root in the realms. These new bastions of Order, founded since the opening of the gates of Azyr, welcome the aid of Sigmar's chosen, but have staunch warriors of their own that march to their defence and that of their allies.

# DEVOTED OF SIGMAR

**The God-King Sigmar rules over Azyrheim like a blazing golden sun, and in his light mortals venerate his holy name. As the Stormcast Eternals conquer and capture gateways in the Mortal Realms, the Devoted march out in their wake, consecrating the ground in the name of the Heldenhammer.**

Sigmar has always inspired faith and fanaticism in his followers, and the citizens of Azyrheim are no exception. From the glittering Hallowhammer Cathedrals that fill the Devotional Districts of the city to the wayshrines that litter the roads the length and breadth of Azyr, there worship men and women willing to do anything for their celestial lord.

As the Storm of Sigmar rolls across the Mortal Realms it is the Devoted who follow closest in its shadow. Across the tortured land they march in huge chanting processions. Most are dressed only in rags, for there can be no possession more important than their faith in Sigmar. Throngs of Flagellants bless the ground with bloody feet and chanted prayer. When they encounter men or beasts corrupted by Chaos, they fall upon them with rabid fervour.

Alongside the zealous ranks of the Devoted stand the Witch Hunters of the Order of Azyr. Hardened trackers, they root out the taint of Chaos in the newfound kingdoms of the realms. Like vengeful shadows they move among the cities of the Azyrite peoples, whispering in the ears of the Devoted and the city lords. Together, Devoted and Witch Hunters serve as willing warriors in Sigmar's armies of reconquest, ever eager to purge the stain Chaos has left upon the Mortal Realms.

### DEVOTED OF SIGMAR
# PILGRIMAGE OF WRATH

**Lashing the ground upon which they march, the Pilgrimage of Wrath cleanses the realms through bloody sacrifice, its warriors tearing apart the foe as its priests chant the word of the Heldenhammer.**

## ORGANISATION

A Pilgrimage of Wrath consists of the following units:

- 1 War Altar of Sigmar
- 2 Warrior Priests
- 1 Witch Hunter
- 2 units of Flagellants

## ABILITIES

**Slay the Unbelievers!:** The close proximity of a War Altar and the rousing oratory of Warrior Priests drives Flagellants into a righteous fury. Such is their zeal that they hurl themselves at nearby enemies with crazed abandon. Roll a dice in your hero phase for each unit of Flagellants from the Pilgrimage that is within 12" of their War Altar and within 3" of an enemy unit. Add 1 to the dice roll for each Warrior Priest from the same battalion that is within 6" of the unit you are rolling for. The total is the number of models from that unit of Flagellants that lash out at the foe (this cannot exceed the number of models left in the unit). Roll a dice for each of these models; for each result of 4 or more, the closest enemy unit to the Flagellants suffers a mortal wound.

# WAR ALTAR OF SIGMAR

| MISSILE WEAPONS | Range | Attacks | To Hit | To Wound | Rend | Damage |
|---|---|---|---|---|---|---|
| Light of Banishment | 20" | D3 | 3+ | ✸ | -1 | 3 |
| MELEE WEAPONS | Range | Attacks | To Hit | To Wound | Rend | Damage |
| Sigmarite Greathammer | 1" | 3 | 4+ | 3+ | -1 | 1 |
| Sigmarite Warhammer | 1" | 4 | 4+ | 4+ | - | 1 |
| Staff of Sigmar | 1" | 1 | 4+ | 3+ | - | D3 |
| Warhorses' Steel-shod Hooves | 1" | 4 | 4+ | 4+ | - | 1 |

MOVE ✸ SAVE 4+
WOUNDS 11
7
BRAVERY

| DAMAGE TABLE | | | |
|---|---|---|---|
| Wounds Suffered | Move | Sigmar's Shield | Light of Banishment |
| 0-2 | 10" | 15" | 2+ |
| 3-4 | 9" | 12" | 3+ |
| 5-6 | 8" | 9" | 3+ |
| 7-8 | 7" | 6" | 4+ |
| 9+ | 6" | 3" | 4+ |

## DESCRIPTION

A War Altar of Sigmar is a single model. It is a vast battle altar pulled into battle by a pair of Warhorses who trample those in their path with Steel-shod hooves. Atop the altar is a Golden Griffon – a vast statue imbued with holy magic that can cast forth the burning Light of Banishment. On a platform at the War Altar's fore stands an Arch Lector – a senior Warrior Priest who smites the foes even as he prays to mighty Sigmar for aid. Most Arch Lectors are armed with a mighty double-handed Sigmarite Greathammer, but a few instead carry a Warhammer alongside a Staff of Sigmar which serves as both a weapon and a badge of office. The War Altar also mounts a Devotional Horn, that heralds the foe's doom.

## ABILITIES

**Divine Power:** The Arch Lector atop a War Altar of Sigmar can attempt to unbind 2 spells in each enemy hero phase as if it were a wizard.

**Sigmar's Shield:** You can roll a dice each time a **Devoted of Sigmar** model from your army is slain within range of this model (as shown on the damage table above). On a 6, that model has been miraculously saved from harm and ignores the wound that slew it.

**The Power of Faith: Devoted of Sigmar** units from your army do not need to take battleshock tests if they are within 10" of a War Altar.

**Light of Banishment:** The holy light that emanates from the Golden Griffon is anathema to the followers of the Dark Gods. When you make a Light of Banishment attack against a **Chaos** unit, double any wounds it suffers. The holy light is especially dangerous to **Chaos Daemons**, who cannot abide its searing touch. Furthermore, attacks against these units are resolved with a Rend of -2 instead of -1.

**Devotional Horn:** Once per battle, the Devotional Horn can be blown in a battleshock phase. When it is blown, all enemy units within 10" of the War Altar must subtract 1 from their Bravery until the end of that phase.

**Battle Prayers:** In your hero phase, the Arch Lector can pray to Sigmar. If he does so, pick a **Devoted of Sigmar** unit within 10", select one of the following blessings and roll a dice. On a 1 or a 2, his prayers go unanswered, but on a 3 or more they have been heard:

*Soulfire:* Roll a dice for each enemy unit within 3" of the unit you picked; on a 4 or more it is struck by soulfire and suffers a mortal wound.

*Righteous Fury:* Until your next hero phase you can re-roll failed hit rolls for the unit in the combat phase.

*Holy Fervour:* Until your next hero phase, you can add 1 to the unit's run rolls, charge rolls, and hit rolls in the combat phase.

| KEYWORDS | ORDER, HUMAN, CELESTIAL, DEVOTED OF SIGMAR, TOTEM, HERO, PRIEST, WAR ALTAR OF SIGMAR |
|---|---|

# WARRIOR PRIEST

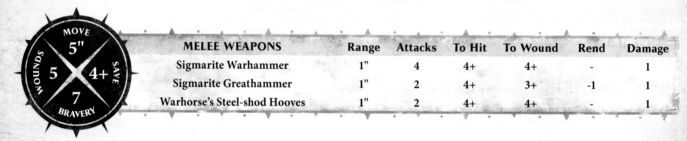

| MELEE WEAPONS | Range | Attacks | To Hit | To Wound | Rend | Damage |
|---|---|---|---|---|---|---|
| Sigmarite Warhammer | 1" | 4 | 4+ | 4+ | - | 1 |
| Sigmarite Greathammer | 1" | 2 | 4+ | 3+ | -1 | 1 |
| Warhorse's Steel-shod Hooves | 1" | 2 | 4+ | 4+ | - | 1 |

MOVE 5"
WOUNDS 5
SAVE 4+
BRAVERY 7

## DESCRIPTION

A Warrior Priest is a single model. Some Warrior Priests are armed with a Sigmarite Warhammer in one hand and a Sigmarite Shield in the other. Others wield a Warhammer in each hand, or pummel the enemy with swings of a double-handed Sigmarite Greathammer.

## WARHORSE

A Warrior Priest can be mounted on a barded Warhorse, granting them a Move of 12" and the Steel-shod Hooves attack.

## ABILITIES

**Sigmarite Shield:** A Warrior Priest with a Sigmarite Shield has a Save of 3+.

**Sigmarite Warhammers:** You can re-roll hit rolls of 1 for a Warrior Priest armed with two Sigmarite Warhammers.

**Divine Power:** A Warrior Priest can attempt to unbind 1 spell in each enemy hero phase, as if he were a wizard.

**Battle Prayers:** In your hero phase, a Warrior Priest can pray to Sigmar. If he does so, pick a **DEVOTED OF SIGMAR** unit within 10", select one of the following blessings and roll a dice. On a 1 or a 2, his prayers go unanswered, but on a 3 or more they have been heard:

*Shield of Faith:* Until your next hero phase, you can roll a dice each time the unit suffers a wound or a mortal wound. On a 6, that wound is ignored.

*Hammer of Sigmar:* Until your next hero phase you can re-roll failed wound rolls for the unit in the combat phase.

*Healing Hands:* One model in the unit immediately heals D3 wounds.

| KEYWORDS | ORDER, HUMAN, CELESTIAL, DEVOTED OF SIGMAR, HERO, PRIEST, WARRIOR PRIEST |
|---|---|

# WITCH HUNTER

| MISSILE WEAPONS | Range | Attacks | To Hit | To Wound | Rend | Damage |
|---|---|---|---|---|---|---|
| Baroque Pistol | 9" | 1 | 3+ | 3+ | -1 | 1 |
| MELEE WEAPONS | Range | Attacks | To Hit | To Wound | Rend | Damage |
| Blessed Rapier | 1" | 3 | 3+ | 4+ | - | 1 |
| Silver Greatsword | 1" | 3 | 3+ | 3+ | -1 | 1 |

**MOVE** 5"
**WOUNDS** 5
**SAVE** 5+
**BRAVERY** 7

## DESCRIPTION

A Witch Hunter is a single model. All Witch Hunters carry a Baroque Pistol. Some Witch Hunters carry a second Baroque Pistol and a Blessed Rapier to despatch their quarry, while others prefer the surety of a double-handed Silver Greatsword.

## ABILITIES

**Baroque Pistols:** A Witch Hunter equipped with two Baroque Pistols makes 2 attacks in the shooting phase.

**Grim Resolve:** Roll a dice if a Witch Hunter is targeted or affected by an enemy spell. On a 5 of more, that spell has no effect on the Witch Hunter (but it may affect other units normally).

**Sigmar's Judgement:** A Witch Hunter's attacks inflict D3 Damage instead of 1 if the target of the attack is a **WIZARD** or a **DAEMON**.

**KEYWORDS** | ORDER, HUMAN, CELESTIAL, DEVOTED OF SIGMAR, HERO, WITCH HUNTER

# FLAGELLANTS

| | MOVE **6"** | | | | | | |
|---|---|---|---|---|---|---|---|
| **WOUNDS 1** | | **SAVE -** | | | | | |
| | **BRAVERY 8** | | | | | | |

| MELEE WEAPONS | Range | Attacks | To Hit | To Wound | Rend | Damage |
|---|---|---|---|---|---|---|
| Castigating Flails and Clubs | 1" | 2 | 5+ | 4+ | - | 1 |

## DESCRIPTION

A unit of Flagellants has 10 or more models. Flagellants march into war waving signs proclaiming their faith and ringing bells to terrify the unbelievers. Units of Flagellants launch themselves at the foe armed with a mixture of Castigating Flails and Clubs.

## PROPHET

The leader of this unit is a Prophet. You can re-roll failed hit rolls for a Prophet.

## ABILITIES

**Glorious Martyrs:** Flagellants make one additional attack in the combat phase if any models from their unit have been slain earlier in this turn. If 5 or more models have been slain earlier in the turn, then they instead make two additional attacks.

**Fanatical Fury:** You can re-roll hit rolls and wound rolls of 1 for Flagellants if they charged during the same turn.

**Reckless Abandon:** When all hope is lost a Flagellant will fling himself at the enemy with reckless abandon, heedless of his own survival. Each time a Flagellant flees, select an enemy unit within 6" and roll a dice; on a 4 or more that unit suffers a mortal wound before the foe can slay the frenzied Flagellant. If there are no enemy units within 6", then the Flagellant instead bashes himself to death with his own flail and is removed from play as normal.

| KEYWORDS | ORDER, HUMAN, CELESTIAL, DEVOTED OF SIGMAR, FLAGELLANTS |
|---|---|

# FREE PEOPLES

**When the Gates of Azyr were closed, the city of Azyrheim became the last bastion of the Free Peoples. Having lost their kingdoms, continents and lands they made a new home in the city. Now they are returning to the Mortal Realms as conquerors and relearning the ancient arts of war.**

War calls to the Free Peoples and they answer its summons in their countless thousands. Vast armies muster before the gates of Azyrheim and march out into the lands retaken by the Stormcast Eternals. Where the Devoted have purged the curse of Chaos from the land, the Free Peoples raise mighty fortresses and begin settling the realms once more. Led by martial city lords, their ranks are filled out by the Freeguilds. Each one is the remnant of an ancient tribe, proudly bearing symbols like the Crowned Skull of Penumbra, the Sanguine Lady of Flames, or the Stonehearted Blood Bull. Drawn from the citizens of Azyrheim and the foundling cities, the soldiers of the Freeguilds are quickly learning the ways of war.

Among the numerous hosts of the Free Peoples, veterans and heroes strengthen the ranks. Greatsword-wielding city guard are regiments that have faced the tribes of Chaos and emerged victorious. Then there are the Outriders and Pistoliers – these skilled horsemen patrol the outer districts of their cities, where their deadly firearms and swift steeds can get them out of trouble quick enough to summon aid. When the Freeguilds march out a Freeguild General himself might accompany them. Atop his griffon mount he is often joined by his finest soldiers, each one riding a demigryph, and together they eagerly exact their revenge upon the servants of the Dark Gods.

## FREE PEOPLES
# FREEGUILD REGIMENT

When the cities of the Free Peoples are threatened they can call upon the disciplined ranks of the Freeguilds, stalwart warriors that stand shoulder to shoulder against enemies of Order.

## ORGANISATION

A Freeguild Regiment consists of the following units:

- 1 Freeguild General or Freeguild General on Griffon
- 1 unit of Demigryph Knights
- 1 unit of Freeguild Greatswords
- 3 units of Freeguild Guard
- 3 units of Freeguild Archers, Crossbowmen or Handgunners, in any combination
- 1 unit of Freeguild Outriders
- 1 unit of Freeguild Pistoliers

## ABILITIES

**Stand Together, Fight Together:** The warriors in this battalion are trained to fight together to overcome their foes. You can add 1 to all hit rolls for a unit in a Freeguild Regiment if it is within 6" of another unit from the regiment when the attack rolls are made.

**Regimental Discipline:** The troops in this battalion are drilled to hold in the face of even the most terrifying enemies. Units from a Freeguild Regiment have +1 Bravery whilst they are within 10" of their Freeguild General. In addition, if you roll a 1 when taking a battleshock test for a unit from a Freeguild Regiment, no models flee from that unit regardless of the result. If that unit includes any standard bearers, no models flee if you roll a 1 or a 2.

# FREEGUILD GENERAL ON GRIFFON

| MELEE WEAPONS | Range | Attacks | To Hit | To Wound | Rend | Damage |
|---|---|---|---|---|---|---|
| Freeguild Lance | 2" | 3 | 3+ | 4+ | -1 | 2 |
| Sigmarite Runesword | 1" | 5 | 3+ | 4+ | -1 | 1 |
| Sigmarite Greathammer | 1" | 3 | 3+ | 3+ | -2 | D3 |
| Griffon's Deadly Beak | 2" | 2 | 3+ | 3+ | -2 | ✹ |
| Griffon's Razor Claws | 2" | ✹ | 4+ | 3+ | -1 | 2 |

**MOVE** ✹ | WOUNDS 13 | SAVE 4+ | BRAVERY 7

| DAMAGE TABLE | | | |
|---|---|---|---|
| Wounds Suffered | Move | Deadly Beak | Razor Claws |
| 0-3 | 15" | D6 | 6 |
| 4-6 | 13" | D6 | 5 |
| 7-9 | 11" | D3 | 4 |
| 10-11 | 9" | D3 | 3 |
| 12+ | 7" | 1 | 2 |

## DESCRIPTION

A Freeguild General on Griffon is a single model. Many Freeguild Generals ride to war armed with a Freeguild Lance to skewer their foes on the charge. Others prefer to carry a Sigmarite Runesword or Greathammer in battle. A Freeguild General may also carry a Freeguild Shield to protect himself in battle. The General's Griffon fights with savage fury with its Deadly Beak and Razor Claws.

## FLY

A Freeguild General on Griffon can fly.

## ABILITIES

**Charging Lance:** Add 1 to the Damage of this model's Lance if it charged this turn.

**Freeguild Shield:** A Freeguild General with a Freeguild Shield has a Save of 3+.

**Piercing Bloodroar:** In the battleshock phase, a Griffon can loose a piercing Bloodroar at a unit within 8". If it does, that unit must roll two dice and use the highest result if it has to take a battleshock test that phase.

## COMMAND ABILITY

**Rousing Battle Cry:** If a Freeguild General on Griffon uses this ability, pick a FREE PEOPLES unit within 15". Until your next hero phase you can add 2 to that unit's Bravery and 1 to its charge rolls and hit rolls.

| KEYWORDS | ORDER, HUMAN, GRIFFON, FREE PEOPLES, MONSTER, HERO, FREEGUILD GENERAL |
|---|---|

# FREEGUILD GENERAL

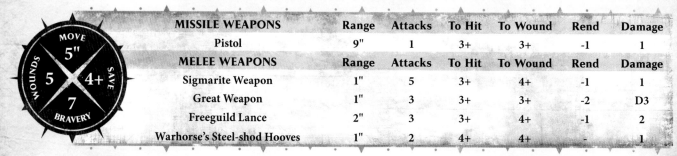

| MISSILE WEAPONS | Range | Attacks | To Hit | To Wound | Rend | Damage |
|---|---|---|---|---|---|---|
| Pistol | 9" | 1 | 3+ | 3+ | -1 | 1 |
| **MELEE WEAPONS** | **Range** | **Attacks** | **To Hit** | **To Wound** | **Rend** | **Damage** |
| Sigmarite Weapon | 1" | 5 | 3+ | 4+ | -1 | 1 |
| Great Weapon | 1" | 3 | 3+ | 3+ | -2 | D3 |
| Freeguild Lance | 2" | 3 | 3+ | 4+ | -1 | 2 |
| Warhorse's Steel-shod Hooves | 1" | 2 | 4+ | 4+ | - | 1 |

**MOVE** 5"
**WOUNDS** 5
**SAVE** 4+
**BRAVERY** 7

## DESCRIPTION
A Freeguild General is a single model. Some Generals favour the heft of a two-handed Great Weapon in battle, but others prefer a magical single-handed Sigmarite Weapon which they can wield alongside a Freeguild Shield. If riding to war, a General may instead slay his foes with a Freeguild Lance. Many Freeguild Generals carry a pistol instead of a shield to shoot their foes from afar. Occasionally, a Freeguild General will have the honour of carrying a Stately War Banner to battle.

## WARHORSE
A Freeguild General can be mounted on a barded Warhorse, granting them a Move of 12" and the Steel-shod Hooves attack.

## ABILITIES
**Stately War Banner:** A General with a Stately War Banner gains the **TOTEM** keyword. You may roll two dice and choose the lowest when taking battleshock tests for **FREE PEOPLES** units from your army within 24" of a Stately War Banner.

**Charging Lance:** Add 1 to the Damage of this model's Lance if it charged this turn.

**Freeguild Shield:** A Freeguild General with a Freeguild Shield has a Save of 3+.

## COMMAND ABILITY
**Hold the Line!:** If a Freeguild General uses this ability, pick up to three **FREE PEOPLES** units within 15". These units cannot move or charge during your turn, but you can add 1 to all hit and wound rolls for them until your next hero phase.

**KEYWORDS** | ORDER, HUMAN, FREE PEOPLES, HERO, FREEGUILD GENERAL

# DEMIGRYPH KNIGHTS

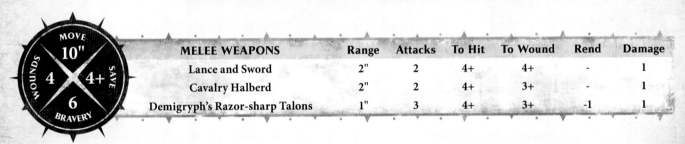

**MOVE** 10"
**WOUNDS** 4
**SAVE** 4+
**BRAVERY** 6

| MELEE WEAPONS | Range | Attacks | To Hit | To Wound | Rend | Damage |
|---|---|---|---|---|---|---|
| Lance and Sword | 2" | 2 | 4+ | 4+ | - | 1 |
| Cavalry Halberd | 2" | 2 | 4+ | 3+ | - | 1 |
| Demigryph's Razor-sharp Talons | 1" | 3 | 4+ | 3+ | -1 | 1 |

## DESCRIPTION

A unit of Demigryph Knights has 3 or more models. Some units of Demigryph Knights wield Lances and Swords, while others are armed with Cavalry Halberds. In either case, the Knights carry Shields and ride upon fearsome Demigryphs that attack with their Razor-sharp Talons.

## PRECEPTOR

The leader of this unit is a Preceptor. A Preceptor makes 1 extra attack with either his Lance and Sword or Cavalry Halberd.

## STANDARD BEARER

Models in this unit may be Standard Bearers. If the unit includes any Standard Bearers, it only needs to take a battleshock test if two or more of its models were slain during the turn.

## HORNBLOWER

Models in this unit may be Hornblowers. If the unit includes any Hornblowers, add 2 to its charge rolls.

## ABILITIES

**Shield:** You can re-roll save rolls of 1 for a unit equipped with Shields.

**Charging Lance:** Add 1 to the wound rolls and Damage for this unit's Lances and Swords if it charged in the same turn.

**Savage Ferocity:** If the wound roll for a Demigryph's Razor-sharp Talons is a 6 or more, then that attack inflicts D3 damage instead of 1.

| KEYWORDS | ORDER, HUMAN, FREE PEOPLES, DEMIGRYPH KNIGHTS |
|---|---|

# FREEGUILD GREATSWORDS

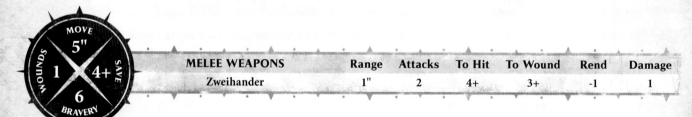

| | | MOVE 5" | | |
|---|---|---|---|---|
| WOUNDS 1 | | | SAVE 4+ | |
| | | 6 BRAVERY | | |

| MELEE WEAPONS | Range | Attacks | To Hit | To Wound | Rend | Damage |
|---|---|---|---|---|---|---|
| Zweihander | 1" | 2 | 4+ | 3+ | -1 | 1 |

## DESCRIPTION
A unit of Freeguild Greatswords has 5 or more models. Units of Freeguild Greatswords are armed with large, double-handed swords called Zweihanders.

## GUILD CHAMPION
The leader of this unit is a Guild Champion. A Guild Champion makes 3 attacks rather than 2.

## STANDARD BEARER
Models in this unit may be Standard Bearers. If you roll a 1 when taking a battleshock test for a unit that includes any Standard Bearers none of its models flee.

## HORNBLOWER
Models in this unit may be Hornblowers. If the unit includes any Hornblowers, it can counter-charge after your opponent has finished moving all his charging units, so long as no enemy models are within 3". A counter-charging unit charges D6".

## ABILITIES
**Oathsworn Honour Guard:** If a unit of Freeguild Greatswords is within 14" of a **FREE PEOPLES HERO** from your army when they attack, you can add 1 to all of their hit rolls.

| KEYWORDS | ORDER, HUMAN, FREE PEOPLES, FREEGUILD GREATSWORDS |
|---|---|

# FREEGUILD CROSSBOWMEN

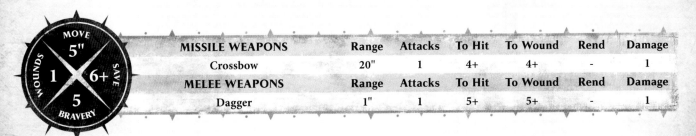

| MOVE 5" |
| WOUNDS 1 |
| SAVE 6+ |
| BRAVERY 5 |

| MISSILE WEAPONS | Range | Attacks | To Hit | To Wound | Rend | Damage |
|---|---|---|---|---|---|---|
| Crossbow | 20" | 1 | 4+ | 4+ | - | 1 |
| MELEE WEAPONS | Range | Attacks | To Hit | To Wound | Rend | Damage |
| Dagger | 1" | 1 | 5+ | 5+ | - | 1 |

## DESCRIPTION
A unit of Freeguild Crossbowmen has 10 or more models. Units of Freeguild Crossbowmen are armed with Crossbows and Daggers.

## MARKSMAN
The leader of this unit is a Marksman. Add 1 to the hit rolls for a Marksman using a Crossbow.

## STANDARD BEARER
Models in this unit may be Standard Bearers. If you roll a 1 when taking a battleshock test for a unit that includes any Standard Bearers none of its models flee.

## PIPERS
Models in this unit may be Pipers. Once per turn, if an enemy unit ends its charge move within 3" of a unit that includes any Pipers, they can signal their unit to stand and shoot; each model can then shoot its Crossbow at the charging unit.

## ABILITIES
**Piercing Bolts:** Each time you roll a wound roll of a 6 or more for a Crossbow, that attack is resolved with a Rend of -1 instead of '-'.

**Reload, Fire:** Freeguild Crossbowmen can shoot twice if their unit has 20 or more models, they did not move in their preceding movement phase and there are no enemy models within 3".

| KEYWORDS | ORDER, HUMAN, FREE PEOPLES, FREEGUILD CROSSBOWMEN |

# FREEGUILD HANDGUNNERS

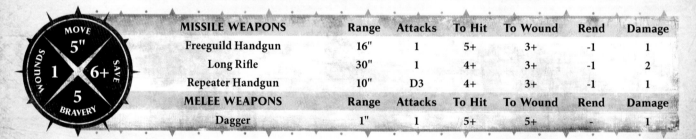

| MISSILE WEAPONS | Range | Attacks | To Hit | To Wound | Rend | Damage |
|---|---|---|---|---|---|---|
| Freeguild Handgun | 16" | 1 | 5+ | 3+ | -1 | 1 |
| Long Rifle | 30" | 1 | 4+ | 3+ | -1 | 2 |
| Repeater Handgun | 10" | D3 | 4+ | 3+ | -1 | 1 |
| MELEE WEAPONS | Range | Attacks | To Hit | To Wound | Rend | Damage |
| Dagger | 1" | 1 | 5+ | 5+ | - | 1 |

**MOVE** 5"
**WOUNDS** 1
**SAVE** 6+
**BRAVERY** 5

## DESCRIPTION
A unit of Freeguild Handgunners has 10 or more models. Units of Freeguild Handgunners are armed with Freeguild Handguns and Daggers.

## MARKSMAN
The leader of this unit is a Marksman. A Marksman is armed with either a Freeguild Handgun, a Long Rifle or a Repeater Handgun. You can add 2 to hit rolls for a Marksman with a Freeguild Handgun in the shooting phase.

## STANDARD BEARER
Models in this unit may be Standard Bearers. If you roll a 1 when taking a battleshock test for a unit that includes any Standard Bearers none of its models flee.

## PIPERS
Models in this unit may be Pipers. Once per turn, if an enemy unit ends its charge move within 3" of a unit that includes any Pipers, they can signal their unit to stand and shoot; each model then can then shoot its missile weapon at the charging unit.

## ABILITIES
**Steady Aim:** You can add 1 to the hit rolls for a Freeguild Handgunner in your shooting phase so long as its unit did not move in the preceding movement phase and there are no enemy models within 3" of its unit.

**Handgun Volley:** You can add 1 to hit rolls for a Freeguild Handgunner when it shoots its missile weapons if its unit includes at least 20 models.

| KEYWORDS | ORDER, HUMAN, FREE PEOPLES, FREEGUILD HANDGUNNERS |
|---|---|

# FREEGUILD ARCHERS

| MOVE | |
|---|---|
| 5" | |
| WOUNDS 1 | SAVE 6+ |
| 5 | |
| BRAVERY | |

| MISSILE WEAPONS | Range | Attacks | To Hit | To Wound | Rend | Damage |
|---|---|---|---|---|---|---|
| Bow | 18" | 1 | 4+ | 4+ | - | 1 |
| MELEE WEAPONS | Range | Attacks | To Hit | To Wound | Rend | Damage |
| Shortsword | 1" | 1 | 5+ | 4+ | - | 1 |

## DESCRIPTION
A unit of Freeguild Archers has 10 or more models. Units of Freeguild Archers are armed with Bows and Shortswords.

## MARKSMAN
The leader of this unit is a Marksman. Add 1 to the hit rolls for a Marksman using a Bow.

## ABILITIES
**Huntsmen:** After set-up is complete, you can make a bonus move with this unit as if it were moving in the movement phase.

**Ordered Volleys:** You can re-roll hit rolls of 1 for Freeguild Archers in the shooting phase. You can re-roll hit rolls of 1 or 2 instead if the unit has 20 or more models, or re-roll any failed hit roll if it has 30 or more models.

| KEYWORDS | ORDER, HUMAN, FREE PEOPLES, FREEGUILD ARCHERS |
|---|---|

# FREEGUILD PISTOLIERS

| MISSILE WEAPONS | Range | Attacks | To Hit | To Wound | Rend | Damage |
|---|---|---|---|---|---|---|
| Brace of Pistols | 9" | 2 | 5+ | 3+ | -1 | 1 |
| Repeater Handgun | 14" | D3 | 4+ | 3+ | -1 | 1 |
| MELEE WEAPONS | Range | Attacks | To Hit | To Wound | Rend | Damage |
| Brace of Pistols | 1" | 2 | 5+ | 3+ | -1 | 1 |
| Cavalry Sabre | 1" | 1 | 4+ | 4+ | - | 1 |
| Steed's Stamping Hooves | 1" | 2 | 4+ | 5+ | - | 1 |

MOVE 12"
WOUNDS 2
SAVE 5+
BRAVERY 5

## DESCRIPTION
A unit of Freeguild Pistoliers has 5 or more models. Units of Freeguild Pistoliers are armed with Braces of Pistols, which they use to slay their foes at range and in melee They are mounted on Steeds that trample the foe with their Stamping Hooves.

## TRUMPETERS
Models in this unit may be Trumpeters. A unit that includes any Trumpeters can shoot and charge in its turn even if it ran during its movement phase.

## OUTRIDER
The leader of this unit is an Outrider. An Outrider has Bravery 6 instead of 5. Some Outriders are armed with a Brace of Pistols – you can add 1 to hit rolls for these Outriders – but many prefer to wield a Repeater Handgun. Some Outriders ride to war equipped with a Repeater Pistol, which they wield alongside a regular Pistol. Outriders are also equipped with a Cavalry Sabre for fighting in close quarters.

## ABILITIES
**Repeater Pistol:** An Outrider equipped with a Repeater Pistol makes 3 attacks instead of 2 when attacking with his Brace of Pistols.

**Reckless Riders:** When this unit runs, roll two dice and pick the highest instead of rolling a single dice when determining how much extra they move. However, when Pistoliers run, they must run as close as possible towards the nearest visible enemy unit.

---

**KEYWORDS**  ORDER, HUMAN, FREE PEOPLES, FREEGUILD PISTOLIERS

# FREEGUILD OUTRIDERS

| MISSILE WEAPONS | Range | Attacks | To Hit | To Wound | Rend | Damage |
|---|---|---|---|---|---|---|
| Repeater Handgun | 14" | D3 | 5+ | 3+ | -1 | 1 |
| Brace of Pistols | 9" | 2 | 4+ | 3+ | -1 | 1 |
| Grenade Launching Blunderbuss | 10" | 1 | 4+ | 3+ | -2 | D3 |
| **MELEE WEAPONS** | **Range** | **Attacks** | **To Hit** | **To Wound** | **Rend** | **Damage** |
| Cavalry Sabre | 1" | 1 | 4+ | 4+ | - | 1 |
| Brace of Pistols | 1" | 2 | 5+ | 3+ | -1 | 1 |
| Steed's Stamping Hooves | 1" | 2 | 4+ | 5+ | - | 1 |

**MOVE** 12"
**WOUNDS** 2
**SAVE** 5+
**BRAVERY** 6

## DESCRIPTION

A unit of Freeguild Outriders has 5 or more models. Units of Freeguild Outriders are armed with Repeater Handguns and Cavalry Sabres. They are mounted on Steeds that trample the foe with their Stamping Hooves.

## TRUMPETERS

Models in this unit may be Trumpeters. A unit that includes any Trumpeters can shoot and charge in its turn even if it ran during its movement phase.

## SHARPSHOOTER

The leader of this unit is a Sharpshooter. Some Sharpshooters shoot the foe with a Repeater Handgun – you can add 1 to hit rolls for these Sharpshooters in the shooting phase – but others ride to war equipped with a Brace of Pistols, one of which will typically be a Repeater Pistol. A few Sharpshooters, usually those that have a Gunmaster as a patron, instead carry a Grenade Launching Blunderbuss. Sharpshooters also make 2 attacks with their Cavalry Sabres instead of 1.

## ABILITIES

**Expert Gunners:** You can add 1 to hit rolls for Outriders in the shooting phase if their unit did not move in their preceding movement phase and there are no enemy models within 3".

**Repeater Pistol:** A Sharpshooter equipped with a Repeater Pistol makes 3 attacks instead of 2 when attacking with his Brace of Pistols.

**KEYWORDS** | ORDER, HUMAN, FREE PEOPLES, FREEGUILD OUTRIDERS

# FREEGUILD GUARD

| MISSILE WEAPONS | Range | Attacks | To Hit | To Wound | Rend | Damage |
|---|---|---|---|---|---|---|
| Militia Weapons | 14" | 1 | 5+ | 4+ | - | 1 |
| MELEE WEAPONS | Range | Attacks | To Hit | To Wound | Rend | Damage |
| Militia Weapons | 1" | 1 | 4+ | 4+ | - | 1 |
| Halberd | 1" | 1 | 4+ | 4+ | -1 | 1 |
| Spear | 2" | 1 | 4+ | 4+ | - | 1 |
| Sword | 1" | 1 | 4+ | 4+ | - | 1 |

MOVE 5"
WOUNDS 1
SAVE 5+
BRAVERY 5

## DESCRIPTION
A unit of Freeguild Guard has 10 or more models. Most units of Freeguild Guard are either armed with Halberds, Spears, or Swords; these units may also carry Shields to battle. Some units of Freeguild Guard are far less uniformly equipped and are instead armed with Militia Weapons – an assortment of blades, clubs, bows, crossbows and even the occasional blackpowder firearm.

## SERGEANT
The leader of this unit is a Sergeant. A Sergeant makes 2 Attacks instead of 1.

## STANDARD BEARER
Models in this unit may be Standard Bearers. If you roll a 1 when taking a battleshock test for a unit that includes any Standard Bearers none of its models flee.

## DRUMMERS
Models in this unit may be Drummers. If the unit includes any Drummers, it can counter-charge after your opponent has finished moving all of their charging units, so long as no enemy models are within 3". A counter-charging unit charges D6".

## ABILITIES
**Massed Ranks:** Add 1 to hit rolls for Freeguild Guard if their unit contains 20 or more models. Add 2 instead if their unit contains 30 or more models, and add 3 if it contains 40 or more models.

**Shield:** You can re-roll save rolls of 1 for a unit equipped with Shields.

**Parry:** You can add 1 to save rolls for Freeguild Guard equipped with Swords in the combat phase.

| KEYWORDS | ORDER, HUMAN, FREE PEOPLES, FREEGUILD GUARD |
|---|---|

# COLLEGIATE ARCANE

**In the sky towers of Azyrheim dwell the Collegiate Arcane. Sorcerous artisans, they create wondrous devices to channel and siphon the magic of the realms into devastating spells of destruction. When Azyrite armies need magical support, it is to the Battlemages of the Collegiate they turn.**

Men long ago mastered the ways of drawing out the magic of the Mortal Realms. When the people fled to Azyrheim before the hosts of Chaos, countless thaumaturges, soothsayers and astromancers were amongst them. These wizards brought their knowledge of the realms with them, and continued to work their magic within the celestial city. In time they constructed vast towers, some breaking free of their moorings to hover over Azyrheim like glimmering stone candles. As the Age of Sigmar dawns, their sorceries and enchantments now aid the Stormhosts, Freeguilds and other armies of Order against the many enemies that assail them across the realms.

Unlike the seers of the Eldritch Council, a Battlemage's talents are not instinctive; they require arcane foci and esoteric machineries to channel their sorcerous powers. Using celestial orreries, etheric lenses and enchanted objects like masks, orbs, staves and hourglasses, they work their spells. In the raging heat of battle they loose searing balls of flame, snaking bolts of lightning or murderous shadows, while many are adept at conjuring protective wards or shimmering shields around their allies. Lord-Celestants can contact the sky towers to summon the aid of the Battlemages, whether it is to counter daemonic chicanery or master the fickle energies of a Realmgate.

COLLEGIATE ARCANE
# WAR COUNCIL

When the Battlemages of the Collegiate gather in great numbers the air shimmers and sparks with the might of their magic, each spell-caster augmenting the powers of their fellow scholars.

## ORGANISATION

A War Council consists of the following units:

- 1 Battlemage on Griffon
- 3-8 Battlemages
- 1 Luminark of Hysh
- 1 Celestial Hurricanum

## ABILITIES

**Augmented Might:** Any Battlemages in a War Council can choose to forgo casting a spell in their hero phase in order to augment a spell cast by another model from the same battalion that is within 6". Declare that they will do so before making the casting roll. Add 1 to the casting roll and 6" to the range of the spell for each Battlemage that helps to augment it.

# BATTLEMAGE

MOVE **5"**
WOUNDS **5**
SAVE **6+**
BRAVERY **6**

| MELEE WEAPONS | Range | Attacks | To Hit | To Wound | Rend | Damage |
|---|---|---|---|---|---|---|
| Battlemage's Staff | 2" | 1 | 4+ | 3+ | -1 | D3 |

## DESCRIPTION

A Battlemage is a single model. All Battlemages specialise in mastering one of the Lores of Magic – Heavens, Bright, Amethyst, White, Gold, Grey, Amber or Jade. They are adorned with the trappings and arcana associated with that Lore. All Battlemages carry a Battlemage's Staff.

## ABILITIES

**Magic Specialisation:** When setting up this model, you can pick one of the following schools of magic for the Battlemage to specialise in: Heavens, Bright, Amethyst, White, Gold, Grey, Amber or Jade.

## MAGIC

A Battlemage can attempt to cast one spell in each of your hero phases, and attempt to unbind a spell in each enemy hero phase. All Battlemages know the Arcane Bolt and Mystic Shield spells. A Battlemage also knows one more spell depending upon his magical specialisation:

| Specialisation | Spell |
|---|---|
| Heavens | Chain Lightning |
| Bright | Fireball |
| Amethyst | Soul Steal |
| White | Light of Battle |
| Gold | Final Transmutation |
| Grey | Mystifying Miasma |
| Amber | Wildform |
| Jade | Lifesurge |

## CHAIN LIGHTNING

Lightning bursts from the wizard's fingertips and arcs towards the enemy with crackling fury. Chain Lightning has a casting value of 6. If successfully cast, pick a visible enemy unit within 18". That unit suffers D3 mortal wounds. Then, roll a dice for every other enemy unit within 6" of the original target; on a 6 the lightning has leapt to that unit and it also suffers D3 mortal wounds.

## FIREBALL

The wizard conjures a ball of flame and hurls it at his foes. Fireball has a casting value of 5. If successfully cast, pick a visible enemy unit within 18" and roll a dice. On a 1 or a 2 that unit suffers a mortal wound, on a 3 or a 4 it suffers D3 mortal wounds and on a 5 or a 6 it suffers D6 mortal wounds.

## SOUL STEAL

The wizard extends a hand and leeches his victim's souls from their bodies. Soul Steal has a casting value of 5. If successfully cast, pick a visible enemy unit within 18". You and your opponent then both roll a dice; add the caster's Bravery to your dice roll and add the Bravery of the target to your opponent's. If your score is the highest, the enemy unit suffers a number of mortal wounds equal to the difference in the scores (for example, if your score was 10 and your opponent's 8, the unit suffers 2 mortal wounds).

## LIGHT OF BATTLE

The wizard infuses his allies with Light energies, filling them with courage. Light of Battle has a casting value of 4. If successfully cast, pick a unit within 18". That unit does not need to take battleshock tests until your next hero phase. The magical aura surrounding that unit also ennobles nearby allies until your next hero phase; other units from your army within 6" of this unit in the battleshock phase add 1 to their Bravery.

## FINAL TRANSMUTATION

With a gesture the wizard transmutes the flesh of his foe into unliving metal. Final Transmutation has a casting value of 6. If successfully cast, pick a visible enemy unit within 18". Your opponent then picks any model in that unit and rolls a dice; if the result is more than that model's remaining number of wounds, it is transformed into a gleaming golden statue and slain.

## MYSTIFYING MIASMA

The wizard creates a fog that numbs his foes' battle skills. Mystifying Miasma has a casting value of 6. If successfully cast, pick a visible enemy unit within 18". Until your next hero phase your opponent must subtract 1 from all hit rolls for that unit.

## WILDFORM

With a roar the wizard infuses his allies' battle spirits with the savage strength of wild creatures. Wildform has a casting value of 6. If successfully cast, pick a unit within 18". Until your next hero phase you can add 1 to all wound rolls for that unit in the combat phase.

## LIFESURGE

The wizard infuses his allies with healing energies. Lifesurge has a casting value of 5. If successfully cast, pick a unit within 18". One model in that unit heals D3 wounds. In addition, until your next hero phase the energies of this spell persist; roll a dice each time a model in the unit suffers a wound or mortal wound. On a 6, that wound is instantly healed and is ignored.

| KEYWORDS | ORDER, HUMAN, COLLEGIATE ARCANE, HERO, WIZARD, BATTLEMAGE |
|---|---|

# BATTLEMAGE ON GRIFFON

| | | | | |
|---|---|---|---|---|
| MOVE | | | | |
| WOUNDS 13 | SAVE 5+ | | | |
| 6 | | | | |
| BRAVERY | | | | |

| MELEE WEAPONS | Range | Attacks | To Hit | To Wound | Rend | Damage |
|---|---|---|---|---|---|---|
| Beaststaff | 2" | 1 | 4+ | 3+ | -1 | D3 |
| Griffon's Twin Beaks | 2" | 4 | 3+ | 3+ | -1 | ✹ |
| Griffon's Razor Claws | 2" | ✹ | 4+ | 3+ | -1 | 2 |

| DAMAGE TABLE | | | |
|---|---|---|---|
| Wounds Suffered | Move | Twin Beaks | Razor Claws |
| 0-3 | 15" | 3 | 6 |
| 4-6 | 13" | D3 | 5 |
| 7-9 | 11" | D3 | 4 |
| 10-11 | 9" | 1 | 3 |
| 12+ | 7" | 1 | 2 |

## DESCRIPTION

A Battlemage on Griffon is a single model. The Battlemage is armed with a Beaststaff, and rides a twin-headed Griffon to battle, which savages its prey with its Twin Beaks and Razor Claws.

## FLY

A Battlemage on Griffon can fly.

## ABILITIES

**Amber Battlemage:** You can add 1 to casting rolls for a Battlemage if the battle is taking place in the Realm of Beasts.

**Two Headed:** You can re-roll hit rolls of 1 when attacking with a Griffon's Twin Beaks.

## MAGIC

A Battlemage can attempt to cast one spell in each of your hero phases, and attempt to unbind one spell in each enemy hero phase. He knows the Arcane Bolt, Mystic Shield and Amber Spear spells.

## AMBER SPEAR

The wizard conjures a magical amber spear that he hurls at his foes with uncanny accuracy, punching through the ranks of his foes without effort. Amber Spear has a casting value of 7. If successfully cast, pick a visible model within 18". Draw a straight line between that model and the caster; the target model's unit, and each other unit that this line passes though, suffers D3 mortal wounds.

| KEYWORDS | ORDER, HUMAN, GRIFFON, COLLEGIATE ARCANE, MONSTER, HERO, WIZARD, BATTLEMAGE |
|---|---|

# LUMINARK OF HYSH

| MISSILE WEAPONS | Range | Attacks | To Hit | To Wound | Rend | Damage |
|---|---|---|---|---|---|---|
| Searing Beam of Light | 30" | 1 | 3+ | 3+ | -2 | ✹ |
| MELEE WEAPONS | Range | Attacks | To Hit | To Wound | Rend | Damage |
| Battlemage's Staff | 2" | 1 | 4+ | 3+ | -1 | D3 |
| Acolytes' Arcane Tools | 1" | 4 | 5+ | 5+ | - | 1 |
| Warhorses' Steel-shod Hooves | 1" | 4 | 4+ | 4+ | - | 1 |

| DAMAGE TABLE | | | |
|---|---|---|---|
| Wounds Suffered | Move | Aura of Protection | Searing Beam of Light |
| 0-2 | 10" | 10" | 6 |
| 3-4 | 9" | 8" | D6 |
| 5-6 | 8" | 6" | D6 |
| 7-8 | 7" | 4" | D3 |
| 9+ | 6" | 2" | D3 |

## DESCRIPTION
A Luminark of Hysh is a single model. The magical lens array mounted upon the battle altar can be used to fire Searing Beams of Light across the battlefield, as well as acting as a focus for magical energy to the benefit of nearby wizards. The Luminark is pulled into battle by two Warhorses that stamp at the enemy with their Steel-shod Hooves, and is manned by Acolytes that protect their charge using Arcane Tools as improvised weapons.

## WHITE BATTLEMAGE
Some Luminarks of Hysh are attended by White Battlemages. These gain the Battlemage's Staff melee weapon.

## ABILITIES
**Locus of Hysh:** Add 1 to unbinding rolls for **Collegiate Arcane Wizards** from your army within 10" of any Luminarks of Hysh.

**Aura of Protection:** Luminarks of Hysh are surrounded by a magical aura that protects those nearby from harm. You can roll a dice each time an **Order** model from your army suffers a wound or mortal wound whilst within range of a Luminark's Aura of Protection ability; on a 6 that attack is deflected by the aura and that wound is ignored. The range of this ability is shown in the Damage Table above.

## MAGIC
The White Battlemage atop a Luminark can attempt to cast one spell in each of your hero phases, and attempt to unbind one spell in each enemy hero phase. He knows the Arcane Bolt, Mystic Shield and Burning Gaze spells.

## BURNING GAZE
Bolts of burning light fly from the wizard's eyes, searing all caught in their path. Burning Gaze has a casting value of 6. If successfully cast, pick a visible unit within 18". That unit suffers D3 mortal wounds. Double the number of wounds inflicted if the target has 10 or more models, and triple them if the target has 20 or more.

## LUMINARK OF HYSH
| KEYWORDS | ORDER, HUMAN, COLLEGIATE ARCANE, LUMINARK OF HYSH |
|---|---|

## LUMINARK OF HYSH WITH WHITE BATTLEMAGE
| KEYWORDS | ORDER, HUMAN, COLLEGIATE ARCANE, HERO, WIZARD, LUMINARK OF HYSH |
|---|---|

# CELESTIAL HURRICANUM

| MISSILE WEAPONS | Range | Attacks | To Hit | To Wound | Rend | Damage |
|---|---|---|---|---|---|---|
| Storm of Shemtek | 18" | ☀ | | See below | | |
| MELEE WEAPONS | Range | Attacks | To Hit | To Wound | Rend | Damage |
| Battlemage's Staff | 2" | 1 | 4+ | 3+ | -1 | D3 |
| Acolytes' Arcane Tools | 1" | 4 | 5+ | 5+ | - | 1 |
| Warhorses' Steel-shod Hooves | 1" | 4 | 4+ | 4+ | - | 1 |

**MOVE** · **WOUNDS 11** · **SAVE 4+** · **BRAVERY 6**

| DAMAGE TABLE | | | |
|---|---|---|---|
| Wounds Suffered | Move | Portents of Battle | Storm of Shemtek |
| 0-2 | 10" | 10" | 3 |
| 3-4 | 9" | 8" | 2 |
| 5-6 | 8" | 6" | 2 |
| 7-8 | 7" | 4" | 1 |
| 9+ | 6" | 2" | 1 |

## DESCRIPTION
A Celestial Hurricanum is a single model. The magical orrery mounted upon the battle altar can be used to unleash a terrifying Storm of Shemtek upon the enemy, as well as acting as a focus for magical energy to the benefit of nearby wizards. The Hurricanum is pulled into battle by two Warhorses that stamp at the enemy with their Steel-shod Hooves, and manned by Acolytes that protect their charge using Arcane Tools as improvised weapons.

## CELESTIAL BATTLEMAGE
Some Celestial Hurricanums are tended by Celestial Battlemages. These gain the Battlemage's Staff attack.

## ABILITIES
**Locus of Azyr:** Add 1 to casting rolls for **COLLEGIATE ARCANE WIZARDS** from your army within 10" of any Celestial Hurricanums in the hero phase.

**Portents of Battle:** Celestial Hurricanums leak magical power, and nearby soldiers marching beside them often report seeing visions of the imminent future. With such knowledge they are able to predict the actions of the foe and land their blows with uncanny accuracy. You can add 1 to the hit rolls of any **ORDER** units from your army within range of any Celestial Hurricanum's Portents of Battle ability when they attack; the range of this ability is shown in the Damage Table above.

**Storm of Shemtek:** A Celestial Hurricanum can summon a magical storm to batter the foe. Each time you make a Storm of Shemtek attack, select a target unit that is visible and in range, then roll a dice to see what kind of fury is unleashed from the heavens:

1-3 **Iceshard Tempest.** The target suffers a mortal wound.

4-5 **Lightning Strike.** The target suffers D3 mortal wounds.

6 **Meteor Strike.** The target suffers D6 mortal wounds.

## MAGIC
A Battlemage tending a Celestial Hurricanum can attempt to cast one spell in each of your hero phases, and attempt to unbind one spell in each enemy hero phase. He knows the Arcane Bolt, Mystic Shield and Comet of Casandora spells.

### COMET OF CASANDORA
Reaching out to the heavens, the wizard draws a wandering comet and sends it crashing down upon the battlefield. Comet of Casandora has a casting value of 6. If successfully cast, pick a unit within 18" of the caster. Your opponent must then select one of his units that is within 18" of the caster (this can be the same unit as the one you chose). Then, roll a dice; on a 1, 2 or 3 the unit your opponent picked is struck by the falling comet, and on a 4 or more the unit you picked is struck – that unit suffers D6 mortal wounds.

## CELESTIAL HURRICANUM

**KEYWORDS** — ORDER, HUMAN, COLLEGIATE ARCANE, CELESTIAL HURRICANUM

## CELESTIAL HURRICANUM WITH CELESTIAL BATTLEMAGE

**KEYWORDS** — ORDER, HUMAN, COLLEGIATE ARCANE, HERO, WIZARD, CELESTIAL HURRICANUM

# IRONWELD ARSENAL

**The workshops and factories of Azyrheim are filled with technological marvels and mechanical war engines largely forgotten by the rest of the Mortal Realms. Crafted and crewed by the engineers of the Ironweld they rain fire and death upon the enemies of Azyrheim and the free cities.**

There are few races as skilled at creating war machines as men and duardin. For centuries the smiths of the Ironweld have dwelt within Azyrheim stockpiling firearms, cannons, armoured war constructs and even flying machines. When the armies of Azyrheim and Sigmar's Stormhosts march to war, vast Ironweld artillery trains rumble after them. The Ironweld Arsenal's weapons are an array of some of the most ingenious devices ever created by mortals. Clockwork engines and gear-driven riding beasts stand alongside wheel lock long rifles and repeating pistols of careful and cunning design. Few inventions of the Ironweld are exactly alike, due to the varied genius of their creators, and it is for this reason the Arsenal was formed – so that men and duardin might share their knowledge for the betterment of Azyrheim. From the minds of the engineers amazing feats of mechanics have been born, like massive Steam Tanks and flying Gyrocopters. However, of all their creations the most useful remain the many black powder weapons. Volley guns, duardin cannon and organ guns rain a storm of shot down upon the foe, while helstorm rockets turn the battlefield into a sea of fire. These guns line the walls of the Eternal City, and, now, as new keeps are raised in the realms, the Ironweld Arsenal is furnishing the lords of these foundling cities with their own artillery.

## IRONWELD ARSENAL
# ARTILLERY DETACHMENT

The war machines of the Ironweld hammer the battlefield as the armies of Azyrheim advance, often leaving nought but smouldering corpses and shattered ruins for the city's soldiers to conquer.

## ORGANISATION

An Artillery Detachment consists of the following units:

- 1 Gunmaster
- 1 Cogsmith
- 1 Helblaster Volley Gun
- 1 Helstorm Rocket Battery
- 1 Cannon
- 1 Organ Gun
- 1 Steam Tank
- 1 unit of Gyrocopters
- 1 unit of Gyrobombers

## ABILITIES

**Preliminary Bombardment:** In your hero phase, pick an enemy unit that is visible to either the battalion's Gunmaster or Cogsmith. Then, roll a dice for each other unit in this battalion; on a 6 that unit can immediately shoot at the nominated enemy unit as if it were the shooting phase.

# GUNMASTER

| MISSILE WEAPONS | Range | Attacks | To Hit | To Wound | Rend | Damage |
|---|---|---|---|---|---|---|
| Artisan Pistol | 9" | 1 | 3+ | 3+ | -1 | 1 |
| Repeater Pistols | 9" | 3 | 4+ | 3+ | -1 | 1 |
| Masterwork Long Rifle | 30" | 1 | 3+ | 3+ | -1 | 2 |
| MELEE WEAPONS | Range | Attacks | To Hit | To Wound | Rend | Damage |
| Engineer's Telescope or Tools | 1" | 2 | 4+ | 5+ | - | 1 |

**MOVE** 5"
**WOUNDS** 5
**SAVE** 6+
**BRAVERY** 6

## DESCRIPTION

A Gunmaster is a single model. All Gunmasters carry a telescope or other range-finding tools, which can also make for improvised weapons in close combat. However, Gunmasters prefer to shoot their foes; they carry a pair of experimental Repeater Pistols into battle alongside a tried and trusted Artisan Pistol. Some Gunmasters also supplement their collection of pistols with a Masterwork Long Rifle to snipe the foe.

## ABILITIES

**Range-finding Optics:** You can re-roll hit rolls of 1 for a Gunmaster in the shooting phase if he did not move in his preceding movement phase and there are no enemy models within 3" of him.

**KEYWORDS** | ORDER, HUMAN, IRONWELD ARSENAL, HERO, ENGINEER, GUNMASTER

# COGSMITH

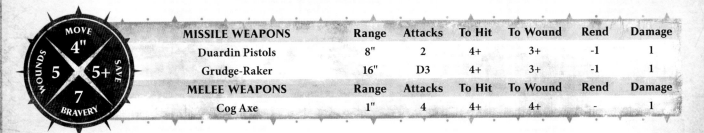

| MISSILE WEAPONS | Range | Attacks | To Hit | To Wound | Rend | Damage |
|---|---|---|---|---|---|---|
| Duardin Pistols | 8" | 2 | 4+ | 3+ | -1 | 1 |
| Grudge-Raker | 16" | D3 | 4+ | 3+ | -1 | 1 |
| MELEE WEAPONS | Range | Attacks | To Hit | To Wound | Rend | Damage |
| Cog Axe | 1" | 4 | 4+ | 4+ | - | 1 |

**MOVE** 4"
**WOUNDS** 5
**SAVE** 5+
**BRAVERY** 7

## DESCRIPTION

A Cogsmith is a single model. He is equipped with a veritable arsenal of weapons, including a brace of trusty Duardin Pistols and a handgun known as a Grudge-Raker to despatch his foes from a distance. He is also armed with his Cog Axe for when things get up close and personal.

## ABILITIES

**Engineer:** In your hero phase, a Cogsmith can repair a single **WAR MACHINE** within 4". That model repairs 1 wound.

| KEYWORDS | ORDER, DUARDIN, IRONWELD ARSENAL, HERO, ENGINEER, COGSMITH |
|---|---|

# HELBLASTER VOLLEY GUN

## WAR MACHINE

| MISSILE WEAPONS | Range | Attacks | To Hit | To Wound | Rend | Damage |
|---|---|---|---|---|---|---|
| Volley of Shots | 26" | D6 | ☀ | 3+ | -1 | 1 |

| WAR MACHINE CREW TABLE | | |
|---|---|---|
| Crew within 1" | Move | Volley of Shots |
| 3 models | 4" | 3+ |
| 2 models | 3" | 4+ |
| 1 model | 2" | 5+ |
| No models | 0" | - |

## WAR MACHINE

| KEYWORDS | ORDER, WAR MACHINE, HELBLASTER VOLLEY GUN |
|---|---|

## CREW

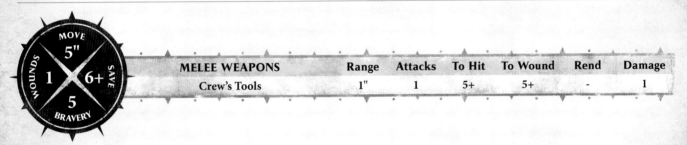

| MELEE WEAPONS | Range | Attacks | To Hit | To Wound | Rend | Damage |
|---|---|---|---|---|---|---|
| Crew's Tools | 1" | 1 | 5+ | 5+ | - | 1 |

**MOVE** 5"
**WOUNDS** 1
**SAVE** 6+
**BRAVERY** 5

### DESCRIPTION

A Helblaster Volley Gun consists of a lethal war machine that fires a Volley of Shots at the foe, and a unit of 3 Ironweld Crew. The Crew load and fire the Volley Gun and can defend it in melee using their Tools as improvised weapons.

### ABILITIES

**Point Blank:** You can add 1 to hit rolls for this model's Volley of Shots if the target unit is within 13".

**Crewed Artillery:** A Helblaster Volley Gun can only move if its Crew are within 1" at the start of the movement phase. If its Crew are within 1" of the Volley Gun in the shooting phase, they can fire the war machine. The war machine cannot make charge moves, does not need to take battleshock tests and is unaffected by any attack or ability that uses Bravery. The Crew are in cover while they are within 1" of their war machine.

**Helblaster Volley:** In the shooting phase the Helblaster Volley Gun's Crew can attempt to load and fire 1, 2, or 3 gun decks. If they loaded 2 gun decks, the war machine makes 2D6 attacks when it fires its Volley of Shots instead of D6, and if

they loaded 3 gun decks, it will make 3D6 attacks. However, if any doubles are rolled when determining how many attacks are made when firing a Volley of Shot, the Helblaster Volley Gun jams and no shots are fired this phase.

**Working Like Clockwork:** Engineers know just how to tinker with Volley Guns to ensure they work at maximum efficiency and do not jam in the heat of battle. You can re-roll all the dice when determining how many attacks are made with a Volley of Shots if there is an **ENGINEER** from your army within 1" of this war machine.

### CREW

| KEYWORDS | ORDER, HUMAN, IRONWELD ARSENAL, CREW |
|---|---|

# HELSTORM ROCKET BATTERY

**WAR MACHINE**

| MISSILE WEAPONS | Range | Attacks | To Hit | To Wound | Rend | Damage |
|---|---|---|---|---|---|---|
| Helstorm Rocket Salvo | 10-36" | 3 | 5+ | 3+ | -2 | ✹ |

| | WAR MACHINE CREW TABLE | |
|---|---|---|
| **Crew within 1"** | **Move** | **Helstorm Rocket Salvo** |
| 3 models | 4" | D6 |
| 2 models | 3" | D3 |
| 1 model | 2" | 1 |
| No models | 0" | 0 |

**WAR MACHINE**

| KEYWORDS | ORDER, WAR MACHINE, HELSTORM ROCKET BATTERY |
|---|---|

## CREW

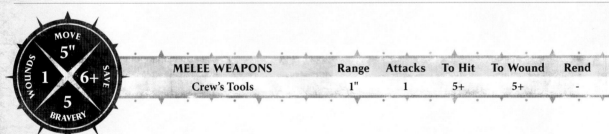

| | MOVE 5" |
|---|---|
| WOUNDS 1 | SAVE 6+ |
| BRAVERY 5 | |

| MELEE WEAPONS | Range | Attacks | To Hit | To Wound | Rend | Damage |
|---|---|---|---|---|---|---|
| Crew's Tools | 1" | 1 | 5+ | 5+ | - | 1 |

## DESCRIPTION

A Helstorm Rocket Battery consists of an artillery piece that launches wildly inaccurate but deadly Helstorm Rockets, and a unit of 3 Ironweld Crew who operate their war machine. The Crew can use their Tools as improvised weapons.

## ABILITIES

**Crewed Artillery:** A Helstorm Rocket Battery can only move if its Crew are within 1" at the start of the movement phase. If its Crew are within 1" of the Rocket Battery in the shooting phase, they can fire the war machine. The war machine cannot make charge moves, does not need to take battleshock tests and is unaffected by any attack or ability that uses Bravery. The Crew are in cover while they are within 1" of their war machine.

**Arcing Ordnance:** A Helstorm Rocket Battery can fire Helstorm Rocket Salvoes at units that are not visible to it.

**Rocket Salvo:** Before firing their war machine, a Helstorm Rocket Battery crew can choose to fire all their Rocket Salvos at the same target. If they do, you can add 1 to the hit rolls for the shots.

**I Meant to Hit That One, Honest:** Engineers are excellent judges of wind speed and other factors and can vastly improve a Rocket Battery's chances of hitting the foe, if not the original target. If there is an ENGINEER from your army within 1" of this war machine and you fail to hit with a Helstorm Rocket Salvo, you may pick a different unit within 10" of the original target and roll a dice; on a 6 that shot hits that unit instead.

## CREW

| KEYWORDS | ORDER, HUMAN, IRONWELD ARSENAL, CREW |
|---|---|

# CANNON

## WAR MACHINE

| MISSILE WEAPONS | Range | Attacks | To Hit | To Wound | Rend | Damage |
|---|---|---|---|---|---|---|
| Cannon Shell | 32" | ☀ | 4+ | 2+ | -2 | D6 |

| | WAR MACHINE CREW TABLE | |
|---|---|---|
| Crew within 1" | Move | Cannon Shell |
| 3 models | 4" | 2 |
| 2 models | 3" | 2 |
| 1 model | 2" | 1 |
| No models | 0" | 0 |

## WAR MACHINE

| KEYWORDS | ORDER, WAR MACHINE, CANNON |
|---|---|

## CREW

| | MOVE **4"** | |
|---|---|---|
| WOUNDS **1** | | SAVE **5+** |
| | **6** | |
| | BRAVERY | |

| MELEE WEAPONS | Range | Attacks | To Hit | To Wound | Rend | Damage |
|---|---|---|---|---|---|---|
| Crew's Tools | 1" | 1 | 4+ | 5+ | - | 1 |

## DESCRIPTION

A Cannon consists of a war machine and a unit of 3 Duardin Crew. The war machine fires deadly explosive Cannon Shells into the enemy's ranks and the Crew can defend their charge using their Tools as improvised weapons.

## ABILITIES

**Duardin Artillery:** A Cannon can only move if its Crew are within 1" at the start of the movement phase. If its Crew are within 1" of the Cannon in the shooting phase, they can fire the war machine. The war machine cannot make charge moves, does not need to take battleshock tests and is unaffected by any attack or ability that uses Bravery. The Crew are in cover while they are within 1" of their war machine.

**Explosive Shells:** You can re-roll the damage inflicted by a Cannon Shell if the target unit has 10 or more models.

**Rune of Accuracy:** Engineers can inscribe Cannon Shells with magical runes to guide them to their target. You can re-roll failed hit rolls when firing a Cannon Shell if there is an **ENGINEER** from your army within 1" of the war machine.

## CREW

| KEYWORDS | ORDER, DUARDIN, IRONWELD ARSENAL, CREW |
|---|---|

# ORGAN GUN

## WAR MACHINE

MOVE
*
WOUNDS 4 X 4+ SAVE
-
BRAVERY

| MISSILE WEAPONS | Range | Attacks | To Hit | To Wound | Rend | Damage |
|---|---|---|---|---|---|---|
| Barrage of Shots | 28" | D6 | * | 3+ | -1 | 1 |

| WAR MACHINE CREW TABLE | | |
|---|---|---|
| Crew within 1" | Move | Barrage of Shots |
| 3 models | 4" | 3+ |
| 2 models | 3" | 4+ |
| 1 model | 2" | 5+ |
| No models | 0" | - |

## WAR MACHINE

| KEYWORDS | ORDER, WAR MACHINE, ORGAN GUN |
|---|---|

## CREW

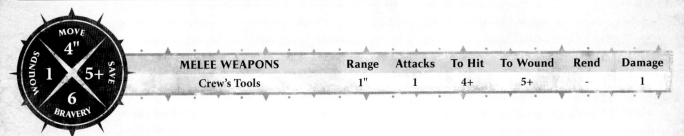

| | MELEE WEAPONS | Range | Attacks | To Hit | To Wound | Rend | Damage |
|---|---|---|---|---|---|---|---|
| | Crew's Tools | 1" | 1 | 4+ | 5+ | - | 1 |

**MOVE** 4"
**WOUNDS** 1
**SAVE** 5+
**BRAVERY** 6

## DESCRIPTION
An Organ Gun consists of a four-barrelled war machine that fires a lethal Barrage of Shots and a unit of 3 Duardin Crew equipped with Tools.

## ABILITIES
**Duardin Artillery:** An Organ Gun can only move if its Crew are within 1" at the start of the movement phase. If its Crew are within 1" of the Organ Gun in the shooting phase, they can fire the war machine. The war machine cannot make charge moves, does not need to take battleshock tests and is unaffected by any attack or ability that uses Bravery. The Crew are in cover while they are within 1" of their war machine.

**Organ Fire:** In the shooting phase the Organ Gun's Crew can load 1, 2, 3 or 4 barrels. If they load 2 or more barrels, roll a dice; if the result is equal to or greater than the number of loaded barrels, make one Barrage of Shots attack for each loaded barrel (roll separately to determine the number of Barrage of Shots attacks made for each barrel being fired). However, if the result is less than the number of loaded barrels, the Organ Gun jams and no shots are fired this phase.

**Rune of Forging:** These runes are used by Engineers to ensure that their war machine stays true and does not misfire in the heat of battle. You can re-roll the dice rolled to see if an Organ Gun jams if there is an ENGINEER from your army within 1" of the war machine.

## CREW

| KEYWORDS | ORDER, DUARDIN, IRONWELD ARSENAL, CREW |
|---|---|

# STEAM TANK

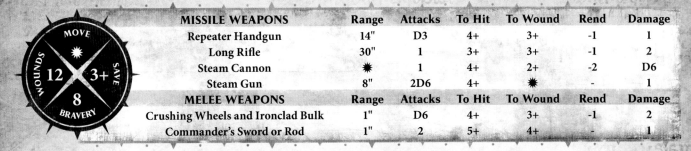

| MISSILE WEAPONS | Range | Attacks | To Hit | To Wound | Rend | Damage |
|---|---|---|---|---|---|---|
| Repeater Handgun | 14" | D3 | 4+ | 3+ | -1 | 1 |
| Long Rifle | 30" | 1 | 3+ | 3+ | -1 | 2 |
| Steam Cannon | ✹ | 1 | 4+ | 2+ | -2 | D6 |
| Steam Gun | 8" | 2D6 | 4+ | ✹ | - | 1 |
| MELEE WEAPONS | Range | Attacks | To Hit | To Wound | Rend | Damage |
| Crushing Wheels and Ironclad Bulk | 1" | D6 | 4+ | 3+ | -1 | 2 |
| Commander's Sword or Rod | 1" | 2 | 5+ | 4+ | - | 1 |

| DAMAGE TABLE | | | |
|---|---|---|---|
| Wounds Suffered | Move | Steam Cannon | Steam Gun |
| 0-2 | 2D6" | 30" | 2+ |
| 3-4 | 2D6" | 24" | 3+ |
| 5-7 | D6" | 18" | 4+ |
| 8-9 | D6" | 12" | 5+ |
| 10+ | D3" | 6" | 6+ |

## DESCRIPTION

A Steam Tank is a single model. The Steam Tank Commander in the Steam Tank's turret can fight with a Commander's Sword or Rod. Some Commanders may also carry a Repeater Handgun, and some may also man a Long Rifle attached to the Steam Tank's cupula. The Steam Tank itself is armed with a Steam Cannon and Steam Gun, and uses its Crushing Wheels and Ironclad Bulk to grind its foes into paste.

## ABILITIES

**More Pressure!:** In your hero phase, the Steam Tank Commander can attempt to overpressure the Steam Tank's Boiler. If he does, roll two dice. If the total is less than the number of wounds the Steam Tank has suffered, valves start to crack and mechanisms break – the Steam Tank immediately suffers D3 mortal wounds. Otherwise, the overpressure of steam means that until your next hero phase you can re-roll any random values for this model (with the exception of the Commander's Repeater Handgun, which isn't connected to the Steam Tank's boiler!).

**Steel Behemoth:** After a Steam Tank completes a charge move, you may select an enemy unit within 1"; that unit suffers D3 mortal wounds.

**Bouncing Cannon Balls:** You can add 1 to hit rolls for a Steam Cannon if the target unit has 10 or more models.

**I'll Fix It:** Instead of using the More Pressure! ability, the Steam Tank Commander can attempt to make repairs to the Steam Tank in your hero phase. If he does, roll a dice; on a 4 or more he repairs one wound.

| KEYWORDS | ORDER, HUMAN, IRONWELD ARSENAL, WAR MACHINE, STEAM TANK |
|---|---|

# GYROCOPTERS

| MISSILE WEAPONS | Range | Attacks | To Hit | To Wound | Rend | Damage |
|---|---|---|---|---|---|---|
| Brimstone Gun | 16" | 3 | 3+ | 3+ | -1 | 1 |
| Steam Gun | 6" | See below | 3+ | 4+ | -1 | 1 |
| MELEE WEAPONS | Range | Attacks | To Hit | To Wound | Rend | Damage |
| Rotor Blades | 1" | D3 | 5+ | 4+ | - | 1 |

**MOVE** 14"
**WOUNDS** 4
**SAVE** 4+
**BRAVERY** 6

## DESCRIPTION

A Gyrocopters unit can have any number of models. Some Gyrocopters are fitted with a nose-mounted Steam Gun, whilst others are armed with a Brimstone Gun. In either case, Gyrocopters have a pair of Guild Bombs that they can drop onto the foe. Each Gyrocopter is piloted by a duardin, who can, in desperate times, use his Gyrocopter's Rotor Blades in a melee.

## FLY

Gyrocopters can fly.

## ABILITIES

**Steam Gun:** When firing a Steam Gun, select a target unit. You can then make one attack against that unit for each model in it that is within range.

**Guild Bombs:** Once per battle, a unit of Gyrocopters can drop their Guild Bombs. To do so, pick one enemy unit that the Gyrocopters flew over in the movement phase. Then, roll two dice for each Gyrocopter in the unit; each time you roll a 4 or more, the unit being bombed suffers a mortal wound.

| KEYWORDS | ORDER, DUARDIN, IRONWELD ARSENAL, WAR MACHINE, GYROCOPTERS |
|---|---|

# GYROBOMBERS

| MISSILE WEAPONS | Range | Attacks | To Hit | To Wound | Rend | Damage |
|---|---|---|---|---|---|---|
| Clattergun | 20" | 4 | 4+ | 3+ | -1 | 1 |
| MELEE WEAPONS | Range | Attacks | To Hit | To Wound | Rend | Damage |
| Rotor Blades | 1" | D3 | 5+ | 4+ | - | 1 |

## DESCRIPTION

A Gyrobombers unit can have any number of models. Gyrobombers are fitted with nose-mounted Clatterguns and carry a rack of Grudgebuster Bombs to obliterate enemy formations as they fly over them. Each Gyrobomber is piloted by a duardin, who can, in desperate times, use his machine's Rotor Blades in a melee.

## FLY

Gyrobombers can fly.

## ABILITIES

**Grudgebuster Bombs:** A unit of Gyrobombers can drop Grudgebuster Bombs as they fly over enemy units. To do so, pick one enemy unit that the Gyrobombers flew over in the movement phase. Then, roll one dice for each Gyrobomber in the unit; each time you roll a 4 or more, the unit being bombed suffers D3 mortal wounds.

| KEYWORDS | ORDER, DUARDIN, IRONWELD ARSENAL, WAR MACHINE, GYROBOMBERS |
|---|---|

# DISPOSSESSED

**Resolute and resilient warriors, the Dispossessed are the remnants of a once great duardin empire. Master builders and servants of Order, the towering walls of Azyrheim and the newly raised cities of the realms owe much to their skill.**

From the flames of the dying Khazalid empires marched the Warden Kings, their duardin people in tow. Bloodied, bearded warriors, wise runelords and loyal clansmen all entered the vaulted gates of Azyrheim. There they created huge ordered cavern kingdoms below the city, where they kept their metal crafts and rune-making alive. It is said that in those first years the smith god Grungni wept tears of molten lead to see that so few of his children had survived.

The domains and fortresses of the Dispossessed are all hard lines and unyielding angles, as rigid and unforgiving as the warriors that created them. As the armies of Order spread out into the Mortal Realms, the Dispossessed are there to carve the rule of law back into the ground. While the Devoted bless the earth and the Freeguilds garrison the cities, the Dispossessed help the Stormcast Eternals and the armies of Azyr to bring down the bastions of Chaos.

Over the ruins the duardin fashion new cities. Every Dispossessed who toils upon these constructs is also a hardened warrior, whether they are veteran Longbeard, heavily armoured Ironbreaker or resolute Hammerer. Even the crazed Unforged, those whose minds have been broken by their encounters with Chaos, have their role to play against enemy beasts and champions. Where the free cities take root once more, so too march the Warden Kings and their warriors.

## DISPOSSESSED
# GRUDGEBOUND WAR THRONG

The Dispossessed warriors still keenly remember the destruction of their empire, and are more than willing to sell their lives against their ancient enemies if it means a chance of settling old scores.

## ORGANISATION

A Grudgebound War Throng consists of the following units:

- 1 Warden King
- 1 Runelord
- 1 Unforged
- Any 4 units from the following list: Warriors, Thunderers, Quarrellers, Longbeards.
- Any 3 units from the following list: Irondrakes, Ironbreakers, Hammerers.

## ABILITIES

**Ancient Grudges:** The warriors of a Grudgebound War Throng hold deep-rooted grudges. When a Grudgebound War Throng goes to war, these sparks of bitterness are fanned into seething flames of vengeance that will only be extinguished when old scores are settled. You can re-roll all hit rolls of 1 for models in a Grudgebound War Throng.

**Stubborn to the End:** The Dispossessed are renowned for their stubborn refusal to admit defeat, especially in the face of overwhelming odds. If you roll a 1, 2 or a 3 when taking a battleshock test for a unit in a Grudgebound War Throng, that unit stubbornly refuses to yield and is treated as having passed the battleshock test irrespective of any penalties on their Bravery or the number of casualties they have suffered that turn.

# WARDEN KING

| | MOVE 4" |
|---|---|
| WOUNDS 5 | SAVE 4+ |
| | BRAVERY 8 |

| MELEE WEAPONS | Range | Attacks | To Hit | To Wound | Rend | Damage |
|---|---|---|---|---|---|---|
| Rune Weapon | 1" | 4 | 3+ | 3+ | -1 | D3 |

## DESCRIPTION

A Warden King is a single model. They wield a Rune Weapon in one hand and an Ancestor Shield in the other. Warden Kings also march to war with an oath stone upon which they defiantly stand to inspire their fellow warriors.

## ABILITIES

**Ancestor Shield:** You can re-roll all failed saves for a Warden King.

**Oath Stone:** In the hero phase, a Warden King can stand atop his oath stone to increase the resolve of his followers. If he does so, he cannot move until his next hero phase, but all DISPOSSESSED units from your army within 18" in the battleshock phase may use the Warden King's Bravery instead of their own.

## COMMAND ABILITY

**Ancestral Grudge:** If a Warden King uses this ability, pick one enemy unit within 16". Until your next hero phase, you can add 1 to wound rolls for all attacks made by DISPOSSESSED models that target that unit.

| KEYWORDS | ORDER, DUARDIN, DISPOSSESSED, HERO, WARDEN KING |
|---|---|

# RUNELORD

| | MOVE | |
|---|---|---|
| | 4" | |
| WOUNDS 5 | | SAVE 4+ |
| | 7 | |
| | BRAVERY | |

| MELEE WEAPONS | Range | Attacks | To Hit | To Wound | Rend | Damage |
|---|---|---|---|---|---|---|
| Rune Staff | 1" | 1 | 4+ | 3+ | - | D3 |
| Forgehammer | 1" | 2 | 4+ | 4+ | - | 1 |

## DESCRIPTION

A Runelord is a single model. He is armed with a Rune Staff and a Forgehammer.

## ABILITIES

**Runes of Spellbreaking:** A Runelord can attempt to unbind one enemy spell in the enemy hero phase as if he were a wizard. You can add 2 to any unbinding rolls for a Runelord.

**Rune Lore:** In your hero phase a Runelord can pray to the Ancestor Gods to imbue his allies' weapons and armour with power. If he does so, pick a **DISPOSSESSED** unit within 16", select a power and roll a dice; on a 1 the Runelord has failed and nothing happens. On a roll of 2 or more the runes hammered into his allies' wargear glow white-hot with rune magic and the power takes effect.

*Ancestral Shield:* Until your next hero phase, you can roll a dice whenever a model in this unit suffers a wound or a mortal wound. On a 6, that wound or mortal wound is ignored.

*Forgefire:* Until your next hero phase, increase the Rend characteristics of the unit's weapons by 1 (i.e. '-' becomes -1, -1 becomes -2 and so on).

| KEYWORDS | ORDER, DUARDIN, DISPOSSESSED, HERO, PRIEST, RUNELORD |
|---|---|

# UNFORGED

| | MELEE WEAPONS | Range | Attacks | To Hit | To Wound | Rend | Damage |
|---|---|---|---|---|---|---|---|
| | Runic Axes | 1" | 6 | 3+ | 3+ | -1 | 1 |

MOVE **4"**
WOUNDS **5**
SAVE **6+**
BRAVERY **10**

## DESCRIPTION
An Unforged is a single model. The Unforged march to seek their doom in battle armed with a pair of Runic Axes.

## ABILITIES
**Runic Axes:** The Unforged launches a deadly flurry of blows. You can re-roll all hit rolls of 1 for an Unforged.

**Epic Deathblow:** If an Unforged is slain in the combat phase, roll a dice before it is removed. On a roll of 4 or more, you can inflict D3 mortal wounds on the enemy unit that struck the fatal blow (inflict D6 mortal wounds instead if a **CHAOS** model struck the final blow).

**Nemesis:** Attacks made by an Unforged inflict double Damage against **CHAOS** units.

**The Bigger They Are...:** You can add 1 to any wound rolls for an Unforged if the target of the attack has a Wounds characteristic of more than 1.

| KEYWORDS | ORDER, DUARDIN, DISPOSSESSED, HERO, UNFORGED |
|---|---|

# WARRIORS

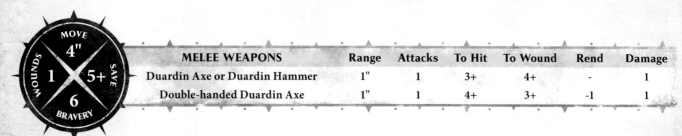

| | MELEE WEAPONS | Range | Attacks | To Hit | To Wound | Rend | Damage |
|---|---|---|---|---|---|---|---|
| | Duardin Axe or Duardin Hammer | 1" | 1 | 3+ | 4+ | - | 1 |
| | Double-handed Duardin Axe | 1" | 1 | 4+ | 3+ | -1 | 1 |

MOVE 4"
WOUNDS 1
SAVE 5+
BRAVERY 6

## DESCRIPTION

A unit of Warriors has 10 or more models. Most Warriors enter battle armed with either a Duardin Axe or a Duardin Hammer, but some units prefer instead to wield Double-handed Duardin Axes to cut down their foes with mighty swings. Many units also carry sturdy Duardin Shields.

## VETERAN

The leader of this unit is the Veteran. A Veteran makes 2 attacks rather than 1.

## STANDARD BEARERS

Models in this unit may be Standard Bearers. Standard Bearers can carry either a Runic Icon or a Clan Banner.

## HORNBLOWERS

Models in this unit can be Hornblowers. When a unit containing any Hornblowers runs, they can 'Sound the Advance'. If they do so, do not roll a dice to see how far the unit runs; instead, they can move up to an extra 4".

## ABILITIES

**Resolute in Defence:** You can re-roll failed wound rolls of 1 when attacking with a Warrior in your opponent's combat phase. You can instead re-roll all failed wound rolls for a Warrior if its unit has 20 or more models when it attacks in your opponent's combat phase.

**Duardin Shields:** A unit equipped with Duardin Shields can create a shield wall instead of running or charging in its turn. If it does so, re-roll all failed save rolls for the unit in the combat phase until its next movement phase.

**Runic Icon:** Roll a dice if a spell affects a unit with any Runic Icons. On a roll of a 5 or more, that spell has no affect on the unit (but it will affect other units normally).

**Clan Banner:** If you fail a battleshock test for a unit that has any Clan Banners, halve the number of models that flee (rounding up).

| KEYWORDS | ORDER, DUARDIN, DISPOSSESSED, WARRIORS |
|---|---|

# IRONDRAKES

**MOVE** 4"
**WOUNDS** 1
**SAVE** 4+
**BRAVERY** 7

| MISSILE WEAPONS | Range | Attacks | To Hit | To Wound | Rend | Damage |
|---|---|---|---|---|---|---|
| Drakegun | 16" | 1 | 3+ | 3+ | -1 | 1 |
| Grudgehammer Torpedo | 20" | 1 | 3+ | 3+ | -2 | D3 |
| Drakefire Pistol | 8" | 1 | 4+ | 3+ | -1 | 1 |
| MELEE WEAPONS | Range | Attacks | To Hit | To Wound | Rend | Damage |
| Drakefire Pistol | 1" | 1 | 4+ | 4+ | - | 1 |
| Mailed Fist | 1" | 1 | 4+ | 5+ | - | 1 |

## DESCRIPTION

A unit of Irondrakes has 5 or more models. Irondrakes are clad in suits of Gromril Armour and are armed with Drakeguns to shoot the foe at range. Irondrakes can punch foes in close combat with their Mailed Fists.

## IRONWARDEN

The leader of this unit is an Ironwarden. Some Ironwardens wield a Drakegun, whilst others prefer to go into battle with a Grudgehammer Torpedo. These Ironwardens are more than happy to punch foes in the face with their Mailed Fists. You can add 1 to hit rolls for an Ironwarden shooting a Drakegun.

Other Ironwardens are instead equipped with a single Drakefire Pistol – with which they can shoot the foe at range or club them in close combat – and a Cinderblast bomb, whilst some prefer to fight with a Drakefire Pistol in each hand.

## ICON BEARER

Models in this unit may be Icon Bearers. Roll a dice if a spell affects a unit with any Icon Bearers. On a roll of a 5 or more, that spell has no affect on the unit (but it will affect other units normally).

## HORNBLOWERS

Models in this unit can be Hornblowers. When a unit containing any Hornblowers runs, they can 'Sound the Advance'. If they do so, do not roll a dice to see how far the unit runs; instead, they can move up to an extra 4".

## ABILITIES

**Brace of Drakefire Pistols:** You can make 2 attacks for an Ironwarden armed with more than one Drakefire Pistol in both the shooting and the combat phases.

**Grudgehammer Torpedo:** A Grudgehammer Torpedo inflicts D6 Damage instead of D3 if the target has the **MONSTER** keyword.

**Cinderblast Bomb:** Once per battle, an Ironwarden with a Cinderblast Bomb can throw it in your shooting phase. To do so, pick a unit within 6" and roll a dice; on a 2 or more, that unit suffers D3 mortal wounds.

**Forge-proven Gromril Armour:** When you make save rolls for this unit, ignore the enemy's Rend characteristic unless it is -2 or better.

**Blaze Away:** Irondrakes can shoot twice with their Drakeguns if they did not move in their preceding movement phase and there are no enemy models within 3".

| KEYWORDS | ORDER, DUARDIN, DISPOSSESSED, IRONDRAKES |
|---|---|

# LONGBEARDS

| MELEE WEAPONS | Range | Attacks | To Hit | To Wound | Rend | Damage |
|---|---|---|---|---|---|---|
| Ancestral Axe or Ancestral Hammer | 1" | 1 | 3+ | 4+ | - | 1 |
| Ancestral Great Axe | 1" | 1 | 4+ | 3+ | -1 | 1 |

## DESCRIPTION

A unit of Longbeards has 10 or more models. Some units of Longbeards wield treasured Ancestral Axes or Ancestral Hammers. Other units prefer to march to war wielding double-handed Ancestral Great Axes to cut down the foe. In addition, some units carry sturdy Gromril Shields.

## OLD GUARD

The leader of this unit is the Old Guard. An Old Guard makes 2 attacks.

## STANDARD BEARER

Models in this unit may be Standard Bearers. If you fail a battleshock test for a unit that has any Standard Bearers, halve the number of models that flee (rounding up).

## THRONG MUSICIAN

Models in this unit can be Hornblowers or Drummers. When a unit containing any Hornblowers or Drummers runs, they can 'Sound the Advance'. If they do so, do not roll a dice to see how far the unit runs; instead, they can move up to an extra 4".

## ABILITIES

**Gromril Shields:** This unit can create a shield wall instead of running or charging in its turn. If it does so, re-roll all failed save rolls for the unit in the combat phase until its next movement phase.

**Old Grumblers:** Longbeards are always grumbling about something, from the hardships they endured when they were younger and how the youth of today don't respect their elders, to how expensive beer is these days. In your hero phase, this unit will complain about something in a suitably duardin manner. When they do, pick one of the grumblings listed below. The effects last until your next hero phase.

*'I thought duardin were made of sterner stuff!':* Roll a dice each time a **Dispossessed** model from your army flees whilst within 8" of this unit; on a 5 or more that model stands firm under the Longbeards' stern gaze and does not flee.

*'Who does this beardling think he is?':* **Dispossessed Heroes** from your army within 8" of this unit in the hero phase can use their command abilities even if they are not your general.

*'Grots are weedier these days!':* You can re-roll wound rolls of 1 for **Dispossessed** models from your army that are within 8" of this unit when they attack in the combat phase.

---

**KEYWORDS** | ORDER, DUARDIN, DISPOSSESSED, LONGBEARDS

# IRONBREAKERS

| MISSILE WEAPONS | Range | Attacks | To Hit | To Wound | Rend | Damage |
|---|---|---|---|---|---|---|
| Drakefire Pistol | 8" | 1 | 4+ | 3+ | -1 | 1 |
| MELEE WEAPONS | Range | Attacks | To Hit | To Wound | Rend | Damage |
| Drakefire Pistol | 1" | 1 | 4+ | 4+ | - | 1 |
| Ironbreaker Axe or Hammer | 1" | 2 | 3+ | 4+ | - | 1 |

**MOVE** 4"
**WOUNDS** 1
**SAVE** 4+
**BRAVERY** 7

## DESCRIPTION

A unit of Ironbreakers has 5 or more models. Ironbreakers are clad in suits of Gromril Armour. Each Ironbreaker goes to war armed with an Ironbreaker Axe or Hammer in one hand and a sturdy Gromril Shield in the other.

## IRONBEARD

The leader of this unit is an Ironbeard. Some Ironbeards choose to wield an Ironbreaker Axe or Hammer and a Gromril Shield. An Ironbeard makes 3 attacks with an Ironbreaker Axe or Hammer instead of 2. Other Ironbeards are armed with a single Drakefire Pistol – with which they can shoot the foe at range or club them in close combat – and a Cinderblast bomb, whilst some prefer to fight with a Drakefire Pistol in each hand.

## ICON BEARER

Models in this unit may be Icon Bearers. Roll a dice if an enemy spell affects a unit with any Icon Bearers. On a roll of a 5 or more, that spell has no affect on the unit (but it will affect other units normally).

## DRUMMER

Models in this unit can be Drummers. When a unit containing any Drummers runs, they can 'Sound the Advance'. If they do so, do not roll a dice to see how far the unit runs; instead, they can move up to an extra 4".

## ABILITIES

**Brace of Drakefire Pistols:** You can make 2 attacks for an Ironbeard armed with more than one Drakefire Pistol in both the shooting and the combat phases.

**Cinderblast Bomb:** Once per battle, a model with a Cinderblast Bomb can throw it in your shooting phase. To do so, pick a unit within 6" and roll a dice; on a 2 or more, that unit suffers D3 mortal wounds.

**Gromril Shields:** This unit can create a shield wall instead of running or charging in its turn. If it does so, re-roll all failed save rolls for the unit in the combat phase until its next movement phase.

**Forge-proven Gromril Armour:** When you make save rolls for this unit, ignore the enemy's Rend characteristic unless it is -2 or better.

| KEYWORDS | ORDER, DUARDIN, DISPOSSESSED, IRONBREAKERS |
|---|---|

# HAMMERERS

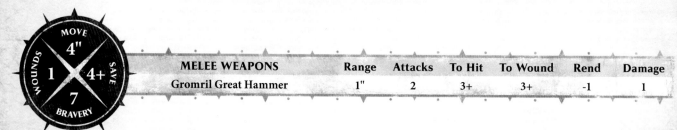

| | MOVE | | | | | |
|---|---|---|---|---|---|---|
| | 4" | | | | | |
| WOUNDS 1 | | SAVE 4+ | | | | |
| | 7 | | | | | |
| | BRAVERY | | | | | |

| MELEE WEAPONS | Range | Attacks | To Hit | To Wound | Rend | Damage |
|---|---|---|---|---|---|---|
| Gromril Great Hammer | 1" | 2 | 3+ | 3+ | -1 | 1 |

## DESCRIPTION
A unit of Hammerers has 5 or more models. They are armed with Gromril Great Hammers.

## THRONG MUSICIAN
Models in this unit can be Hornblowers or Drummers. When a unit containing any Hornblowers or Drummers runs, they can 'Sound the Advance'. If they do so, do not roll a dice to see how far the unit runs; instead, they can move up to an extra 4".

## STANDARD BEARER
Models in this unit may be Standard Bearers. If you fail a battleshock test for a unit that has any Standard Bearers, halve the number of models that flee (rounding up).

## KEEPER OF THE GATE
The leader of this unit is the Keeper of the Gate. A Keeper of the Gate makes 3 attacks rather than 2.

## ABILITIES
**Kingsguard:** You do not need to take battleshock tests for this unit if it is within 16" of a **DISPOSSESSED HERO** from your army in the battleshock phase.

| KEYWORDS | ORDER, DUARDIN, DISPOSSESSED, HAMMERERS |
|---|---|

# THUNDERERS

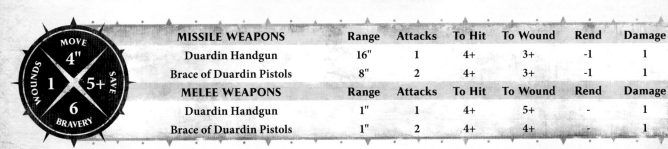

| | MOVE 4" | | |
|---|---|---|---|
| WOUNDS 1 | | SAVE 5+ | |
| | BRAVERY 6 | | |

| MISSILE WEAPONS | Range | Attacks | To Hit | To Wound | Rend | Damage |
|---|---|---|---|---|---|---|
| Duardin Handgun | 16" | 1 | 4+ | 3+ | -1 | 1 |
| Brace of Duardin Pistols | 8" | 2 | 4+ | 3+ | -1 | 1 |
| MELEE WEAPONS | Range | Attacks | To Hit | To Wound | Rend | Damage |
| Duardin Handgun | 1" | 1 | 4+ | 5+ | - | 1 |
| Brace of Duardin Pistols | 1" | 2 | 4+ | 4+ | - | 1 |

## DESCRIPTION

A unit of Thunderers has 10 or more models. They go to war armed with Duardin Handguns, which at a pinch can be used to bludgeon foes in close combat. Some units of Thunderers are also equipped with Duardin Bucklers.

## STANDARD BEARER

Models in this unit may be Standard Bearers. Standard Bearers can carry either a Runic Icon or a Clan Banner.

## VETERAN

The leader of this unit is the Veteran. Some Veterans fight with a Duardin Handgun, but others prefer a Brace of Duardin Pistols. You can add 1 to hit rolls for a Veteran when he fires a Duardin Handgun.

## DRUMMERS

Models in this unit can be Drummers. When a unit containing any Drummers runs, they can 'Sound the Advance'. If they do so, do not roll a dice to see how far the unit runs; instead, they can move up to an extra 4".

## ABILITIES

**Precision Fire:** You can add 1 to all hit rolls for a Thunderer if its unit has 20 or more models and there are no enemy models within 3".

**Runic Icon:** Roll a dice if a spell affects a unit with any Runic Icons. On a roll of a 5 or more, that spell has no affect on the unit (but it will affect other units normally).

**Clan Banner:** If you fail a battleshock test for a unit that has any Clan Banners, halve the number of models that flee (rounding up).

**Duardin Bucklers:** If a unit is equipped with Duardin Bucklers, it can create a shield wall instead of running or charging in its turn. If it does so, re-roll all failed save rolls for the unit in the combat phase until its next movement phase.

| KEYWORDS | ORDER, DUARDIN, DISPOSSESSED, THUNDERERS |
|---|---|

# QUARRELLERS

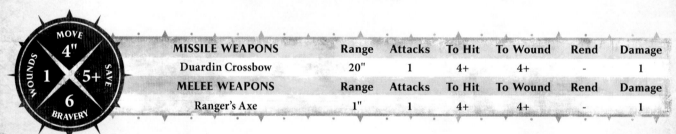

| MISSILE WEAPONS | Range | Attacks | To Hit | To Wound | Rend | Damage |
|---|---|---|---|---|---|---|
| Duardin Crossbow | 20" | 1 | 4+ | 4+ | - | 1 |
| MELEE WEAPONS | Range | Attacks | To Hit | To Wound | Rend | Damage |
| Ranger's Axe | 1" | 1 | 4+ | 4+ | - | 1 |

**MOVE** 4"
**WOUNDS** 1
**SAVE** 5+
**BRAVERY** 6

## DESCRIPTION
A unit of Quarrellers has 10 or more models. They go to war armed with Duardin Crossbows and Ranger's Axes. Some units of Quarrellers are also equipped with Duardin Bucklers.

## VETERAN
The leader of this unit is the Veteran. You can add 1 to hit rolls for a Veteran when he fires his Duardin Crossbow.

## STANDARD BEARER
Models in this unit may be Standard Bearers. Standard Bearers can carry either a Runic Icon or a Clan Banner.

## DRUMMERS
Models in this unit can be Drummers. When a unit containing any Drummers runs, they can 'Sound the Advance'. If they do so, do not roll a dice to see how far the unit runs; instead, they can move up to an extra 4".

## ABILITIES
**Volley Fire:** Quarrellers can shoot twice if their unit has 20 or more models and there are no enemy models within 3".

**Runic Icon:** Roll a dice if a spell affects a unit with any Runic Icons. On a roll of a 5 or more, that spell has no affect on the unit (but it will affect other units normally).

**Clan Banner:** If you fail a battleshock test for a unit that has any Clan Banners, halve the number of models that flee (rounding up).

**Duardin Bucklers:** If a unit is equipped with Duardin Bucklers, it can create a shield wall instead of running or charging in its turn. If it does so, re-roll all failed save rolls for the unit in the combat phase until its next movement phase.

| KEYWORDS | ORDER, DUARDIN, DISPOSSESSED, QUARRELLERS |
|---|---|

# ELDRITCH COUNCIL

**Aelf sorcerers are among the most mysterious and inscrutable of their race. Elemental wizards of the highest order, each one is born with the power to shape the Mortal Realms, casting spells that raise up pillars of ethereal flame that burn without end or domes of shimmering force no blade can break.**

Dotted throughout Azyrheim and the foundling cities of the Mortal Realms stand the White Towers. Within their alabaster halls gather the wizards of the Eldritch Council. Masters of flame, frost and gale, their power is that of the elements, be it black ice from the depths of Shyish or the flickering soul-fire of Aqshy. Fighting with Sigmar's Stormcast Eternals, they lend potent magical attacks and inviolate wards to the celestial warriors. They also work alongside the Devoted to purge the curse of Chaos that rests heavy upon the realms. While faith and blood consecrate the ground itself, aelf magic shatters Chaos runes and unbinds hellish spell-traps.

The Eldritch Council rarely gathers its full might – more often just one or two of these aelven wizards will grace the armies of Azyr with their sorceries, wreaking ruin in the ranks of the enemy. When the Eldritch Council gathers in its entirety, the very air thrums with energy, and it is said the High Star burns brighter to see so many master elementalists marching to battle. In these exceptional times of total war the council will also call forth its fearsome Drakeseers. From the backs of majestic beasts they ride into battle, hurling sorceries as the creature lets loose its flaming breath, leaving naught but spell-ravaged corpses and smouldering remains in their wake.

# ARCHMAGE

| MELEE WEAPONS | Range | Attacks | To Hit | To Wound | Rend | Damage |
|---|---|---|---|---|---|---|
| Seerstaff | 2" | 1 | 4+ | 3+ | -1 | 1 |
| Aelven Steed's Swift Hooves | 1" | 2 | 4+ | 5+ | - | 1 |

## DESCRIPTION

An Archmage is a single model. He wields a mystical Seerstaff that channels his arcane abilities. Almost every Archmage also carries a Talisman of Arcane Power, be it a tome of spells or a magical amulet, to aid them in dispelling the fell sorceries of their foes.

## AELVEN STEED

An Archmage can ride an Aelven Steed. If he does so, his Move is increased to 14" and he gains the Swift Hooves attack.

## ABILITIES

**Talisman of Arcane Power:** You can add 1 to any unbinding rolls for an Archmage with a Talisman of Arcane Power.

## MAGIC

An Archmage is a wizard. He can attempt to cast one spell in each of your own hero phases, and attempt to unbind one spell in each enemy hero phase. He knows the Arcane Bolt, Mystic Shield and Elemental Shield spells.

## ELEMENTAL SHIELD

The Archmage weaves a dome of magical energy around himself and his allies. Elemental Shield has a casting value of 6. If successfully cast, until your next hero phase, you can roll a dice each time the Archmage, or a model in your army within 18" of him, suffers a wound or a mortal wound. On the roll of a 6 that hit is deflected by the magical barrier surrounding the Archmage and is ignored.

| KEYWORDS | ORDER, AELF, ELDRITCH COUNCIL, HERO, WIZARD, ARCHMAGE |
|---|---|

# ARCHMAGE ON DRAGON

| MELEE WEAPONS | Range | Attacks | To Hit | To Wound | Rend | Damage |
|---|---|---|---|---|---|---|
| Magestaff | 2" | 1 | 4+ | 3+ | -1 | D3 |
| Sorcerous Blade | 1" | 3 | 4+ | 4+ | - | 1 |
| Dragon's Claws | 2" | ✸ | 4+ | 3+ | -1 | 2 |
| Dragon's Fearsome Jaws | 3" | 3 | 4+ | ✸ | -2 | D6 |

**MOVE** ✸ 14
**WOUNDS** 14 / **SAVE** 5+
**BRAVERY** 7

| DAMAGE TABLE | | | |
|---|---|---|---|
| Wounds Suffered | Move | Claws | Fearsome Jaws |
| 0-3 | 14" | 6 | 2+ |
| 4-6 | 12" | 5 | 3+ |
| 7-9 | 10" | 4 | 3+ |
| 10-12 | 8" | 3 | 4+ |
| 13+ | 6" | 2 | 4+ |

## DESCRIPTION

An Archmage on Dragon is a single model. Archmages wield a Magestaff. Some also carry an Arcane Tome, to aid them in casting spells, while others instead prefer to wield a Sorcerous Blade alongside their Magestaff to smite their foes in combat. Almost every Archmage also carries a Talisman of Arcane Power to aid him in dispelling the fell sorceries of his foes.

An Archmage's Dragon mount devours enemies in its Fearsome Jaws and tears them apart with its Claws. The Dragon can also unleash a deadly torrent of Dragonfire to immolate its foes.

### FLY

An Archmage on Dragon can fly.

## ABILITIES

**Talisman of Arcane Power:** You can add 1 to any unbinding rolls for an Archmage on Dragon with a Talisman of Arcane Power.

**Dragonfire:** A Dragon can unleash a blast of Dragonfire in your shooting phase. When it does so, pick a visible unit within 12" and roll a dice; on a 1 or 2 that unit suffers a mortal wound, on a 3 or 4 that unit suffers D3 mortal wounds, and on a 5 or 6 that unit suffers D6 mortal wounds.

## MAGIC

An Archmage on Dragon is a wizard. He can attempt to cast one spell in each of your own hero phases, and attempt to unbind two spells in each enemy hero phase. An Archmage with an Arcane Tome can attempt to cast two different spells in each of your hero phases instead of just one, and attempt to unbind two spells in each enemy hero phase. An Archmage on Dragon knows the Arcane Bolt, Mystic Shield and Drain Magic spells.

### DRAIN MAGIC

The Archmage conjures a vortex of anti-magic, dispelling enemy conjurations and banishing daemons from the battlefield. Drain Magic has a casting value of 4. If successfully cast, select a visible unit within 18". Any spells that are affecting that unit immediately cease. Furthermore, if that unit is a **DAEMON** unit, it suffers D3 mortal wounds as the magic sustaining their forms is ripped away and dissipated by the vortex.

# DRAKESEER

| | | | | | | |
|---|---|---|---|---|---|---|
| **MELEE WEAPONS** | **Range** | **Attacks** | **To Hit** | **To Wound** | **Rend** | **Damage** |
| Drakeseer's Sunstaff | 2" | 1 | 4+ | 3+ | -1 | D3 |
| Dragon's Claws | 2" | ✸ | 4+ | 3+ | -1 | 2 |
| Dragon's Fearsome Jaws | 3" | 3 | 4+ | ✸ | -2 | D6 |

MOVE ✸ / SAVE 5+ / WOUNDS 14 / BRAVERY 7

| DAMAGE TABLE | | | |
|---|---|---|---|
| **Wounds Suffered** | **Move** | **Claws** | **Fearsome Jaws** |
| 0-3 | 14" | 6 | 2+ |
| 4-6 | 12" | 5 | 3+ |
| 7-9 | 10" | 4 | 3+ |
| 10-12 | 8" | 3 | 4+ |
| 13+ | 6" | 2 | 4+ |

## DESCRIPTION
A Drakeseer is a single model. The Drakeseer rider wields a Sunstaff alight with magical flame, while his Dragon mount devours enemies in its Fearsome Jaws and tears them apart with its Claws. The Dragon can also unleash a deadly torrent of Dragonfire to immolate its foes.

## FLY
A Drakeseer can fly.

## ABILITIES
**Warrior Mage:** A Drakeseer makes 3 attacks with his Sunstaff instead of 1 if he charged in the same turn.

**Dragonfire:** A Dragon can unleash a blast of Dragonfire in your shooting phase. When it does so, pick a visible unit within 12" and roll a dice; on a 1 or 2 that unit suffers a mortal wound, on a 3 or 4 that unit suffers D3 mortal wounds, and on a 5 or 6 that unit suffers D6 mortal wounds.

## MAGIC
A Drakeseer is a wizard. He can attempt to cast one spell in each of your own hero phases, and attempt to unbind one spell in each enemy hero phase. He knows the Arcane Bolt, Mystic Shield, and Flames of the Phoenix spells.

## FLAMES OF THE PHOENIX
The Drakeseer summons forth flames out of the air to immolate the unworthy, and with every passing second they grow hotter. Flames of the Phoenix has a casting value of 7. If successfully cast, pick a visible enemy unit within 18". That unit suffers a mortal wound as it is set ablaze. Then, roll another dice – if the result is a 3 or less the flames die out and this spell ends. On a 4 or more, however, the unit suffers an additional 2 mortal wounds and continues to burn; roll another dice – if the result is a 3 or less the fire dies out, but on a 4 or more, the unit suffers an additional 3 mortal wounds and the conflagration continues. Keep rolling extra dice in this way, inflicting 1 more mortal wound than last time you rolled, until either the flames die out or the unit does!

| KEYWORDS | ORDER, AELF, DRAGON, ELDRITCH COUNCIL, HERO, WIZARD, MONSTER, DRAKESEER |
|---|---|

# LOREMASTER

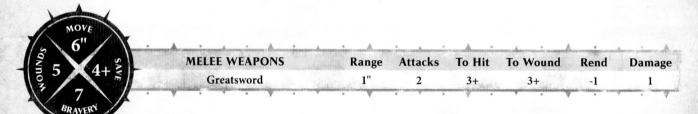

**MOVE** 6"
**WOUNDS** 5
**SAVE** 4+
**BRAVERY** 7

| MELEE WEAPONS | Range | Attacks | To Hit | To Wound | Rend | Damage |
|---|---|---|---|---|---|---|
| Greatsword | 1" | 2 | 3+ | 3+ | -1 | 1 |

## DESCRIPTION

A Loremaster is a single model. He wields a Greatsword.

## ABILITIES

**Deflect Shots:** Such is his skill that a Loremaster can deflect arrows in mid-air. You can re-roll failed save rolls for this model in the shooting phase.

## MAGIC

A Loremaster is a wizard. He can attempt to cast one spell in each of your hero phases, and attempt to unbind one spell in each enemy hero phase. He knows the Arcane Bolt, Mystic Shield and Hand of Glory spells.

## HAND OF GLORY

With a simple sign the Loremaster grants his allies the might of old. Hand of Glory has a casting value of 5. If successfully cast, pick a model within 18". Until your next hero phase you can re-roll all failed hit rolls and wound rolls for that model.

**KEYWORDS** | ORDER, AELF, ELDRITCH COUNCIL, HERO, WIZARD, LOREMASTER

# SWORDMASTERS

| MELEE WEAPONS | Range | Attacks | To Hit | To Wound | Rend | Damage |
|---|---|---|---|---|---|---|
| Greatsword | 1" | 2 | 3+ | 3+ | -1 | 1 |

**MOVE** 6"
**SAVE** 4+
**WOUNDS** 1
**BRAVERY** 7

## DESCRIPTION
A unit of Swordmasters has 5 or more models. They wield mighty Greatswords.

## BLADELORD
The leader of this unit is a Bladelord. A Bladelord makes 3 attacks rather than 2.

## HORNBLOWER
Models in this unit may be Hornblowers. You can re-roll any dice rolls of 1 when determining how far this unit can run or charge if it includes any Hornblowers.

## STANDARD BEARER
Models in this unit may be Standard Bearers. If the unit includes any Standard Bearers, add 1 to the Bravery of its models. Add 2 to their Bravery instead if the unit is within 8" of another **Eldritch Council** unit from your army that includes a Standard Bearer.

## ABILITIES
**A Blur of Blades:** Swordmasters wield and spin their blades so deftly that they can almost always land a fatal blow. You can re-roll hit rolls of 1 when attacking with a Swordmaster.

**Deflect Shots:** Such is their skill that Swordmasters can deflect arrows in mid-air. You can re-roll failed save rolls for this unit in the shooting phase.

**KEYWORDS** | ORDER, AELF, ELDRITCH COUNCIL, SWORDMASTERS

# PHOENIX TEMPLE

**The Phoenix is a potent symbol for the aelves, for it is an enchanted creature that has risen from the ashes to take its revenge. The Phoenix Temple is a warrior conclave dedicated to the great Ur-Phoenix and her children, its soldiers scouring Chaos-corrupted lands with flame and frost.**

To enter the Phoenix Temple an aelf must have walked through the blistering flame and freezing winds of war. Scarred by battle, broken in spirit and mind, they will be borne by their brethren to a shrine to be healed. Deathly silent warriors take the dying aelf and carry them into the shrouded heart of the shrine to the Ur-Phoenix, one of the great godbeasts of the realms. In a ceremony that can last for days, a Flamespyre or Frostheart Phoenix wraps its wings around the aelf. Finally, like the magical creature, they rise again, restored in body, mind and spirit. The price of this restoration is high, and from this day on the aelf must join the ranks of the Phoenix Guard.

When the drums and horns of war sound, the Phoenix Temple is swift to answer the call. The magical creatures and redoubtable warriors of the temple cleanse regions that even the faith of the Devoted or the sorcery of the Eldritch Council cannot reach, for only the enchanted fires of the Phoenixes are strong enough to reduce the deepest corruption of Chaos to nought but ash and frozen shards. In terrifying silence, ranks of Phoenix Guard march forth across befouled lands to cut down their foes with shimmering halberds, while the magic of the Ur-Phoenix protects them from harm. Overhead the skies glimmer with flights of Phoenix riders, blazing orange and brilliant blue, burning and freezing all that fall under their shadows.

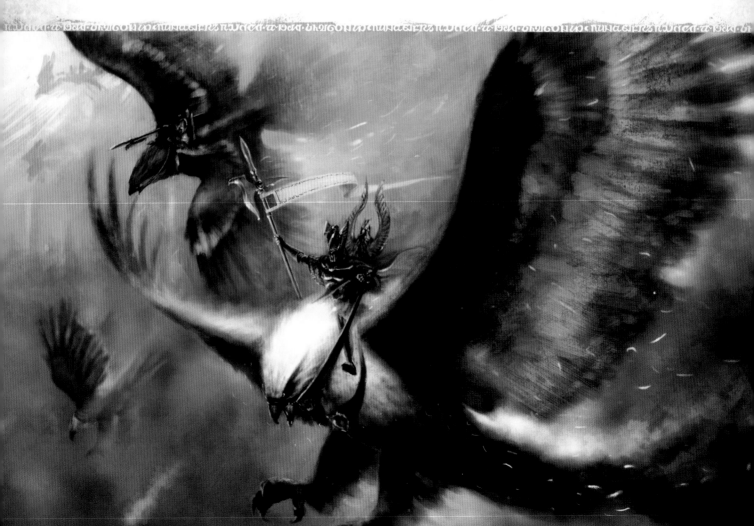

## PHOENIX TEMPLE
# SPYREHEART WARHOST

Wreathed in ice and flame, the warriors of the Spyreheart Warhost emanate the elemental power of their god, which when fanned by the wings of the Phoenix blasts their enemies to ash and ruin.

### ORGANISATION

A Spyreheart Warhost consists of the following units:

- 2-4 units chosen from the following, in any combination:
  - Flamespyre Phoenix
  - Frostheart Phoenix
- 1 Anointed
- 2 units of Phoenix Guard

### ABILITIES

**Elemental Nova:** A flight of Phoenixes can beat their wings in unison to batter the foe with freezing blizzards or searing firestorms. In the hero phase, select one enemy unit and roll a dice for each Flamespyre and/or Frostheart Phoenix from this battalion that is within 9" of it. For each result of 4 or more, that unit suffers D3 mortal wounds.

# FLAMESPYRE PHOENIX

| MELEE WEAPONS | Range | Attacks | To Hit | To Wound | Rend | Damage |
|---|---|---|---|---|---|---|
| Flaming Talons | 2" | ☀ | 4+ | 3+ | -1 | 2 |
| Great Phoenix Halberd | 2" | 4 | 3+ | 3+ | -1 | 1 |

| DAMAGE TABLE | | | |
|---|---|---|---|
| Wounds Suffered | Move | Flaming Talons | Wake of Fire |
| 0-2 | 16" | 6 | D6 mortal wounds |
| 3-4 | 14" | 5 | D3 mortal wounds |
| 5-7 | 12" | 4 | D3 mortal wounds |
| 8-9 | 10" | 3 | 1 mortal wound |
| 10+ | 8" | 2 | 1 mortal wound |

FLAMESPYRE PHOENIX

| KEYWORDS | ORDER, PHOENIX TEMPLE, MONSTER, FLAMESPYRE PHOENIX |
|---|---|

## DESCRIPTION

A Flamespyre Phoenix is a single model. It attacks with its Flaming Talons while enemies burn in its Wake of Fire.

### ANOINTED

Some Flamespyre Phoenixes are ridden by an Anointed. Flamespyre Phoenixes ridden by an Anointed gain the Great Phoenix Halberd, the Witness to Destiny ability and the Captain of the Phoenix Guard command ability.

### FLY

A Flamespyre Phoenix can fly.

## ABILITIES

**Phoenix Reborn:** If this model is slain, roll a dice in your next hero phase. On a result of 4 or more, it is reborn with all its wounds restored! Set up the model anywhere on the battlefield that is more than 9" from the enemy. This counts as the model's move for that turn's movement phase.

**Wake of Fire:** A Flamespyre Phoenix can attack enemies with a Wake of Fire as it flies over them. To do so, pick one enemy unit that the Flamespyre Phoenix flew over in the movement phase. Then, consult the damage table opposite to see how many mortal wounds are inflicted on the unit as they are engulfed in flame.

**Attuned to Magic:** If a model within 12" of this model successfully casts a spell, whether or not the spell is unbound, roll a dice. If the result is 2 or more, you can add 1 to all save rolls for the Flamespyre Phoenix until your next hero phase.

**Witness to Destiny:** Whenever a Flamespyre Phoenix ridden by an Anointed suffers a wound or mortal wound, roll a dice. If the result is 4 or more, the wound or mortal wound is ignored.

## COMMAND ABILITY

**Captain of the Phoenix Guard:** If the Anointed uses this ability, then until your next hero phase you can re-roll failed wound rolls for **PHOENIX TEMPLE** units from your army if they are within 8" of this model when they attack in the combat phase.

## ANOINTED ON FLAMESPYRE PHOENIX

| KEYWORDS | ORDER, AELF, FLAMESPYRE PHOENIX, PHOENIX TEMPLE, HERO, MONSTER, ANOINTED |
|---|---|

# FROSTHEART PHOENIX

| MELEE WEAPONS | Range | Attacks | To Hit | To Wound | Rend | Damage |
|---|---|---|---|---|---|---|
| Ice-hard Talons | 2" | ☀ | 3+ | 3+ | -1 | 2 |
| Great Phoenix Halberd | 2" | 4 | 3+ | 3+ | -1 | 1 |

| DAMAGE TABLE | | | |
|---|---|---|---|
| Wounds Suffered | Move | Ice-cold Talons | Blizzard Aura |
| 0-2 | 16" | 8 | 9" |
| 3-4 | 14" | 6 | 6" |
| 5-7 | 12" | 5 | 3" |
| 8-9 | 10" | 4 | 2" |
| 10+ | 8" | 3 | 1" |

MOVE ☀ · WOUNDS 12 · SAVE 5+ · BRAVERY 9

## FROSTHEART PHOENIX

| KEYWORDS | ORDER, PHOENIX TEMPLE, MONSTER, FROSTHEART PHOENIX |
|---|---|

## DESCRIPTION

A Frostheart Phoenix is a single model. It attacks with its Ice-hard Talons while enemies freeze solid in its Blizzard Aura.

### ANOINTED

Some Frostheart Phoenixes are ridden by an Anointed. Frostheart Phoenixes ridden by an Anointed gain the Great Phoenix Halberd, the Witness to Destiny ability and the Captain of the Phoenix Guard command ability.

### FLY

A Frostheart Phoenix can fly.

## ABILITIES

**Blizzard Aura:** Enemy models are chilled within this model's Blizzard Aura, which extends out from it a number of inches as shown on the damage table opposite. Your opponent must subtract 1 from any wound rolls for models within range of any Blizzard Auras when they attack.

**Attuned to Magic:** If a model within 12" of this model successfully casts a spell, whether or not the spell is unbound, roll a dice. If the result is 2 or more, you can add 1 to all save rolls for the Frostheart Phoenix until your next hero phase.

**Witness to Destiny:** Whenever a Frostheart Phoenix ridden by an Anointed suffers a wound or mortal wound, roll a dice. If the result is 4 or more, the wound or mortal wound is ignored.

## COMMAND ABILITY

**Captain of the Phoenix Guard:** If the Anointed uses this ability, then until your next hero phase you can re-roll failed wound rolls for PHOENIX TEMPLE units from your army if they are within 8" of this model when they attack in the combat phase.

## ANOINTED ON FROSTHEART PHOENIX

| KEYWORDS | ORDER, AELF, FROSTHEART PHOENIX, PHOENIX TEMPLE, HERO, MONSTER, ANOINTED |
|---|---|

# ANOINTED

| | MOVE 6" | | MELEE WEAPONS | Range | Attacks | To Hit | To Wound | Rend | Damage |
|---|---|---|---|---|---|---|---|---|---|
| WOUNDS 5 | | SAVE 4+ | Great Phoenix Halberd | 2" | 4 | 3+ | 3+ | -1 | 1 |
| | BRAVERY 7 | | | | | | | | |

## DESCRIPTION

An Anointed is a single model. He wields an ornate but deadly Great Phoenix Halberd.

## ABILITIES

**Witness to Destiny:** Whenever an Anointed suffers a wound or mortal wound, roll a dice. If the result is 4 or more, the wound or mortal wound is ignored.

**Blessing of the Ur-Phoenix:** An Anointed can attempt to unbind one spell in each enemy hero phase as if he were a wizard.

## COMMAND ABILITY

**Captain of the Phoenix Guard:** If the Anointed uses this ability, then until your next hero phase you can re-roll failed wound rolls for PHOENIX TEMPLE units from your army if they are within 8" of this model when they attack in the combat phase.

| KEYWORDS | ORDER, AELF, PHOENIX TEMPLE, HERO, ANOINTED |
|---|---|

# PHOENIX GUARD

| | MOVE 6" | | |
|---|---|---|---|
| WOUNDS 1 | | SAVE 4+ | |
| | 7 BRAVERY | | |

| MELEE WEAPONS | Range | Attacks | To Hit | To Wound | Rend | Damage |
|---|---|---|---|---|---|---|
| Phoenix Halberd | 2" | 2 | 3+ | 3+ | - | 1 |

## DESCRIPTION
A unit of Phoenix Guard has 5 or more models. They wield finely crafted Phoenix Halberds.

## KEEPER OF THE FLAME
The leader of this unit is a Keeper of the Flame. A Keeper of the Flame makes 3 attacks rather than 2.

## STANDARD BEARER
Models in this unit may be Standard Bearers. If the unit includes any Standard Bearers, add 1 to the Bravery of its models. Add 2 to their Bravery instead if the unit is within 8" of another **PHOENIX TEMPLE** unit from your army that includes a Standard Bearer.

## DRUMMERS
Models in this unit may be Drummers. You can re-roll any dice rolls of 1 when determining how far this unit can run or charge if it includes any Drummers.

## ABILITIES
**Witness to Destiny:** Whenever a Phoenix Guard suffers a wound or mortal wound, roll a dice. If the result is 4 or more, the wound or mortal wound is ignored.

**Aura of Dread:** If an enemy unit within 3" of any Phoenix Guard fails a battleshock test, one extra model will flee.

**Emboldened:** This unit does not need to take battleshock tests whilst it is within 8" of a **PHOENIX TEMPLE HERO** from your army.

| KEYWORDS | ORDER, AELF, PHOENIX TEMPLE, PHOENIX GUARD |
|---|---|

# LION RANGERS

**The monastic order of the Lion Rangers temper their spirits and sharpen their war axes until their minds and blades are both razor-sharp. Clad in the pelts of celestial lions they stride into battle, the precise blows of their masterwork weapons leaving a path of red ruin in their wake.**

The ancient order of the Lion Rangers are a warrior brotherhood that claim that their origins can be traced back to the Age of Myth. Masters of close-quarters battle, the order's aelf warriors carry huge war axes that can slay a foe with a single spine-cleaving blow. In ancient times they dwelt in forbidding monasteries, always built in inaccessible places like the peaks of sky-piercing mountains or islands far out among storm-wracked oceans. In times of war they would come to the aid of other aelves, or provide them shelter in their fortresses.

For all their skill at arms and mighty keeps, however, the order could not resist the minions of the Dark Gods during the first years of the Age of Chaos. Like a grinding tide of blades the servants of the Ruinous Powers swept across their lands, and one monastery after another fell to flame and ruin. It is a testament to how hard and long the Lion Rangers fought that when the Gates of Azyr closed only the barest handful of their warriors made it to the safety of Azyrheim.

These survivors did not dwell upon their defeats, and set about making a new home in the Realm of Heavens. The order quickly departed from Azyrheim, living as wandering warrior-mystics, roaming the surrounding glimmering glades – after the defeats of

the Age of Chaos the order of the Lion Rangers remain deeply distrustful of walls and cities, given that these barriers failed them so utterly in the past.

The Lion Rangers fight alongside the armies of the Free Peoples, aelves and duardin, ranging ahead of the celestial hosts with the other scouting forces. Their wilderness survival skills and warrior patience serve them well in this role. If speed is required they can call upon their chariots, each one drawn by lions tamed and trained for war. When enemies are found, the Lion Rangers do not hesitate to attack, displaying a focussed vengeance tempered over centuries.

Lord Leto – master of the Bullheart Guilds, Prefect of the Hammerweld District and High Magistrate of Outriders – shifted uncomfortably on the floor of the tent. In the gloom, he could see his Freeguild captains likewise fidgeting with their cloaks or beards, each one feeling just as out of place as him. But the needs of war demanded the armies of the Eternal City march out into the realms and for this expedition Leto had left the walls of Azyrheim behind to seek the aid of the legendary Lion Rangers.

The fur-clad aelf stooped as he entered, his silver hair mingling with the pale lion pelt that hung from his shoulder. With a grace Leto and his captains could never match, the newcomer sat down cross-legged opposite the men. In his grip was a huge double-headed axe which rested easily in his hand, its gleaming edge another witness to the proceedings.

'My lord aelf, I bring you greetings from the Eternal City,' Leto began, preparing himself for the lengthy negotiations to follow.

'Your cities weep, human, your foundling kingdoms flounder and the darkness nips at your heels,' the aelf said, his voice barely above a whisper.

'Yes, of course, the new provinces are indeed threatened, my men have–'

'My warriors will quiet the wailing of these tormented lands,' interrupted the aelf. 'And worry not, city dweller – we do not fear what lies beyond the Gates of Azyr…'

# WHITE LIONS

MOVE 6"
WOUNDS 1
SAVE 4+
BRAVERY 7

| MELEE WEAPONS | Range | Attacks | To Hit | To Wound | Rend | Damage |
|---|---|---|---|---|---|---|
| Ranger Great Axe | 1" | 2 | 3+ | 3+ | -1 | 1 |

## DESCRIPTION

A unit of White Lions has 5 or more models. They are armed with hefty Ranger Great Axes and wear enchanted Lion Cloaks to protect them from enemy arrow fire.

## GUARDIAN

The leader of this unit is a Guardian. A Guardian makes 3 attacks rather than 2.

## HORNBLOWER

Models in this unit may be Hornblowers. You can re-roll any dice rolls of 1 when determining how far this unit can run or charge if it includes any Hornblowers.

## STANDARD BEARER

Models in this unit may be Standard Bearers. If the unit includes any Standard Bearers, add 1 to the Bravery of its models. Add 2 to their Bravery instead if the unit is within 8" of another **LION RANGERS** unit from your army that includes a Standard Bearer.

## ABILITIES

**Lion Cloak:** You can re-roll save rolls of 1 for White Lions in the shooting phase.

**Unflinching Courage:** Roll a dice each time a White Lion flees; on a 4 or more that model's courage stirs up within him and he returns to the battle – he does not flee.

| KEYWORDS | ORDER, AELF, LION RANGERS, WHITE LIONS |
|---|---|

# WHITE LION CHARIOTS

| MELEE WEAPONS | Range | Attacks | To Hit | To Wound | Rend | Damage |
|---|---|---|---|---|---|---|
| Ranger Great Axes | 1" | 4 | 3+ | 3+ | -1 | 1 |
| War Lions' Fangs and Claws | 1" | 4 | 4+ | 3+ | - | 1 |

## DESCRIPTION

A unit of White Lion Chariots can have any number of models. Each Chariot is crewed by a pair of White Lions that fight with Ranger Great Axes and wear enchanted Lion Cloaks to protect them from enemy arrow fire. Each chariot is drawn by two ferocious War Lions that savage their hapless victims with their Fangs and Claws.

## ABILITIES

**Lion Cloak:** You can re-roll save rolls of 1 for White Lion Chariots in the shooting phase.

**Unbridled Ferocity:** A White Lion Chariot's War Lions make 8 attacks with their Fangs and Claws instead of 4 if this model charged in the same turn.

| KEYWORDS | ORDER, AELF, LION RANGERS, WHITE LION CHARIOTS |
|---|---|

# ORDER DRACONIS

**The dragons of the Order Draconis descend into battle as vengeful shadows against skies riven by dark energies. Upon the ground their cavalry thunder over scorched plains in a blur of shimmering armour and gleaming lances, counted among the first and last defenders of the realms.**

Few of Azyrheim's shock troops can match the majesty of the Order Draconis. Heroic aelves, they ride to war upon the backs of immortal Dragons and pure-blooded steeds. A wall of glimmering drake-steel plate, lances and blades, they sweep into the midst of their opponents, possessed of a skill and strength unmatched outside the Stormhosts.

Once the aelf dragon orders ruled over kingdoms across the realms. When the Gates of Azyr crashed closed, some of their orders endured behind the walls of Azyrheim, though many other knightly hosts were also left in the Mortal Realms to fend for themselves. Now the descendants of the Azyrite orders are fighting to reunite their lost brethren. Ranging out into the ruined landscapes of the realms is no easy task, and the knights must use not just their blades but also their speed and bravery to stay alive.

In the wild lands still claimed by Chaos, these knights spread the word of Sigmar's return. As the boldest of the soldiers of Azyrheim, the Order Draconis offer to fight alongside Devoted and Dispossessed alike whenever these allies venture forth from their gates. Following the roiling celestial storms sent by Sigmar, they even take to wing and hoof to fight alongside the God-King's Stormhosts.

## ORDER DRACONIS
# DRAGONLORD HOST

A beacon of martial discipline, each Order Draconis Dragonlord is the flame that forges his knights into an unbreakable blade, the shadow of the aelf hero and his steed guiding his brothers to the fray.

## ORGANISATION

A Dragonlord Host consists of the following units:

- 1 Dragonlord
- 2-3 units of Dragon Blades

## ABILITIES

**Martial Pride:** When a Dragonlord Host goes to war the ancient martial discipline and pride of their heritage is roused once again. Once per battle, in any of your hero phases, the Dragonlord Host's Dragonlord, and each other unit from his battalion that is within 8" of him, can make a move as if it were the movement phase (models cannot run as part of this move). If, after a unit moves, there are any enemy units within 12" of it, roll a dice; on a 4 or more that unit can then attempt to charge as if it were the charge phase. On a 4 or more the Dragonlord can instead choose to attack with its Dragonfire as if it were the shooting phase.

# DRAGONLORD

| MISSILE WEAPONS | Range | Attacks | To Hit | To Wound | Rend | Damage |
|---|---|---|---|---|---|---|
| Reaver Bow | 20" | 3 | 3+ | 3+ | - | 1 |
| **MELEE WEAPONS** | **Range** | **Attacks** | **To Hit** | **To Wound** | **Rend** | **Damage** |
| Dragon Lance | 2" | 3 | 3+ | 3+ | -1 | 2 |
| Dragon Blade | 2" | 4 | 3+ | 3+ | -1 | D3 |
| Dragon's Claws | 2" | ✳ | 4+ | 3+ | -1 | 2 |
| Dragon's Fearsome Jaws | 3" | 3 | 4+ | ✳ | -2 | D6 |

| DAMAGE TABLE | | | |
|---|---|---|---|
| **Wounds Suffered** | **Move** | **Claws** | **Fearsome Jaws** |
| 0-3 | 14" | 6 | 2+ |
| 4-6 | 12" | 5 | 3+ |
| 7-9 | 10" | 4 | 3+ |
| 10-12 | 8" | 3 | 4+ |
| 13+ | 6" | 2 | 4+ |

## DESCRIPTION

A Dragonlord is a single model. Many Dragonlords go to war armed with a Dragon Blade and an Enchanted Shield, while others fight with a Dragon Lance and an Enchanted Shield. Some Dragonlords eschew the protection afforded by a shield and wield a Reaver Bow alongside their Dragon Blade or Dragon Lance, so that they might shoot their prey from afar. Some particularly noble Dragonlords carry an Aelven War Horn instead of a shield or bow, to sound the call to arms.

A Dragonlord's mount devours enemies in its Fearsome Jaws and tears them apart with its Claws. The Dragon can also unleash a deadly torrent of Dragonfire to immolate its foes.

## FLY

A Dragonlord can fly.

## ABILITIES

**Dragon Lance:** Add 1 to the wound rolls and Damage of a Dragon Lance if the Dragonlord charged in the same turn.

**Enchanted Shield:** You can re-roll all failed save rolls for a Dragonlord carrying an Enchanted Shield.

**Aelven War Horn:** Once per game, in your hero phase, a Dragonlord with an Aelven War Horn can blow it to sound the attack. When he does so, all models in **ORDER DRACONIS** units from your army within 10" of this model when they attack in your next combat phase make one extra attack with each of their melee weapons.

**Dragonfire:** A Dragon can unleash a blast of Dragonfire in your shooting phase. When it does so, pick a visible unit within 12" and roll a dice; on a 1 or 2 that unit suffers a mortal wound, on a 3 or 4 that unit suffers D3 mortal wounds, and on a 5 or 6 that unit suffers D6 mortal wounds.

## COMMAND ABILITY

**Lord of Dragons:** If a Dragonlord uses this ability, then until your next hero phase you can re-roll failed hit rolls for any **ORDER DRACONIS** unit from your army that is within 10" when it attacks in the combat phase.

| KEYWORDS | ORDER, AELF, DRAGON, ORDER DRACONIS, HERO, MONSTER, DRAGONLORD |
|---|---|

# DRAGON NOBLE

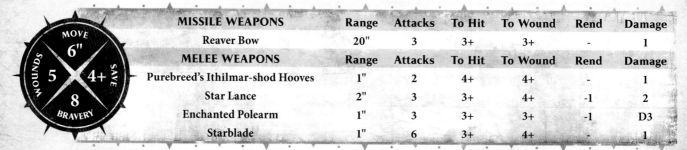

| MISSILE WEAPONS | Range | Attacks | To Hit | To Wound | Rend | Damage |
|---|---|---|---|---|---|---|
| Reaver Bow | 20" | 3 | 3+ | 3+ | - | 1 |
| MELEE WEAPONS | Range | Attacks | To Hit | To Wound | Rend | Damage |
| Purebreed's Ithilmar-shod Hooves | 1" | 2 | 4+ | 4+ | - | 1 |
| Star Lance | 2" | 3 | 3+ | 4+ | -1 | 2 |
| Enchanted Polearm | 1" | 3 | 3+ | 3+ | -1 | D3 |
| Starblade | 1" | 6 | 3+ | 4+ | - | 1 |

**MOVE** 6"
**WOUNDS** 5
**SAVE** 4+
**BRAVERY** 8

## DESCRIPTION
A Dragon Noble is a single model. Some Dragon Nobles are armed with a magical Starblade, while others wield a larger Enchanted Polearm, such as a halberd or a spear. If riding to war, a Dragon Noble may instead slay his foes with a mighty Star Lance. Many Dragon Nobles fight with an Enchanted Shield for protection, while others prefer instead to carry a magical Reaver Bow to shoot their foes from afar. Occasionally, a Dragon Noble will have the honour of carrying a Phoenix Banner.

## AELVEN PUREBRED
Some Dragon Nobles ride to battle on Aelven Purebreeds; these models have Move 12" instead of 6" and gain the steed's Ithilmar-shod Hooves attack.

## ABILITIES
**Phoenix Banner:** A Noble with a Phoenix Banner gains the **Totem** keyword. You can re-roll any dice when determining the charge distance for **Order Draconis** units from your army if they are within 16" of this model when they charge.

**Star Lance:** Add 1 to the wound rolls and Damage of a Star Lance if the Dragon Noble charged in the same turn.

**Enchanted Shield:** You can re-roll all failed save rolls for a Dragon Noble with an Enchanted Shield.

## COMMAND ABILITY
**Might of the Dragon:** If a Noble uses this ability, pick a **Order Draconis** unit within 16". Until your next hero phase you can re-roll all failed hit rolls for that unit.

**KEYWORDS** ORDER, AELF, ORDER DRACONIS, HERO, DRAGON NOBLE

# DRAGON BLADES

| MELEE WEAPONS | Range | Attacks | To Hit | To Wound | Rend | Damage |
|---|---|---|---|---|---|---|
| Drake Lance and Sword | 1" | 2 | 3+ | 4+ | - | 1 |
| Purebreed's Ithilmar-shod Hooves | 1" | 2 | 4+ | 4+ | - | 1 |

**MOVE** 12" — **WOUNDS** 2 — **SAVE** 4+ — **BRAVERY** 7

## DESCRIPTION
A unit of Dragon Blades has 5 or more models. They wield Drake Lances and Swords and carry Drake Shields. Their steeds are graceful Aelven Purebreeds that pummel the enemy with their Ithilmar-shod Hooves.

## DRAKEMASTER
The leader of this unit is a Drakemaster. A Drakemaster makes 3 attacks rather than 2 with his Drake Lance and Sword.

## STANDARD BEARER
Models in this unit may be Standard Bearers. If the unit includes any Standard Bearers, add 1 to the Bravery of its models. Add 2 to their Bravery instead if the unit is within 8" of another **ORDER DRACONIS** unit from your army that includes a Standard Bearer.

## HORNBLOWER
Models in this unit may be Hornblowers. You can re-roll any dice rolls of 1 when determining how far this unit can run or charge if it includes any Hornblowers.

## ABILITIES
**Lance Charge:** Add 1 to the wound rolls and Damage of this unit's Drake Lances and Swords if it charged in the same turn.

**Drake Shield:** You can re-roll save rolls of 1 for a unit with Drake Shields. You can instead re-roll failed save rolls of 1 or 2 for this unit in the shooting phase.

**Ancient Dignity:** This unit does not need to take a battleshock test if it is within 16" of any friendly **ORDER DRACONIS HERO**.

**KEYWORDS** | ORDER, AELF, ORDER DRACONIS, DRAGON BLADES

# SWIFTHAWK AGENTS

**Nimble celestial messengers and scouts, the Swifthawk Agents connect the armies of Azyrheim. In battle they sweep out on the flanks of the city's armies, harrying enemy scouts from above and below, then streaking away before their victims can strike with blade or arrow.**

The aelves have always prized speed in battle, teaching that they who strike first oft strike last. The Swifthawk Agents epitomise this maxim, tearing across the ground on sleek chariots or cutting through the sky aboard airborne war machines. It is said that in the Age of Myth they were the messengers of the aelf empires, travelling between the realms to bring word of wars and strife, but also to deliver missives of hope and coming aid. It was not long before the sight of the Swifthawk Agents became one that stirred the hearts of aelf armies and brought despair to their enemies.

Now they have become an even greater symbol, not just of hope but of defiance. In the wars to reclaim the Mortal Realms the Swifthawk Agents are both messengers and outriders of Azyr. Like an invisible blade cutting the strands of a spider's web they attack their enemies' lines of communication. Outriders are picked off, beacons of damnation brought down and sorcerers put to the sword. The Agents themselves are drawn from many aelf kindreds, and each brings their own skills and tactics to bear in the war for the realms. In the air the sea aelf Skycutters display unrivalled speed, able to outpace even the swiftest beasts of Chaos. Great hawks effortlessly draw these enchanted chariots across the sky, their crews raining arrows into the foe.

The realms are winding and twisting places, filled with mystical kingdoms and tormented lands, but no path is beyond the ability of the Swifthawk Agents to traverse. As Skycutters race across the heavens, elegant chariots and grim Shadow Warriors work their way through subterranean plains and across continents savaged by living tornados. Whether gathered in a host or alone, the Agents' mission remains the same – deliver the missives of Order's armies, and attack the messengers of Chaos wherever they are found.

Long ago, the Swifthawk Agents built waytowers across the Mortal Realms, and many of these alabaster eyries still stand. These were fortresses on the peaks of mountains, hanging from the undersides of floating continents or standing on islands in roiling spirit seas – each one almost impossible to attack from the ground, with cunningly hidden entrances for Shadow Warriors and Agents riding chariots. Here the aelves could rest and sharpen their blades. These bastions now serve to keep the Swifthawk Agents independent as they cross the realms, and they are building a new reputation as havens of Order in a sea of Chaos. Places such as the Weaveweld Spire, which stands over the Dreaming Vales of Hysh, or the Islands of Morn, hidden in the stormwracked skies above the Ashlands, all bear the icons of the Swifthawk Agents. It is these fortresses that are restoring the web that once connected the cities of the Mortal Realms. From their spires the aelves embark on missions both vital and perilous, that will take them far from the light of Azyr.

**'By the light of dying lands, in skies aflame with the tears of stars, through maelstroms of keening souls the Swifthawk Agents fly, ride and run. We are the messengers of heaven, and as the light of Azyr reaches all realms, so too do our warriors roam in every land.'**

*- Engraving upon the Eyrie of the Starhawk in Azyrheim*

# SKYWARDEN

| MOVE 16" | WOUNDS 8 | SAVE 5+ | BRAVERY 7 |
| --- | --- | --- | --- |

| MELEE WEAPONS | Range | Attacks | To Hit | To Wound | Rend | Damage |
| --- | --- | --- | --- | --- | --- | --- |
| Zephyr Trident | 2" | 2 | 4+ | 3+ | - | 2 |
| Skywarden's Ithilmar Blade | 1" | 3 | 4+ | 4+ | - | 1 |
| Agent's Blade | 1" | 1 | 4+ | 4+ | - | 1 |
| Swiftfeather Hawk's Raking Talons | 3" | 3 | 3+ | 4+ | -1 | 1 |

## DESCRIPTION

A Skywarden is a single model. The Skywarden rides a Skycutter, and is armed with an Ithilmar Blade and an Enchanted Shield. Some Skywardens also wield a Zephyr Trident, while others carry a Swifthawk Pennant. The Skycutter is also crewed by an Agent – who carries a Blade – and drawn by a Swiftfeather Hawk with Raking Talons that gouge at the foe.

## FLY

A Skywarden can fly.

## ABILITIES

**Enchanted Shield:** You can re-roll all failed save rolls for this model.

**Swifthawk Pennant:** A Skywarden with a Swifthawk Pennant gains the **TOTEM** keyword. You can add 1 to all wound rolls for all **SWIFTHAWK AGENTS** from your army if they are within 16" of this model when they attack.

**Windrider:** A Skywarden has a Save of 4+ instead of 5+ in the shooting phase.

**Fleet of Wing:** If this model runs, roll two dice instead of one and use the total when determining how much extra it can move.

## COMMAND ABILITY

**Swoop and Attack!:** If a Skywarden uses this ability, **SWIFTHAWK AGENTS** in your army that can fly can charge in your next charge phase even if they ran this turn.

| KEYWORDS | ORDER, AELF, SWIFTHAWK AGENTS, HERO, SKYWARDEN |
| --- | --- |

# SKYCUTTERS

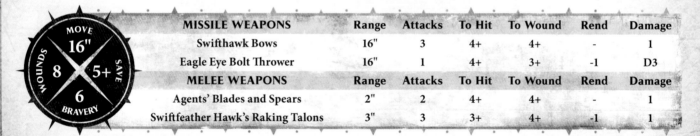

| MISSILE WEAPONS | Range | Attacks | To Hit | To Wound | Rend | Damage |
|---|---|---|---|---|---|---|
| Swifthawk Bows | 16" | 3 | 4+ | 4+ | - | 1 |
| Eagle Eye Bolt Thrower | 16" | 1 | 4+ | 3+ | -1 | D3 |
| MELEE WEAPONS | Range | Attacks | To Hit | To Wound | Rend | Damage |
| Agents' Blades and Spears | 2" | 2 | 4+ | 4+ | - | 1 |
| Swiftfeather Hawk's Raking Talons | 3" | 3 | 3+ | 4+ | -1 | 1 |

**MOVE** 16"
**WOUNDS** 8
**SAVE** 5+
**BRAVERY** 6

## DESCRIPTION

A unit of Skycutters can have any number of models. Each is drawn by a Swiftfeather Hawk that swipes the foe with Raking Talons. Some Skycutters are crewed by a trio of Agents that shoot the foe with Swifthawk Bows, while some are instead crewed by a pair of Agents who fire an Eagle Eye Bolt Thrower. The crew are also armed with Blades and Spears, and Aelven Shields.

## FLY

Skycutters can fly.

## ABILITIES

**Aelven Shield:** You can re-roll save rolls of 1 for a unit with Aelven Shields. You can instead re-roll failed save rolls of 1 or 2 for this unit in the shooting phase.

**Agents' Blades and Spears:** If a Skycutter is crewed by a trio of Agents, it makes 3 attacks with its Agents' Blades and Spears instead of 2.

**Fleet of Wing:** If this model runs, roll two dice instead of one and use the total when determining how much extra it can move.

**Sky Chariot:** Skycutters can shoot even if they ran in their movement phase.

**Swifthawk Discipline:** If you fail a battleshock test for this unit whilst a SWIFTHAWK AGENTS HERO from your army is within 16", halve the number of models that flee (rounding fractions up).

| KEYWORDS | ORDER, AELF, SWIFTHAWK AGENTS, SKYCUTTERS |
|---|---|

# CHARIOTS

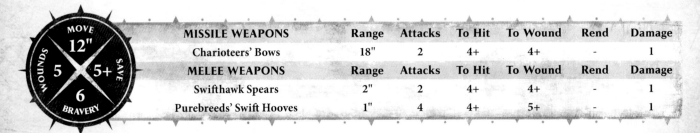

| MISSILE WEAPONS | Range | Attacks | To Hit | To Wound | Rend | Damage |
|---|---|---|---|---|---|---|
| Charioteers' Bows | 18" | 2 | 4+ | 4+ | - | 1 |
| **MELEE WEAPONS** | **Range** | **Attacks** | **To Hit** | **To Wound** | **Rend** | **Damage** |
| Swifthawk Spears | 2" | 2 | 4+ | 4+ | - | 1 |
| Purebreeds' Swift Hooves | 1" | 4 | 4+ | 5+ | - | 1 |

**MOVE** 12"
**WOUNDS** 5
**SAVE** 5+
**BRAVERY** 6

## DESCRIPTION

A unit of Chariots can have any number of models. Each Chariot is crewed by two aelven charioteers who fight with Bows and Swifthawk Spears, and is drawn by a pair of Purebreeds that attack the foe with their Swift Hooves.

## ABILITIES

**Graceful Charge:** You can re-roll all failed wound rolls for a Chariot in the combat phase if it made a charge in the same turn.

**Swift and Deadly:** If a Chariot runs there is no need to roll a dice, it can always move up to an extra 6". In addition, Chariots can pile in up to 6", instead of 3".

**KEYWORDS** | ORDER, AELF, SWIFTHAWK AGENTS, CHARIOTS

# SHADOW WARRIORS

**MOVE** 6"
**SAVE** 5+
**BRAVERY** 6
**WOUNDS** 1

| MISSILE WEAPONS | Range | Attacks | To Hit | To Wound | Rend | Damage |
|---|---|---|---|---|---|---|
| Ranger Bow | 18" | 1 | 3+ | 4+ | - | 1 |
| MELEE WEAPONS | Range | Attacks | To Hit | To Wound | Rend | Damage |
| Shadow Blade | 1" | 2 | 3+ | 4+ | - | 1 |

## DESCRIPTION

A unit of Shadow Warriors has 5 or more models. They wield Ranger Bows and Shadow Blades.

## SHADOW-WALKER

The leader of this unit is a Shadow-walker. A Shadow-walker makes 2 attacks with a Ranger Bow rather than 1.

## ABILITIES

**One With the Shadows:** After set-up is complete, you can move this unit up to 12", as long as no model in the unit moves within 3" of an enemy model.

**Strike Unseen:** If all models from this unit are in cover and are more than 6" from any enemy units, you can re-roll failed hit rolls for their Ranger Bows.

| KEYWORDS | ORDER, AELF, SWIFTHAWK AGENTS, SHADOW WARRIORS |
|---|---|

# SCOURGE PRIVATEERS

**Sailing their vast shadow arks, the Scourge Privateers ply the celestial waters of Azyr. Raiders and pirates, they hunt down misshapen monsters and deadly beasts to slay for rare ingredients or drag back to the Eternal City to sell to its wizards and warlords.**

The Scourge Privateers are master mariners and beast hunters. For generations their aelf crews have travelled the waterways of the realms, wrangling monsters for the armies of Azyr and its most powerful personages. Wrapped in scaled cloaks, corsairs pile forth from their ships, armed with blade and bow. Under the ruthless command of their captains, they run fantastical creatures to ground. Some of these proud creatures, those not twisted by Chaos, are hauled back to Azyrheim where they might be trained to serve, sold off to the Orders Draconis or Serpentis or the armies of the Free Peoples. Others are dissected for their organs, for which the Eldritch Council and Collegiate Arcane will pay well.

Aboard their huge Black Arks they raid the lands held by the forces of Chaos. To aid them in this task the Privateers enslave lumbering sea-borne war-beasts like the Kharibdyss. Able to emit a spine-chilling howl, the aquatic horror drives warriors into the waiting weapons of the Privateers. Against swift-moving foes the Privateers also employ Scourgerunner Chariots. Quick and deadly, these war machines streak ahead of the hunting parties. From the mobile fighting platforms, keen-eyed aelves snare beasts by launching wickedly sharp harpoons. Once a target is so speared, the crew use the speed of their war engine to run the creature to exhaustion, until it collapses and the Privateer crew can cage or kill it.

## SCOURGE PRIVATEERS
# REALM REAVERS

The Scourge Privateers range out into the realms under the harsh leadership of their Fleetmaster, attacking remote settlements and capturing mighty monsters for the beast markets of Azyrheim.

### ORGANISATION

A Realm Reavers battalion consists of the following units:

- 1 Black Ark Fleetmaster
- 2 units of Black Ark Corsairs
- 1 unit of Scourgerunner Chariots
- 1 Kharibdyss

### ABILITIES

**Feared Taskmaster:** The warriors of a Realm Reavers force fear the wrath of their Fleetmaster more than any enemy, and they obey without hesitation whenever he looms nearby barking orders. In your hero phase, this battalion's Black Ark Fleetmaster can bark orders to another unit from this battalion that is within 8". When he does so, the unit can immediately do one of the following things; move as if it were the movement phase (it cannot run as part of this move), shoot as if it were the shooting phase, charge as if it were the charge phase or, if there are any enemy units within 3", pile in and attack as if it were the combat phase.

**Capture That Beast!:** A Fleetmaster can gain both prestige and riches if his Realm Reavers force can capture a large and impressive beast. You can re-roll wound rolls of 1 whenever a model from a Realm Reavers battalion targets a MONSTER.

# BLACK ARK FLEETMASTER

| MELEE WEAPONS | Range | Attacks | To Hit | To Wound | Rend | Damage |
|---|---|---|---|---|---|---|
| Black Ark Cutlass | 1" | 3 | 3+ | 4+ | - | 1 |
| Murder Hook | 1" | 2 | 4+ | 3+ | -1 | 1 |

## DESCRIPTION
A Black Ark Fleetmaster is a single model. He fights with a Black Ark Cutlass in one hand and a Murder Hook in the other. He also wears a Sea Dragon Cloak, whose thick hide protects him from enemy arrows.

## ABILITIES
**Sea Dragon Cloak:** You can re-roll save rolls of 1 for a Black Ark Fleetmaster in the shooting phase.

**Murderous Swashbuckler:** You can re-roll failed hit rolls for this model's Black Ark Cutlass.

## COMMAND ABILITY
**At Them, You Curs!:** If a Black Ark Fleetmaster uses this ability, pick one Scourge Privateers unit within 14". Until your next hero phase you can re-roll all failed hit rolls for that unit.

**KEYWORDS** | ORDER, AELF, SCOURGE PRIVATEERS, HERO, BLACK ARK FLEETMASTER

# BLACK ARK CORSAIRS

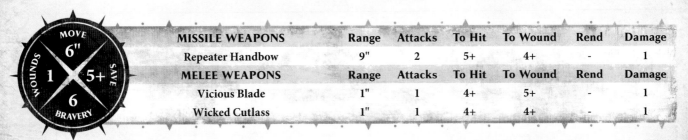

| | MOVE 6" | |
|---|---|---|
| WOUNDS 1 | | SAVE 5+ |
| | 6 | |
| | BRAVERY | |

| MISSILE WEAPONS | Range | Attacks | To Hit | To Wound | Rend | Damage |
|---|---|---|---|---|---|---|
| Repeater Handbow | 9" | 2 | 5+ | 4+ | - | 1 |
| **MELEE WEAPONS** | **Range** | **Attacks** | **To Hit** | **To Wound** | **Rend** | **Damage** |
| Vicious Blade | 1" | 1 | 4+ | 5+ | - | 1 |
| Wicked Cutlass | 1" | 1 | 4+ | 4+ | - | 1 |

## DESCRIPTION

A unit of Black Ark Corsairs has 10 or more models. Some units of Black Ark Corsairs pepper the foe with bolts from their Repeater Handbows before drawing close to attack with their Vicious Blades, while others prefer to attack with a Wicked Cutlass in one hand and a Vicious Blade in the other.

## REAVER

The leader of this unit is a Reaver. You can add 1 to any hit rolls for a Reaver.

## STANDARD BEARER

Models in this unit may be Standard Bearers. If the unit includes any Standard Bearers, add 1 to the Bravery of its models. Add 2 to their Bravery instead if the unit is within 8" of any SCOURGE PRIVATEERS HERO from your army.

## HORNBLOWER

Models in this unit may be Hornblowers. You can re-roll a single dice when determining how far this unit can charge if it includes any Hornblowers.

## ABILITIES

**Sea Dragon Cloaks:** You can re-roll save rolls of 1 for Black Ark Corsairs in the shooting phase.

**Flashing Steel:** You can add 1 to all hit rolls in the combat phase for a Black Ark Corsair if its unit has 20 or more models.

**Notorious Raiders:** Roll a dice each time an enemy model flees within 6" of this unit; on a 6 another model flees from its unit.

| KEYWORDS | ORDER, AELF, SCOURGE PRIVATEERS, BLACK ARK CORSAIRS |
|---|---|

# KHARIBDYSS

| MELEE WEAPONS | Range | Attacks | To Hit | To Wound | Rend | Damage |
|---|---|---|---|---|---|---|
| Fanged Tentacles | 3" | ✹ | 4+ | 3+ | -1 | 2 |
| Clawed Limbs | 1" | 2 | 3+ | 3+ | -1 | 1 |
| Spiked Tail | 2" | D6 | 4+ | ✹ | - | 1 |
| Handlers' Cruel Goads and Whips | 2" | 2 | 4+ | 4+ | - | 1 |

| DAMAGE TABLE | | | |
|---|---|---|---|
| Wounds Suffered | Move | Fanged Tentacles | Spiked Tail |
| 0-1 | 7" | 6 | 2+ |
| 2-3 | 6" | 5 | 3+ |
| 4-5 | 5" | 4 | 4+ |
| 6-7 | 5" | 3 | 5+ |
| 8+ | 4" | 2 | 6+ |

## DESCRIPTION

A Kharibdyss is a single model. Its Fanged Tentacles snatch victims up one after another, while its heavy-set Clawed Limbs stomp and trample. A Kharibdyss can also cut a swathe through its foes with a swipe of its Spiked Tail and unleash an abyssal howl that leaves the foe panicked and terrified. It is goaded into battle by a pair of Beastmaster Handlers whose Cruel Whips crack and snap.

## ABILITIES

**Abyssal Howl:** In your hero phase, a Kharibdyss can unleash an abyssal howl. If it does, pick a unit within 10". That unit must subtract 1 from its Bravery until your next hero phase.

**Feast of Bones:** Roll a dice each time a Kharibdyss slays a model with its Fanged Tentacles; on a 6 it heals a wound.

**Quick With The Lash:** Before a Kharibdyss makes a charge move, its Beastmaster Handlers can apply the lash. If they do so, you can roll three dice and discard the lowest when determining the Kharibdyss' charge distance. However, if you roll a triple then the whips have driven the monster into a wild frenzy – the charge fails and this model suffers a mortal wound as the Beastmasters are savaged by their charge.

**KEYWORDS** ORDER, AELF, SCOURGE PRIVATEERS, MONSTER, KHARIBDYSS

# SCOURGERUNNER CHARIOTS

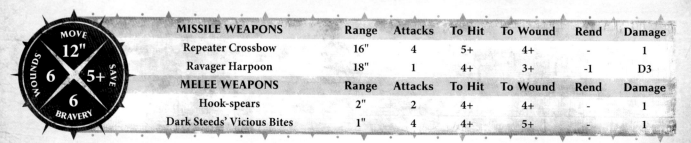

| MISSILE WEAPONS | Range | Attacks | To Hit | To Wound | Rend | Damage |
|---|---|---|---|---|---|---|
| Repeater Crossbow | 16" | 4 | 5+ | 4+ | - | 1 |
| Ravager Harpoon | 18" | 1 | 4+ | 3+ | -1 | D3 |
| MELEE WEAPONS | Range | Attacks | To Hit | To Wound | Rend | Damage |
| Hook-spears | 2" | 2 | 4+ | 4+ | - | 1 |
| Dark Steeds' Vicious Bites | 1" | 4 | 4+ | 5+ | - | 1 |

**MOVE** 12"
**WOUNDS** 6
**SAVE** 5+
**BRAVERY** 6

## DESCRIPTION
A unit of Scourgerunner Chariots can have any number of models. They are crewed by Beastmasters that fight with cruel Hook-spears and a Repeater Crossbow. They can also send barbed Ravager Harpoons whistling towards their prey. Scourgerunner Chariots are drawn by swift Dark Steeds that have an extraordinarily Vicious Bite.

## HIGH BEASTMASTER
The leader of this unit is a High Beastmaster. You can add 1 to hit rolls for a High Beastmaster in the shooting phase.

## ABILITIES
**Lay The Beast Low:** When a Scourgerunner Chariot targets a **MONSTER** with its Ravager Harpoon and the wound roll is 6 or higher, the weapon inflicts D6 Damage rather than D3.

**KEYWORDS** ORDER, AELF, SCOURGE PRIVATEERS, SCOURGERUNNER CHARIOTS

# DAUGHTERS OF KHAINE

**A mysterious exile cult dwells within the Shrouded Districts of Azyrheim. Worshippers of the mythical god Khaine, they crave rapture in battle and seek strength through the taking of life, keeping their deity's memory alive with each swing of their curved blades.**

The Daughters of Khaine are a strange and deadly cult that exists in the shadows of Azyrheim. They worship the god Khaine, an ancient aelf deity of battle and death, a figure whose origins precede even the Age of Myth. Ruled over by warrior queens, they keep their bodies strong and youthful through strange blood rituals. Like pale shadows they dance among their foes, weaving a red path of jetting arteries and opened throats until their flawless skin is drenched in gore. When they gather in great numbers the cult will bring with them huge enchanted cauldrons of blood, believed to be an offering to their god, which impart strength and speed upon their warriors. Alongside these moving altars to Khaine ride darkly cloaked warlocks, the male attendants of the cult, who gallop into battle hurling bolts of shadowy energy. Then there are the Bloodwrack Medusae, sinuous serpentine beasts that are drawn to the immortal magics of the blood queens. A single glance from such a creature causes blood to burst forth from its victim in a shower of gore terrible to behold.

In Azyrheim the Grand Conclave often speak in whispers of the Daughters of Khaine, and of their allegiance with the Darkling Covens. However, not even the lords of the Free Peoples will refuse the cult's aid in battle, such is the fearsome reputation of their warriors.

## DAUGHTERS OF KHAINE
# BLOODWRACK SISTERHOOD

A cold fury burns in the hearts of the Witch Aelves, and as they visit pain and death upon the enemies of Order, they hear the voice of their god cry out for more slaughter.

### ORGANISATION

A Bloodwrack Sisterhood consists of the following units:

- 1 Cauldron of Blood
- 1 unit of Bloodwrack Medusae or 1 Bloodwrack Shrine
- 1 Death Hag
- 3-6 units chosen in any combination from the following list: Witch Aelves, Doomfire Warlocks, Sisters of Slaughter

### ABILITIES

**Delight in Slaughter:** Freshly spilt blood and the prospect of spilling more drives the warriors of a Bloodwrack Sisterhood into a murderous frenzy. In your hero phase, roll a dice for each unit in this battalion that is within 3" of an enemy unit and within 9" of the battalion's Cauldron of Blood; on a 6 it can immediately pile in and attack as if it were the combat phase. This does not stop them from piling in and attacking again later in the turn.

# CAULDRON OF BLOOD

**MOVE** ✷
**WOUNDS** 13
**SAVE** 5+
**BRAVERY** 7

| MELEE WEAPONS | Range | Attacks | To Hit | To Wound | Rend | Damage |
|---|---|---|---|---|---|---|
| Witch Aelves' Sacrificial Knives | 1" | ✷ | 3+ | 4+ | - | 1 |
| Death Hag's Deathsword | 1" | 2 | 3+ | 3+ | -1 | D3 |
| Death Hag's Blade of Khaine | 1" | 4 | 3+ | 4+ | - | 1 |

| DAMAGE TABLE | | | |
|---|---|---|---|
| Wounds Suffered | Move | Sacrificial Knives | Bloodshield |
| 0-2 | 6" | 6 | 9" |
| 3-5 | 5" | 5 | 7" |
| 6-8 | 4" | 4 | 5" |
| 9-10 | 3" | 3 | 3" |
| 11+ | 2" | 2 | 1" |

## DESCRIPTION

A Cauldron of Blood is a single model. It is crewed by two Witch Aelves, who leap from its dais to attack with their Sacrificial Knives, and a Death Hag, who opens the throats of her victims with a Blade of Khaine. Some Death Hags wield Deathswords to shed even more blood, whilst others gift their followers with draughts of Witchbrew from her Chalice.

## ABILITIES

**Bloodshield:** The powerful magic that fuels the Cauldron of Blood grants it and any **Daughters of Khaine** models from your army protection so long as they are within range of the Bloodshield. The range of this ability is shown in the damage table above. If any of these models suffer a wound or a mortal wound, roll a dice. Add 1 to the result if the model is a **Witch Aelf**. If the roll is a 6 or more, that hit has been absorbed by the Bloodshield and the wound or mortal wound is ignored.

**Witchbrew:** Witchbrew drives the imbibers into such an ecstasy of destruction that they will fight on in the face of impossible odds. If the Death Hag has a Witchbrew Chalice, then in your hero phase the Cauldron of Blood's attendants or a unit of Witch Aelves within 3" can drink the Witchbrew. If a unit does so, you can re-roll wound rolls of 1 for the unit and it does not need to take battleshock tests until your next hero phase.

**Pact of Blood:** A Death Hag attending a Cauldron of Blood can attempt to dispel one spell in each enemy hero phase as if she were a wizard.

**Strength of Khaine:** In your hero phase the Cauldron of Blood's Death Hag can pray to Khaine. If she does so, pick a **Daughters of Khaine** unit from your army within 14" and roll a dice; on a 1 the prayer is found unworthy and the Cauldron of Blood suffers a mortal wound. On a roll of 2 or more, the unit you picked is infused with Khaine's strength; until your next hero phase you can add 1 to any wound rolls for that unit in the combat phase.

## COMMAND ABILITY

**Orgy of Slaughter:** If a Death Hag atop a Cauldron of Blood uses this ability, pick a **Daughters of Khaine** unit within 14". That unit is gripped by a bloody frenzy and can be chosen to pile in and attack twice that turn instead of only once.

**KEYWORDS** | ORDER, AELF, DAUGHTERS OF KHAINE, TOTEM, HERO, PRIEST, WITCH AELVES, DEATH HAG, CAULDRON OF BLOOD

# DEATH HAG

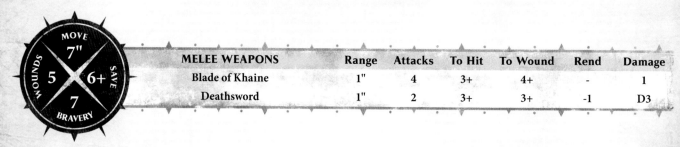

| | MELEE WEAPONS | Range | Attacks | To Hit | To Wound | Rend | Damage |
|---|---|---|---|---|---|---|---|
| | Blade of Khaine | 1" | 4 | 3+ | 4+ | - | 1 |
| | Deathsword | 1" | 2 | 3+ | 3+ | -1 | D3 |

Move 7"
Wounds 5
Save 6+
Bravery 7

## DESCRIPTION

A Death Hag is a single model. She wields a Blade of Khaine in one hand and either a cursed Deathsword or a chalice filled with Witchbrew, in the other.

## ABILITIES

**Priestess of Khaine:** In your hero phase, a Death Hag can pray to Khaine. If she does so, pick a power and roll a dice; on a 1 or a 2 the Death Hag is found unworthy and suffers a mortal wound. On a roll of 3 or more, the power is carried out.

*Rune of Khaine:* The Death Hag's Blade of Khaine inflicts D3 damage instead of 1 until your next hero phase.

*Touch of Death:* Select a unit within 3" and then hide a dice in one of your hands. Ask your opponent to pick a hand; if that hand is holding the dice, the unit you picked suffers D3 mortal wounds.

**Witchbrew:** Distilled from the blood of Hag Queens, Witchbrew drives the imbiber into such an ecstasy of destruction that they will fight on in the face of impossible odds. In your hero phase, either the Death Hag or a unit of Witch Aelves within 3" of her can drink Witchbrew. If a unit does so, you can re-roll wound rolls of 1 for the unit and it does not need to take battleshock tests until your next hero phase.

| KEYWORDS | ORDER, AELF, DAUGHTERS OF KHAINE, HERO, PRIEST, DEATH HAG |
|---|---|

# WITCH AELVES

| MELEE WEAPONS | Range | Attacks | To Hit | To Wound | Rend | Damage |
|---|---|---|---|---|---|---|
| Sacrificial Knives | 1" | 2 | 3+ | 4+ | - | 1 |

**MOVE** 7"
**WOUNDS** 1
**SAVE** -
**BRAVERY** 7

## DESCRIPTION
A unit of Witch Aelves has 5 or more models. They are armed with deadly Sacrificial Knives.

## HAG
The leader of this unit is a Hag. A Hag makes 3 attacks rather than 2.

## STANDARD BEARER
Models in this unit may be Standard Bearers. If the unit includes any Standard Bearers, add 1 to the Bravery of its models. Add 2 to their Bravery instead if the unit is within 8" of any DAUGHTERS OF KHAINE HERO from your army.

## HORNBLOWER
Models in this unit may be Hornblowers. You can re-roll a single dice when determining how far this unit can charge if it includes any Hornblowers.

## ABILITIES
**Frenzied Fervour:** If this unit is within 14" of a DAUGHTERS OF KHAINE HERO from your army when they attack in the combat phase, all of its models make one extra attack with their Sacrificial Knives.

**Sacrificial Knives:** Witch Aelves attack with such a flurry of blows that one is bound to find its mark. You can re-roll hit rolls of 1 for Witch Aelves. You can re-roll all failed hit rolls instead if this unit has 20 or more models.

| KEYWORDS | ORDER, AELF, DAUGHTERS OF KHAINE, WITCH AELVES |
|---|---|

# BLOODWRACK SHRINE

| MOVE | WOUNDS | SAVE | BRAVERY |
|------|--------|------|---------|
| | 13 | 5+ | 7 |

| MISSILE WEAPONS | Range | Attacks | To Hit | To Wound | Rend | Damage |
|-----------------|-------|---------|--------|----------|------|--------|
| Bloodwrack Stare | 10" | | | See below | | |

| MELEE WEAPONS | Range | Attacks | To Hit | To Wound | Rend | Damage |
|---------------|-------|---------|--------|----------|------|--------|
| Whisperclaw | 1" | 4 | 4+ | 3+ | - | 1 |
| Bloodwrack Spear | 2" | 1 | 3+ | 3+ | -1 | D3 |
| Shrinekeepers' Goadstaves | 2" | ✹ | 4+ | 4+ | - | 1 |

| DAMAGE TABLE | | | |
|---|---|---|---|
| Wounds Suffered | Move | Goadstaves | Aura of Agony |
| 0-2 | 6" | 6 | 9" |
| 3-5 | 5" | 5 | 7" |
| 6-8 | 4" | 4 | 5" |
| 9-10 | 3" | 3 | 3" |
| 11+ | 2" | 2 | 1" |

## DESCRIPTION

A Bloodwrack Shrine is a single model. It is crewed by two Shrinekeepers who stab any who approach with their Goadstaves. Atop the Shrine writhes a Bloodwrack Medusa, who slashes at her enemies with her Whisperclaw before impaling them upon a Bloodwrack Spear. Should a victim's eyes lock with hers for even a second its lifeblood violently rebels, flooding from every pore until its body collapses into a pool of gore.

## ABILITIES

**Bloodwrack Stare:** When making a Bloodwrack Stare attack, pick a visible unit within range and roll a dice for each model in that unit; for each roll of 5 or more that unit suffers a mortal wound as they foolishly meet the Medusa's deadly gaze.

**Aura of Agony:** Bloodwrack Shrines emit an aura that wracks enemies with waves of agony. Roll a dice for each enemy unit in range of the Aura of Agony at the start of your hero phase (the range of this ability is shown in the damage table above). On a 6, that unit suffers a mortal wound as pure agony courses through them.

| KEYWORDS | ORDER, AELF, DAUGHTERS OF KHAINE, BLOODWRACK MEDUSA, BLOODWRACK SHRINE |
|----------|------------------------------------------------------------------------|

# BLOODWRACK MEDUSAE

| MISSILE WEAPONS | Range | Attacks | To Hit | To Wound | Rend | Damage |
|---|---|---|---|---|---|---|
| Bloodwrack Stare | 10" | | | See below | | |
| **MELEE WEAPONS** | **Range** | **Attacks** | **To Hit** | **To Wound** | **Rend** | **Damage** |
| Whisperclaw | 1" | 4 | 4+ | 3+ | - | 1 |
| Bloodwrack Spear | 2" | 1 | 3+ | 3+ | -1 | D3 |

MOVE 8"
WOUNDS 5
SAVE 5+
BRAVERY 6

## DESCRIPTION

A unit of Bloodwrack Medusae can have any number of models. Each slashes at her enemies with her Whisperclaw before impaling them upon a wickedly barbed Bloodwrack Spear. However, a Bloodwrack Medusa's stare is perhaps her most deadly weapon; should a victim's eyes lock with hers for even a second its lifeblood violently rebels, flooding from every pore until its body collapses into a pool of gore.

## ABILITIES

**Bloodwrack Stare:** When making a Bloodwrack Stare attack, pick a visible unit within range and roll a dice for each model in that unit; for each roll of 5 or more that unit suffers a mortal wound as they foolishly meet the Medusa's deadly gaze.

| KEYWORDS | ORDER, DAUGHTERS OF KHAINE, BLOODWRACK MEDUSAE |
|---|---|

# SISTERS OF SLAUGHTER

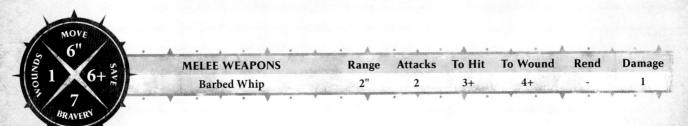

| MELEE WEAPONS | Range | Attacks | To Hit | To Wound | Rend | Damage |
|---|---|---|---|---|---|---|
| Barbed Whip | 2" | 2 | 3+ | 4+ | - | 1 |

**MOVE** 6"
**WOUNDS** 1
**SAVE** 6+
**BRAVERY** 7

## DESCRIPTION
A unit of Sisters of Slaughter has 5 or more models. They are armed with Barbed Whips and carry Bladed Bucklers.

## HANDMAIDEN
The leader of this unit is a Handmaiden. She makes 3 attacks rather than 2.

## STANDARD BEARER
Models in this unit may be Standard Bearers. If the unit includes any Standard Bearers, add 1 to the Bravery of its models. Add 2 to their Bravery instead if the unit is within 8" of any **DAUGHTERS OF KHAINE HERO** from your army.

## HORNBLOWER
Models in this unit may be Hornblowers. You can re-roll a single dice when determining how far this unit can charge if it includes any Hornblowers.

## ABILITIES
**Bladed Buckler:** Roll a dice each time you make a successful save roll of 6 or more for this unit in the combat phase; on a 4 or more a Sister of Slaughter will lash out and slit her assailant's throat with her Bladed Buckler – the attacking model's unit suffers a mortal wound after it has made all of its attacks.

**Dance of Death:** You can add 2 to save rolls for this unit in the combat phase.

| KEYWORDS | ORDER, AELF, DAUGHTERS OF KHAINE, SISTERS OF SLAUGHTER |
|---|---|

# DOOMFIRE WARLOCKS

| MELEE WEAPONS | Range | Attacks | To Hit | To Wound | Rend | Damage |
|---|---|---|---|---|---|---|
| Cursed Scimitar | 1" | 2 | 4+ | 4+ | - | 1 |
| Dark Steed's Vicious Bite | 1" | 2 | 4+ | 5+ | - | 1 |

**MOVE** 14"
**WOUNDS** 2
**SAVE** 5+
**BRAVERY** 6

## DESCRIPTION

A unit of Doomfire Warlocks has 5 or more models. They are armed with Cursed Scimitars and ride Dark Steeds that have a Vicious Bite.

## MASTER OF WARLOCKS

The leader of this unit is a Master of Warlocks. A Master of Warlocks makes 3 attacks with his Cursed Scimitar rather than 2.

## MAGIC

A unit of Doomfire Warlocks can attempt to cast one spell in each of your hero phases, and attempt to unbind one spell in each enemy hero phase. You can add 1 to any casting and unbinding rolls for this unit if it has 10 or more models. Doomfire Warlocks know the Arcane Bolt, Mystic Shield and Doombolt spells.

## DOOMBOLT

The Doomfire Warlocks hurl bolts of blazing black flame at their foes. Doombolt has a casting value of 5. If successfully cast, pick a visible unit within 18". The target unit suffers D3 mortal wounds if the casting unit has less than 5 models, D6 mortal wounds if it has 5 to 9 models, or 6 mortal wounds if it has 10 or more models.

| KEYWORDS | ORDER, AELF, DAUGHTERS OF KHAINE, WIZARD, DOOMFIRE WARLOCKS |
|---|---|

# DARKLING COVENS

**The Darkling Covens are led by aelf spellcasters of prodigious and ancient power. Allied to Azyrheim by proximity rather than design, they continue to practise their dark rites as they dream of reclaiming their shadow empires and stygian keeps.**

When Chaos invaded the Realms of Death and Shadow it drove countless sorceress aelf queens and dark wizards to the safety of Azyrheim. Loath to surrender their armies and knowledge to the Eldritch Council, they formed their own secret cults. Most Darkling Covens centre around a single powerful Sorceress; these despots may have apprentice spellcasters and captains, but their rule is absolute. Such is the supernatural charisma of the mistress of a Darkling Coven that almost anyone might fall under her spell. From free lords to lowly militia soldiers, anyone can be an agent of the coven, and be called upon should the Sorceress need them. For the most part, however, Darkling Sorceresses favour aelves for personal protection, and their standing armies are almost exclusively aelven.

These ensorcelled aelf warriors can range from those completely bewitched by the Sorceress to those that are given a measure of free will, like the famed Black Guard. Utterly loyal, these are the personal protectors of the coven's leader. Many of these Sorceresses are exquisitely paranoid, however, not content to be defended by one military arm alone – their Darkling Covens sometimes number in the thousands. Dreadspears, Bleakswords and Darkshards augment the Sorceress' spells with cold steel on the battlefield.

For reasons that often defy the understanding of the generals of Order, Darkling Covens will appear to aid the armies of Azyrheim. Some cults even have the favour of the Order Serpentis, and it is not unheard of to see an aelf queen swooping into battle astride one of the Order's Black Dragons. Despite these displays of alliance with the Eternal City, though, the covens exist only to further their mistresses' agendas.

## DARKLING COVEN
# THRALL WARHOST

Ensorcelled by the unbreakable will of the Sorceress, the warriors of her warhost hurl themselves into battle, each soldier bound to give their life for their dark and terrible queen if need be.

### ORGANISATION

A Thrall Warhost consists of the following units:

- 1-6 Sorceresses or Sorceresses on Black Dragons
- 1 unit of Black Guard
- 1 unit of Executioners
- 3-6 units chosen in any combination from the following list: Dreadspears, Bleakswords, Darkshards

### ABILITIES

**Kill Them Now!:** The commands of the Sorceress that leads a Thrall Warhost are obeyed instantly. At the beginning of the game, pick one Sorceress in the battalion to be the coven's master. In your hero phase, pick one unit from this battalion that is within 12" of an enemy unit and within 18" of the coven master. The unit you pick can charge as if it were the charge phase, and then pile in and attack as if it were the combat phase. This does not stop them from charging, piling in and attacking again later in the turn.

# SORCERESS ON BLACK DRAGON

**WOUNDS** 14 **SAVE** 5+ **BRAVERY** 7

| MELEE WEAPONS | Range | Attacks | To Hit | To Wound | Rend | Damage |
|---|---|---|---|---|---|---|
| Witch Rod | 1" | 1 | 4+ | 3+ | -1 | D3 |
| Darkling Sword | 1" | 3 | 4+ | 4+ | - | 1 |
| Witch Lash | 2" | 1 | 3+ | 4+ | - | 1 |
| Black Dragon's Claws | 2" | ✷ | 4+ | 3+ | -1 | 2 |
| Black Dragon's Fearsome Jaws | 3" | 3 | 4+ | ✷ | -2 | D6 |

| DAMAGE TABLE | | | |
|---|---|---|---|
| Wounds Suffered | Move | Fearsome Jaws | Claws |
| 0-3 | 14" | 2+ | 6 |
| 4-6 | 12" | 3+ | 5 |
| 7-9 | 10" | 3+ | 4 |
| 10-12 | 8" | 4+ | 3 |
| 13+ | 6" | 4+ | 2 |

## DESCRIPTION

A Sorceress on Black Dragon is a single model. Most Sorceresses wield a Witch Rod – a magical symbol of their office – but more battle-frenzied Sorceresses prefer to wield a Darkling Sword in its place. Some Sorceresses also wield a Witch Lash to inflict even more pain and misery on their foes. All Sorceresses carry a dagger, which they can use to sacrifice their allies and boost their magical powers. The Black Dragon can rend foes apart with its Claws and swallow men whole in its Fearsome Jaws. Black Dragons can also exhale a deadly Noxious Breath to poison and choke their prey.

### FLY

A Sorceress on Black Dragon can fly.

## ABILITIES

**Blood Sacrifice:** In your hero phase, a Sorceress can sacrifice a **DARKLING COVEN** model from your army within 3". If she does, that model is slain, but you can then add 2 to all casting rolls for that Sorceress until the end of the hero phase.

**Noxious Breath:** In your shooting phase, a Black Dragon can breathe a cloud of noxious gas. If it does so, pick a target unit that is visible and roll one dice for each model in that unit that is within 6". For each roll of 6, that unit suffers a mortal wound.

## MAGIC

A Sorceress on Black Dragon is a wizard. She can attempt to cast one spell in each of your own hero phases, and attempt to unbind one spell in each enemy hero phase. She knows the Arcane Bolt, Mystic Shield and Bladewind spells.

### BLADEWIND

The Sorceress summons a cloud of ethereal blades to cut her foes to ribbons. Bladewind has a casting value of 6. If successfully cast, pick a visible enemy unit within 18" and roll 6 dice. Compare these with the unit's best To Hit characteristic of any melee weapon it has; each time you rolled lower than this number the unit fails to parry an ethereal blade and suffers a mortal wound.

**KEYWORDS**  ORDER, AELF, DRAGON, DARKLING COVEN, HERO, WIZARD, MONSTER, SORCERESS

# SORCERESS

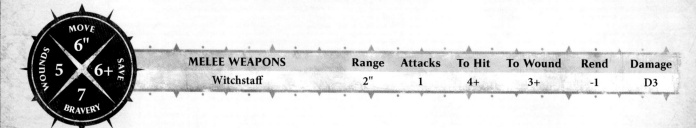

| | MOVE | |
|---|---|---|
| WOUNDS | 6" | SAVE |
| 5 | | 6+ |
| | 7 | |
| | BRAVERY | |

| MELEE WEAPONS | Range | Attacks | To Hit | To Wound | Rend | Damage |
|---|---|---|---|---|---|---|
| Witchstaff | 2" | 1 | 4+ | 3+ | -1 | D3 |

## DESCRIPTION

A Sorceress is a single model. A Sorceress carries a Witchstaff and a dagger, which she can use to sacrifice her allies and boost her magical powers.

## ABILITIES

**Blood Sacrifice:** In your hero phase, the Sorceress can sacrifice a **DARKLING COVEN** model from your army within 3". If she does, that model is slain but you can then add 2 to all casting rolls for that Sorceress until the end of the hero phase.

## MAGIC

A Sorceress is a wizard. She can attempt to cast one spell in each of your own hero phases, and attempt to unbind one spell in each enemy hero phase. She knows the Arcane Bolt, Mystic Shield and Word of Pain spells.

## WORD OF PAIN

As the Sorceress utters a forbidden name, her foes are wracked with agony. Word of Pain has a casting value of 7. If successfully cast, pick a visible unit within 16". That unit suffers a mortal wound. In addition, your opponent must subtract 1 from any hit rolls for that unit until your next hero phase.

| KEYWORDS | ORDER, AELF, DARKLING COVEN, HERO, WIZARD, SORCERESS |
|---|---|

# BLACK GUARD

| | MELEE WEAPONS | Range | Attacks | To Hit | To Wound | Rend | Damage |
|---|---|---|---|---|---|---|---|
| | Ebon Halberd | 2" | 2 | 3+ | 3+ | -1 | 1 |

**MOVE** 6"
**SAVE** 4+
**WOUNDS** 1
**BRAVERY** 8

## DESCRIPTION
A unit of Black Guard has 5 or more models. They fight with Ebon Halberds.

## CAPTAIN
The leader of this unit is a Captain. A Captain makes 3 attacks rather than 2.

## STANDARD BEARER
Models in this unit may be Standard Bearers. If the unit includes any Standard Bearers, add 1 to the Bravery of its models. Add 2 to their Bravery instead if the unit is within 8" of any **DARKLING COVEN HERO** from your army.

## DRUMMERS
Models in this unit may be Drummers. You can re-roll a single dice when determining how far this unit can charge if it includes any Drummers.

## ABILITIES
**Elite Bodyguard:** You can re-roll failed hit rolls of 1 for Black Guard.

**KEYWORDS** | ORDER, AELF, DARKLING COVEN, BLACK GUARD

# EXECUTIONERS

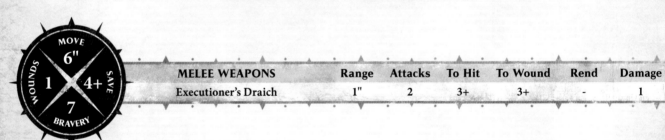

| | MOVE | | | MELEE WEAPONS | Range | Attacks | To Hit | To Wound | Rend | Damage |
|---|---|---|---|---|---|---|---|---|---|---|
| WOUNDS 1 | 6" | SAVE 4+ | | Executioner's Draich | 1" | 2 | 3+ | 3+ | - | 1 |
| | 7 BRAVERY | | | | | | | | | |

## DESCRIPTION
A unit of Executioners has 5 or more models. Each is armed with an Executioner's Draich, a ceremonial weapon of their own forging that can decapitate its victim with one deft blow.

## DRAICH MASTER
The leader of this unit is a Draich Master. A Draich Master makes 3 attacks rather than 2.

## STANDARD BEARER
Models in this unit may be Standard Bearers. If the unit includes any Standard Bearers, add 1 to the Bravery of its models. Add 2 to their Bravery instead if the unit is within 8" of any **Darkling Coven Hero** from your army.

## DRUMMERS
Models in this unit may be Drummers. You can re-roll a single dice when determining how far this unit can charge if it includes any Drummers.

## ABILITIES
**Severing Strike:** If the hit roll for an Executioner is 6 or more, its Executioner's Draich inflicts 2 mortal wounds on the target instead of its normal Damage – no roll to wound is necessary.

| KEYWORDS | ORDER, AELF, DARKLING COVEN, EXECUTIONERS |
|---|---|

# DREADSPEARS

| | MOVE | |
|---|---|---|
| WOUNDS | 6" | SAVE |
| 1 | | 5+ |
| | 6 | |
| | BRAVERY | |

| MELEE WEAPONS | Range | Attacks | To Hit | To Wound | Rend | Damage |
|---|---|---|---|---|---|---|
| Darkling Spear | 2" | 1 | 4+ | 4+ | - | 1 |

## DESCRIPTION
A unit of Dreadspears has 10 or more models. They are armed with Darkling Spears and carry Darkshields.

## LORDLING
The leader of this unit is a Lordling. A Lordling makes 2 attacks instead of 1.

## STANDARD BEARER
Models in this unit may be Standard Bearers. If the unit includes any Standard Bearers, add 1 to the Bravery of its models. Add 2 to their Bravery instead if the unit is within 8" of any **Darkling Coven Hero** from your army.

## HORNBLOWER
Models in this unit may be Hornblowers. You can re-roll a single dice when determining how far this unit can charge if it includes any Hornblowers.

## ABILITIES
**Darkshields:** You can re-roll save rolls of 1 for a unit with Darkshields. You can re-roll failed save rolls of 1 or 2 for this unit in the combat phase instead.

**Coven Guard:** You can add 1 to hit rolls for a Dreadspear if it did not move in its preceding movement phase.

**Formidable Bastion:** You can add 1 to hit rolls for a Dreadspear if its unit has 20 or more models.

| KEYWORDS | ORDER, AELF, DARKLING COVEN, DREADSPEARS |
|---|---|

# BLEAKSWORDS

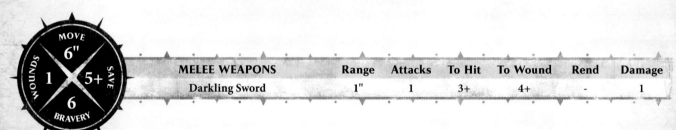

| | MOVE 6" | | MELEE WEAPONS | Range | Attacks | To Hit | To Wound | Rend | Damage |
|---|---|---|---|---|---|---|---|---|---|
| WOUNDS 1 | | SAVE 5+ | Darkling Sword | 1" | 1 | 3+ | 4+ | - | 1 |
| | BRAVERY 6 | | | | | | | | |

## DESCRIPTION
A unit of Bleakswords has 10 or more models. They are armed with Darkling Swords and carry Darkshields.

## LORDLING
The leader of this unit is a Lordling. A Lordling makes 2 attacks rather than 1.

## STANDARD BEARER
Models in this unit may be Standard Bearers. If the unit includes any Standard Bearers, add 1 to the Bravery of its models. Add 2 to their Bravery instead if the unit is within 8" of any **Darkling Coven Hero** from your army.

## HORNBLOWER
Models in this unit may be Hornblowers. You can re-roll a single dice when determining how far this unit can charge if it includes any Hornblowers.

## ABILITIES
**Quicksilver Strike:** Each time you make a hit roll of 6 or more for a Bleaksword, that model can immediately make one extra attack with its Darkling Sword. If its unit has 20 or more models, it can make one extra attack on a hit roll of 5 or more instead.

**Darkshields:** You can re-roll save rolls of 1 for a unit with Darkshields. You can re-roll failed save rolls of 1 or 2 for this unit in the combat phase instead.

| KEYWORDS | ORDER, AELF, DARKLING COVEN, BLEAKSWORDS |
|---|---|

# DARKSHARDS

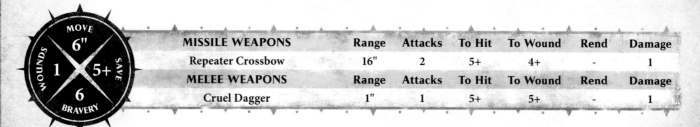

| MOVE 6" | | WOUNDS 1 | SAVE 5+ | BRAVERY 6 |

| MISSILE WEAPONS | Range | Attacks | To Hit | To Wound | Rend | Damage |
|---|---|---|---|---|---|---|
| Repeater Crossbow | 16" | 2 | 5+ | 4+ | - | 1 |
| MELEE WEAPONS | Range | Attacks | To Hit | To Wound | Rend | Damage |
| Cruel Dagger | 1" | 1 | 5+ | 5+ | - | 1 |

## DESCRIPTION
A unit of Darkshards has 10 or more models. Darkshards are armed with fast-firing Repeater Crossbows and Cruel Daggers. Some units of Darkshards also carry Darkshields into battle.

## GUARDMASTER
The leader of this unit is a Guardmaster. You can add 1 to hit rolls for a Guardmaster in the shooting phase.

## STANDARD BEARER
Models in this unit may be Standard Bearers. If the unit includes any Standard Bearers, add 1 to the Bravery of its models. Add 2 to their Bravery instead if the unit is within 8" of any **Darkling Coven Hero** from your army.

## HORNBLOWER
Models in this unit may be Hornblowers. You can re-roll a single dice when determining how far this unit can charge if it includes any Hornblowers.

## ABILITIES
**Storm of Iron-tipped Bolts:** You can add 1 to hit rolls for a Darkshard in the shooting phase if its unit has 20 or more models and there are no enemy models within 3".

**Darkshields:** You can re-roll save rolls of 1 for a unit with Darkshields. You can re-roll failed save rolls of 1 or 2 for this unit in the combat phase instead.

| KEYWORDS | ORDER, AELF, DARKLING COVEN, DARKSHARDS |

# SHADOWBLADES

**Precious little is known about the Shadowblades beyond their hatred of the enemies of Order. Legendary figures born of the shadows, they are expert killers that move through the realms like ghosts, appearing only long enough to despatch their targets before vanishing once more.**

The path of the assassin has a long and proud history among the aelf nations. Though the Free Peoples look down on the profession as the remit of thugs and murderers, the aelves see grace and beauty in the art of taking life swiftly and silently. A skilled aelf assassin is as a thought given form, appearing but for the barest flicker of an eye before receding into darkness leaving their prey lying in a pool of its own blood.

Far beyond even the most skilled human killer, the Shadowblades are true masters of murder. It is said they can change their faces, appearing as any of the myriad mortal races of the realms. Moving through cities while hidden in plain sight, their prey seldom see them coming until it is far too late. Some believe they are immortal soldiers from the Realm of Shadow, servants of some long forgotten god or perhaps the last surviving guardians of a dark and terrible king. Others claim they were warriors bequeathed to Sigmar by one of his godly allies, a relic of the God-King's ancient pantheon. All that is known for sure is that when a sorcerous black mark in the shape of a curved blade appears on a target's flesh, the Shadowblades have singled him or her out for death. Many Chaos Lords have met their end so marked, but so too have traitors and corrupted souls in the Realm of Heavens.

During the years of strife and darkness after the Gates of Azyr closed, it is said that it was the Shadowblades who purged Azyrheim of corruption. Sigmar's noble armies scoured the Realm of Heavens for corrupted beasts and followers of Chaos, but they could not root out every dark soul and traitor that lurked within the Eternal City. This task fell to the aelf assassins. For the better part of a century they did their work. Servants of Chaos both grand and humble

fell to their blades, as did spies hidden among the armies of the Free Peoples and even, it is rumoured, more than one member of the Grand Conclave itself. Of the assassins no sign was ever seen. After a night of blood, dawn would greet a fresh body swinging over one of the grand districts' crossroads, its crimes listed on parchment and hung about its neck. The citizens would look upon such offerings and whisper to each other in horror, though many counted themselves fortunate the shadowy murderers were on their side. To this day, none know for sure how the assassins choose their victims, and all hope only the enemies of Order suffer the Shadowblades' attentions.

Kurgoth slammed a mailed fist down upon the arm of his blood-drenched throne and screamed at his gathered army.

'*Cowards!*' he bellowed.

The legion of hardened Chaos Warriors, each one with an ocean of blood on their calloused hands, flinched back from their raging lord.

'These shadow walkers slit a few throats and you soil yourselves like children. They are just charlatan sorcerers, things of flesh and blood that can be crushed, cut and killed. By the Dark Gods, steel will end their tricks soon enough!'

A gust of frigid air suddenly burst into the ruined throne room. It blew open the massive chamber doors, giving a glimpse of the burning silver city outside and a courtyard littered with gold-armoured corpses. Over the gathered Chaos host it swept, stirring the gore-spattered banners hung on the walls, depicting the long line of kings and queens Kurgoth had violently brought to an end this night. At last it washed over the lord himself, chilling his blood and causing him to raise a hand to shield his eyes. At that moment he caught a glimpse of his flesh, visible between gauntlet and mail. There, as if staring back at him, was a black scythe-like mark. Strange, he had no recollection of it being there before.

'We will crush these assassins just as we–' The rest of Kurgoth's rant was lost in a wash of blood, as a blade like smoke drew across his throat.

# ASSASSIN

| | MOVE 6" |
|---|---|
| WOUNDS 5 | SAVE 5+ |
| | 7 BRAVERY |

| MELEE WEAPONS | Range | Attacks | To Hit | To Wound | Rend | Damage |
|---|---|---|---|---|---|---|
| Poison-coated Blades | 1" | 6 | 3+ | 3+ | - | 1 |

## DESCRIPTION

An Assassin is a single model. He is armed a pair of Poison-coated Blades for slaying his target.

## ABILITIES

**Black Lotus Venom:** Assassins use their deadliest poisons to slay kings and warlords. If the target of an attack made by an Assassin is a **HERO**, its weapons inflict D3 Damage rather than 1.

**Hidden Murderer:** Instead of setting up the Assassin normally, you can place him to one side and say that he is set up in hiding. If you do so, secretly note down one of your units for this Assassin to hide in. At the start of any combat phase you can reveal the Assassin; set him up within 1" of the unit you picked. The Assassin can then pile in and attack, even if it is your opponent's turn to select a unit to attack with. If the unit hiding the Assassin is destroyed before he is revealed, the Assassin is destroyed as well.

| KEYWORDS | ORDER, AELF, SHADOWBLADES, HERO, ASSASSIN |
|---|---|

# DARK RIDERS

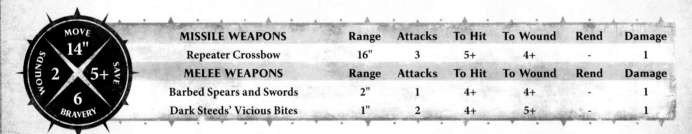

| MOVE 14" | | | | | | | |
| WOUNDS 2 | SAVE 5+ | | | | | | |
| BRAVERY 6 | | | | | | | |

| MISSILE WEAPONS | Range | Attacks | To Hit | To Wound | Rend | Damage |
|---|---|---|---|---|---|---|
| Repeater Crossbow | 16" | 3 | 5+ | 4+ | - | 1 |
| **MELEE WEAPONS** | **Range** | **Attacks** | **To Hit** | **To Wound** | **Rend** | **Damage** |
| Barbed Spears and Swords | 2" | 1 | 4+ | 4+ | - | 1 |
| Dark Steeds' Vicious Bites | 1" | 2 | 4+ | 5+ | - | 1 |

## DESCRIPTION
A unit of Dark Riders has 5 or more models. They are armed with deadly Repeater Crossbows and cruel Barbed Spears and Swords. Dark Riders also carry Darkshields. They ride Dark Steeds that attack with Vicious Bites.

## HERALD
The leader of this unit is a Herald. You can add 1 to any hit rolls for a Herald.

## STANDARD BEARER
Models in this unit may be Standard Bearers. If the unit includes any Standard Bearers, add 1 to the Bravery of its models.

## HORNBLOWER
Models in this unit may be Hornblowers. You can re-roll a single dice when determining how far this unit can charge if it includes any Hornblowers.

## ABILITIES
**Sow Terror and Confusion:** Enemy units within 14" of Dark Riders are terror-struck; if any of these units take a battleshock test and the roll for that test is a 1, you can roll a dice and add its score to the unit's battleshock test result.

**Darkshields:** You can re-roll save rolls of 1 for a unit with Darkshields. You can re-roll failed save rolls of 1 or 2 for this unit in the combat phase instead.

| KEYWORDS | ORDER, AELF, SHADOWBLADES, DARK RIDERS |
|---|---|

# ORDER SERPENTIS

**The Order Serpentis are merciless raiders fighting at the forefront of Azyrheim's armies. Riding terrifying Black Dragons into battle alongside scaled war beasts both great and small, they rip apart their enemies in a storm of razor-sharp fangs, dark steel and wicked lances.**

The Order Serpentis are an ancient organisation. In ages past they were lords of the sky and rode mighty Black Dragons down from the heavens to strike their foes. Now, as the Gates of Azyr open, their armies ride forth, accompanied not just by Dragons, but all manner of scaled mounts, from hissing drakespawn to ferocious War Hydras. Against the vastly more numerous forces of Chaos, the Order Serpentis engage their foes using devastating raids, using the speed of their mounts to stay beyond the reach of the servants of the Dark Gods. Often by the time their enemies react the aelf warriors have retreated into the wilds, leaving only their ravaged kills behind.

The Order Serpentis survived the Age of Chaos because they will do whatever it takes to keep their order alive. As the Black Dragons became scarce, the Order sought new ways to supplement their armies and mount their warriors. The masters of the Order oversaw the creation of many war beasts, using dark sorcery to give draconic offspring new and terrible forms. From these experiments they created the War Hydras, each many-headed beast a horror to behold in battle as they rampage among the enemy ranks. They also gave rise to the ferocious drakespawn, fearsome reptilian steeds that carry knights and draw chariots into combat.

### ORDER SERPENTIS
# EBONDRAKE WARHOST

A scaled shadow upon the land, the Ebondrake Warhost is an army of masterful killers, skilled in the arts of blade and lance, but also driven to war by a fathomless hatred of the enemies of Order.

## ORGANISATION

An Ebondrake Warhost consists of the following units:

- 1 Dreadlord on Black Dragon
- 2-3 units of Drakespawn Knights
- 1-2 units of Drakespawn Chariots
- 1-3 War Hydras

## ABILITIES

**Murderous Prowess:** Ebondrake Warhosts are filled with proficient killers – for these warriors, dealing death is a pleasure and an art as much as it their duty. You can re-roll wound rolls of 1 in the combat phase for models from an Ebondrake Warhost.

**Ancient Hatred:** A pit of hatred lurks in the soul of every knight of the Order Serpentis, and when they march to war this becomes a source of strength that guides them as they give vent to their innermost fury. Once per battle, in any of your hero phases, the warhost's Dreadlord can let loose his hatred in a chilling howl. When he does so, every unit in his warhost that is within 8" of him and within 12" of at least one enemy unit can immediately attempt to charge as if it were the charge phase.

# DREADLORD ON BLACK DRAGON

| MISSILE WEAPONS | Range | Attacks | To Hit | To Wound | Rend | Damage |
|---|---|---|---|---|---|---|
| Repeater Crossbow | 16" | 4 | 4+ | 4+ | - | 1 |
| **MELEE WEAPONS** | **Range** | **Attacks** | **To Hit** | **To Wound** | **Rend** | **Damage** |
| Exile Blade | 1" | 6 | 3+ | 4+ | - | 1 |
| Lance of Spite | 2" | 3 | 3+ | 3+ | -1 | 1 |
| Black Dragon's Claws | 2" | ✹ | 4+ | 3+ | -1 | 2 |
| Black Dragon's Fearsome Jaws | 3" | 3 | 4+ | ✹ | -2 | D6 |

| DAMAGE TABLE | | | |
|---|---|---|---|
| **Wounds Suffered** | **Move** | **Fearsome Jaws** | **Claws** |
| 0-3 | 14" | 2+ | 6 |
| 4-6 | 12" | 3+ | 5 |
| 7-9 | 10" | 3+ | 4 |
| 10-12 | 8" | 4+ | 3 |
| 13+ | 6" | 4+ | 2 |

## DESCRIPTION

A Dreadlord on Black Dragon is a single model. Many Dreadlords go to war armed with an Exile Blade and a Tyrant Shield, while others fight with a Lance of Spite and a Tyrant Shield. Some Dreadlords care not for the protection afforded by a shield and wield a Repeater Crossbow alongside their Exile Blade or Lance of Spite, to shoot their prey from afar. Some particularly bloodthirsty Dreadlords wield an Exile Blade in each hand, the better to shed the blood of their foes.

The Dreadlord's Black Dragon can rend foes apart with its Claws and swallow men whole in its Fearsome Jaws. Black Dragons can also exhale a deadly Noxious Breath to poison and choke their prey.

## FLY

A Dreadlord on Black Dragon can fly.

## ABILITIES

**Noxious Breath:** In your shooting phase, a Black Dragon can belch forth a cloud of noxious gas. If it does so, pick a target unit that is visible and roll one dice for each model in that unit that is within 6". For each roll of 6, that unit suffers a mortal wound.

**The Price of Failure:** If any **ORDER SERPENTIS** models from your army flee whilst within 3" of this Dreadlord, they will be ruthlessly cut apart, flayed or otherwise murdered by him as an example to those who would disappoint him. If this happens, other **ORDER SERPENTIS** units from your army do not need to take battleshock tests in the same phase if they are within 14" of this Dreadlord.

**Tyrant Shield:** You can re-roll failed save rolls for a Dreadlord with a Tyrant Shield.

**Exile Blades:** A Dreadlord can more easily land a killing blow when equipped with two swords. If a Dreadlord has two Exile Blades you can re-roll hit rolls of 1 when he attacks with them.

**Lance of Spite:** A Lance of Spite inflicts 2 Damage instead of 1 if the Dreadlord charged that turn.

## COMMAND ABILITY

**Do Not Disappoint Me:** If a Dreadlord on Black Dragon uses this ability, select an **ORDER SERPENTIS** unit from your army within 14". Until your next hero phase you can re-roll all failed wound rolls for that unit in the combat phase.

| KEYWORDS | ORDER, AELF, DRAGON, ORDER SERPENTIS, HERO, MONSTER, DREADLORD |
|---|---|

# DRAKESPAWN KNIGHTS

MOVE 10"
WOUNDS 2
SAVE 4+
BRAVERY 7

| MELEE WEAPONS | Range | Attacks | To Hit | To Wound | Rend | Damage |
|---|---|---|---|---|---|---|
| Barbed Lance and Blade | 2" | 1 | 3+ | 4+ | - | 1 |
| Drakespawn's Ferocious Jaws | 1" | 2 | 3+ | 4+ | - | 1 |

## DESCRIPTION
A unit of Drakespawn Knights can have 5 or more models. They wield Barbed Lances and Blades and carry Darkshields. They are mounted on foul Drakespawn that tear into the enemy with their Ferocious Jaws.

## DREAD KNIGHT
The leader of this unit is a Dread Knight. A Dread Knight makes 2 attacks rather than 1 with his Barbed Lance and Blade.

## STANDARD BEARER
Models in this unit may be Standard Bearers. If the unit includes any Standard Bearers, add 1 to the Bravery of its models. Add 2 to their Bravery instead if the unit is within 8" of any ORDER SERPENTIS HERO from your army.

## HORNBLOWER
Models in this unit may be Hornblowers. You can re-roll a single dice when determining how far this unit can charge if it includes any Hornblowers.

## ABILITIES
**Lance Charge:** Add 1 to the wound rolls and Damage of a Drakespawn Knight's Barbed Lance and Blade if he charged in the same turn.

**Darkshields:** You can re-roll save rolls of 1 for a unit with Darkshields. You can re-roll failed save rolls of 1 or 2 for this unit in the combat phase instead.

KEYWORDS | ORDER, AELF, ORDER SERPENTIS, DRAKESPAWN KNIGHTS

# DRAKESPAWN CHARIOTS

| MISSILE WEAPONS | Range | Attacks | To Hit | To Wound | Rend | Damage |
|---|---|---|---|---|---|---|
| Repeater Crossbow | 16" | 4 | 5+ | 4+ | - | 1 |
| MELEE WEAPONS | Range | Attacks | To Hit | To Wound | Rend | Damage |
| Charioteers' Barbed Spears and Blades | 2" | 2 | 3+ | 4+ | - | 1 |
| Drakespawn's Ferocious Jaws | 1" | 4 | 3+ | 4+ | - | 1 |

**MOVE** 10"
**WOUNDS** 6
**SAVE** 4+
**BRAVERY** 7

## DESCRIPTION

A unit of Drakespawn Chariots can have any number of models. They are crewed by Charioteers that fight with Barbed Spears and Blades. The Charioteers can also shoot their foes from afar with a Repeater Crossbow. Drakespawn Chariots are drawn by reptilian beasts that tear into foes not cut down by the war machine's scythed runners with their Ferocious Jaws.

## ABILITIES

**Scythed Runners:** If a unit of Drakespawn Chariots charges, roll a dice for each enemy model that is within 1" of the unit after it is has completed its charge move; for each roll of a 6 that model's unit suffers a mortal wound.

**KEYWORDS** ORDER, AELF, ORDER SERPENTIS, DRAKESPAWN CHARIOTS

# WAR HYDRA

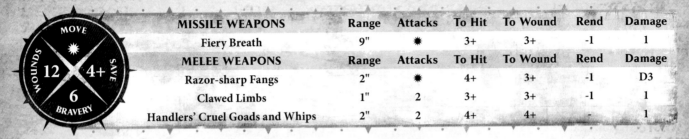

| MISSILE WEAPONS | Range | Attacks | To Hit | To Wound | Rend | Damage |
|---|---|---|---|---|---|---|
| Fiery Breath | 9" | ✴ | 3+ | 3+ | -1 | 1 |
| MELEE WEAPONS | Range | Attacks | To Hit | To Wound | Rend | Damage |
| Razor-sharp Fangs | 2" | ✴ | 4+ | 3+ | -1 | D3 |
| Clawed Limbs | 1" | 2 | 3+ | 3+ | -1 | 1 |
| Handlers' Cruel Goads and Whips | 2" | 2 | 4+ | 4+ | - | 1 |

| DAMAGE TABLE | | | |
|---|---|---|---|
| Wounds Suffered | Move | Fiery Breath | Razor Sharp Fangs |
| 0-2 | 8" | 6 | 6 |
| 3-5 | 7" | 5 | 5 |
| 6-7 | 6" | 4 | 4 |
| 8-9 | 5" | 3 | 3 |
| 10+ | 4" | 2 | 2 |

## DESCRIPTION

A War Hydra is a single model. It tears at the foe with Razor-sharp Fangs, swipes them aside with its massive Clawed Limbs, and incinerates them with its Fiery Breath. The War Hydra is guided by a pair of Beastmaster Handlers whose Cruel Goads and Whips flay flesh from bone.

## ABILITIES

**Sever One Head, Another Takes Its Place:** It is almost impossible to kill a Hydra, for they regenerate wounds and regrow severed heads at an alarming rate. A War Hydra heals 3 wounds in each of your hero phases.

**Quick With The Lash:** Before a War Hydra makes a charge move, its Beastmaster Handlers can apply the lash. If they do so, you can roll three dice and discard the lowest when determining the War Hydra's charge distance. However, if you roll a triple then the whips have driven the monster into a wild frenzy – the charge fails and this model suffers a mortal wound as the Beastmasters are savaged by their charge.

| KEYWORDS | ORDER, AELF, ORDER SERPENTIS, MONSTER, WAR HYDRA |
|---|---|

# WANDERERS

**The Wanderers are warriors of the wilderness who weave spells of bitterthorn and everoak as their lithe soldiers move like shadows among the forest. Attuned to the magic of the Mortal Realms, they strive to connect broken ley lines and return life to the worlds beyond Azyr.**

The Wanderers have ever been servants of Order. Though their lords can be fey and fickle, they despise Chaos in all its forms. When the war horns of Azyrheim sound, the kindreds of the Wanderers gather from the wilderness to aid the Free Peoples and their allies. They dart into battle, peppering their enemies with flights of arrows or calling up the woods to consume them. When their prey is cornered they strike with swift cavalry and lithe soldiers, cutting apart their foes in a graceful and deadly display.

Long ago the Wanderer kings fought for the Realm of Life, and it haunts them still that they were forced to flee and leave Ghyran to its fate. However, it is not this ancient betrayal that feeds the rift between sylvaneth and Wanderers. Alarielle and her children see the Wanderers as divorced from nature – creatures that cannot share the bond of the mythic sylvaneth protectors. Even so, the Wanderer kindreds cherish the magic of life and seek its return to the Mortal Realms. They follow the light of Sigendil as it fragments into hundreds of ley lines. These shimmering cords spill out across the realms, wending their way over continents, mountains and seas. The nomad kindreds trace the paths of this light to hidden lands, laying waystones to amplify and restore its power. Thus do they push back the curse of Chaos upon the realms.

# WANDERERS
# WAYSTONE PATHFINDERS

Moving through the wilds of the realms, the Waystone Pathfinders follow the ley lines, their warriors appearing as if from nowhere to bring down their enemies with swift blades and a hail of arrows.

## ORGANISATION

A Waystone Pathfinders battalion consists of the following units:

- 1 Nomad Prince
- 1 Spellweaver
- Any 3 HEROES from the following list: Wayfinder, Waystrider, Waywatcher.
- Any 4 units from the following list: Eternal Guard, Glade Guard, Wildwood Rangers, Sisters of the Watch.
- Any 2 units from the following list: Wild Riders, Sisters of the Thorn.

## ABILITIES

**Realm Wanderers:** Waystone Pathfinders have travelled the realms for countless years and know many hidden paths. Instead of setting up the units in this battalion on the battlefield, you can place them to one side. In your first movement phase, set up all of these units wholly within 6" of the edges of the battlefield, and more than 9" from any enemy models. This is each unit's move for that movement phase.

**Protective Volley:** Perhaps the greatest weapon of the Waystone Pathfinders lies in their ability to cut down any foes that draw close enough to threaten their leader with devastatingly effective volleys of bow-fire. In your hero phase, pick one enemy unit within 12" of the battalion's Nomad Prince. All other Waystone Pathfinder units can immediately make a shooting attack against that unit as if it were the shooting phase.

# NOMAD PRINCE

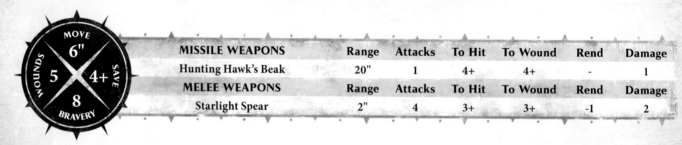

| MOVE 6" | WOUNDS 5 | SAVE 4+ | BRAVERY 8 |
| --- | --- | --- | --- |

| MISSILE WEAPONS | Range | Attacks | To Hit | To Wound | Rend | Damage |
| --- | --- | --- | --- | --- | --- | --- |
| Hunting Hawk's Beak | 20" | 1 | 4+ | 4+ | - | 1 |
| MELEE WEAPONS | Range | Attacks | To Hit | To Wound | Rend | Damage |
| Starlight Spear | 2" | 4 | 3+ | 3+ | -1 | 2 |

## DESCRIPTION

A Nomad Prince is a single model. He is armed with a Starlight Spear and a Deepwood Shield. Each is accompanied by a trusted hawk who can peck out the eyes of his foes with its Beak.

## ABILITIES

**Eye Thief:** If an enemy model suffers any wounds from a Hunting Hawk's Beak and is not slain, the hawk has pecked out one of its eyes. For the rest of the battle, your opponent must subtract 1 from any hit roll made for the affected model.

**Deepwood Shield:** You can re-roll any failed save rolls for a Nomad Prince.

## COMMAND ABILITY

**Lord of the Deepwood Host:** If a Nomad Prince uses this ability, then until your next hero phase you can re-roll all hit rolls of 1 for **WANDERER** units from your army that are within 8" of him when they attack.

| KEYWORDS | ORDER, AELF, WANDERER, HERO, NOMAD PRINCE |
| --- | --- |

# SPELLWEAVER

| | MOVE |
|---|---|
| WOUNDS | 6" |
| 5 | SAVE 6+ |
| | BRAVERY 7 |

| MELEE WEAPONS | Range | Attacks | To Hit | To Wound | Rend | Damage |
|---|---|---|---|---|---|---|
| Blows of Mystic Power | 1" | 3 | 4+ | 3+ | - | 1 |
| Heartwood Staff | 2" | 1 | 4+ | 3+ | -1 | D3 |

## DESCRIPTION

A Spellweaver is a single model. Some Spellweavers carry a Heartwood Staff, while others strike with Blows of Mystic Power.

## ABILITIES

**Ancient Blessings:** Once per game, this model can call upon these blessings when attempting to unbind a spell. When it does so, that attempt is automatically successful.

## MAGIC

A Spellweaver is a wizard. A Spellweaver can attempt to cast one spell in each of your own hero phases, and attempt to unbind one spell in each enemy hero phase. A Spellweaver knows the Arcane Bolt, Mystic Shield and Blessing of Life spells.

## BLESSING OF LIFE

The Spellweaver speaks in the tongue of ancient days, restoring life to the fallen. Blessing of Life has a casting value of 5. If successfully cast, select a **WANDERERS** unit within 16". You can return D3 slain models to that unit.

| KEYWORDS | ORDER, AELF, WANDERER, HERO, WIZARD, SPELLWEAVER |
|---|---|

# WAYSTRIDER

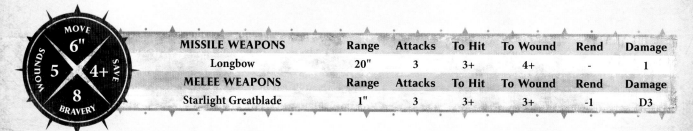

| | MOVE | | |
|---|---|---|---|
| WOUNDS 5 | 6" | 4+ | SAVE |
| | 8 | | |
| | BRAVERY | | |

| MISSILE WEAPONS | Range | Attacks | To Hit | To Wound | Rend | Damage |
|---|---|---|---|---|---|---|
| Longbow | 20" | 3 | 3+ | 4+ | - | 1 |
| **MELEE WEAPONS** | **Range** | **Attacks** | **To Hit** | **To Wound** | **Rend** | **Damage** |
| Starlight Greatblade | 1" | 3 | 3+ | 3+ | -1 | D3 |

## DESCRIPTION

A Waystrider is a single model armed with a double-handed Starlight Greatblade that can bisect a warrior with a single swing. Waystriders also go to war with a magical Longbow to shoot down any who try to escape.

## ABILITIES

**Heartseeker Arrow:** After set-up is complete, roll a dice if the enemy general is visible to at least one Waystrider from your army; on a 5 or more that general suffers a mortal wound.

## COMMAND ABILITY

**Boldest of the Bold:** If a Waystrider uses this ability, then until your next hero phase, WANDERERS from your army that are within 18" of him in the battleshock phase may use his Bravery instead of their own. In addition, if you roll a 1 for any of these units' battleshock tests, that unit can immediately pile in and attack as if it were the combat phase.

| KEYWORDS | ORDER, AELF, WANDERER, HERO, WAYSTRIDER |
|---|---|

# WAYWATCHER

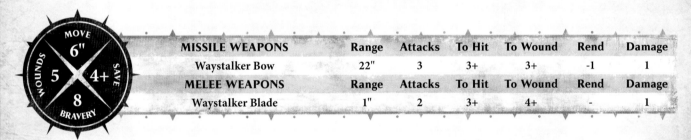

| | MOVE | |
|---|---|---|
| WOUNDS 5 | 6" | SAVE 4+ |
| | 8 | |
| | BRAVERY | |

| MISSILE WEAPONS | Range | Attacks | To Hit | To Wound | Rend | Damage |
|---|---|---|---|---|---|---|
| Waystalker Bow | 22" | 3 | 3+ | 3+ | -1 | 1 |
| **MELEE WEAPONS** | **Range** | **Attacks** | **To Hit** | **To Wound** | **Rend** | **Damage** |
| Waystalker Blade | 1" | 2 | 3+ | 4+ | - | 1 |

## DESCRIPTION
A Waywatcher is a single model. Such is his skill with his Waystalker Bow that he can fire either Fast Shots or Precise Shots to deadly effect. He also carries a Waystalker Blade with which to finish off his prey.

## ABILITIES
**Invisible Hunter:** Your opponent subtracts 1 from any hit rolls that target a model with this ability in the shooting phase.

**Hawk-eyed Archer:** When a Waywatcher shoots his Waystalker Bow, he can choose to make either Fast Shots or Precise Shots (he cannot make Fast and Precise Shots in the same shooting phase):

*Fast Shots:* A Waywatcher firing Fast Shots makes three extra attacks with his Waystalker Bow. In addition, each time you roll a hit roll of 6 or more for this model when making a Fast Shot, it can make one additional attack with its bow.

*Precise Shots:* A Waywatcher firing Precise Shots inflicts double damage with its Waystalker Bow. In addition, each time you roll a wound roll of 6 or more for this model when making Precise Shots, that shot is resolved with a Rend of -2 instead of -1.

**Solitary Marksman:** Add 1 to hit rolls made for a Waywatcher's shooting attacks if it did not move in its preceding movement phase.

## COMMAND ABILITY
**See, But Do Not Be Seen:** If a Waywatcher uses this ability, then until your next hero phase, **Wanderers** from your army that are within 18" of him gain the Invisible Hunter ability (see left).

| KEYWORDS | ORDER, AELF, WANDERER, HERO, WAYWATCHER |
|---|---|

# WAYFINDER

| MISSILE WEAPONS | Range | Attacks | To Hit | To Wound | Rend | Damage |
|---|---|---|---|---|---|---|
| Hunting Falcon's Beak | 18" | 1 | 4+ | 4+ | - | 1 |
| Greatbow | 20" | 3 | 3+ | 3+ | -1 | 1 |
| MELEE WEAPONS | Range | Attacks | To Hit | To Wound | Rend | Damage |
| Kindred Blade | 1" | 3 | 3+ | 4+ | - | 1 |

**MOVE** 6"
**WOUNDS** 5
**SAVE** 4+
**BRAVERY** 8

## DESCRIPTION

A Wayfinder is a single model. These extraordinary archers each carry a lethal Hail of Doom Arrow, as well as a small Kindred Blade for defence in melee, and they are accompanied by a Hunting Falcon which attacks their enemies with its Beak.

## ABILITIES

**Hail of Doom Arrow:** Once per game, a Wayfinder can fire its Hail of Doom Arrow during your shooting phase. When he does so he makes 3D6 attacks with his Greatbow that phase instead of 3.

## COMMAND ABILITY

**Bravest of the Brave:** If a Wayfinder uses this ability, then until your next hero phase, WANDERERS from your army that are within 18" of him in the battleshock phase may use his Bravery instead of their own. In addition, if you roll a 1 for any of these units' battleshock tests, that unit can immediately shoot as if it were the shooting phase.

**KEYWORDS** | ORDER, AELF, WANDERER, HERO, WAYFINDER

# GLADE GUARD

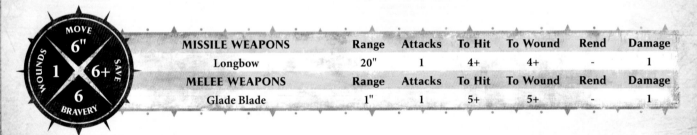

| | MOVE 6" | |
|---|---|---|
| WOUNDS 1 | | SAVE 6+ |
| | BRAVERY 6 | |

| MISSILE WEAPONS | Range | Attacks | To Hit | To Wound | Rend | Damage |
|---|---|---|---|---|---|---|
| Longbow | 20" | 1 | 4+ | 4+ | - | 1 |
| MELEE WEAPONS | Range | Attacks | To Hit | To Wound | Rend | Damage |
| Glade Blade | 1" | 1 | 5+ | 5+ | - | 1 |

## DESCRIPTION
A unit of Glade Guard has 10 or more models. They are armed with Glade Blades and loose deadly volleys of arrows from their Longbows.

## LORD'S BOWMAN
The leader of this unit is the Lord's Bowman. A Lord's Bowman makes 2 attacks rather than 1 with his Longbow.

## PENNANT BEARER
Models in this unit may be Pennant Bearers. If the unit includes any Pennant Bearers, add 1 to the Bravery of its models. Add 2 their Bravery instead if the unit is in cover.

## HORNBLOWER
Models in this unit may be Hornblowers. You can re-roll the dice when determining how far this unit can run if it includes any Hornblowers.

## ABILITIES
**Peerless Archery:** You can add 1 to all hit rolls made for a unit of Glade Guard in the Shooting phase if it has 20 or more models and there are no enemy models within 3".

**Arcane Bodkins:** Once per game, this unit can fire enchanted arrows called arcane bodkins in your shooting phase instead of their normal arrows. If they do, the Rend of their Longbows is -3 until the end of that phase.

| KEYWORDS | ORDER, AELF, WANDERER, GLADE GUARD |
|---|---|

# WILDWOOD RANGERS

**MOVE** 6"
**WOUNDS** 1
**SAVE** 5+
**BRAVERY** 7

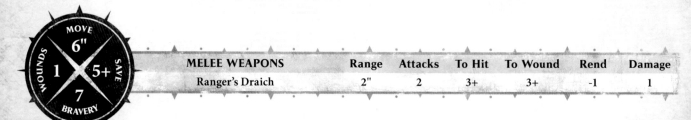

| MELEE WEAPONS | Range | Attacks | To Hit | To Wound | Rend | Damage |
|---|---|---|---|---|---|---|
| Ranger's Draich | 2" | 2 | 3+ | 3+ | -1 | 1 |

## DESCRIPTION
A unit of Wildwood Rangers has 5 or more models. They fight with elegantly crafted Rangers' Draichs.

## WILDWOOD WARDEN
The leader of this unit is a Wildwood Warden. A Wildwood Warden makes 3 attacks rather than 2.

## STANDARD BEARER
Models in this unit may be Standard Bearers. If the unit includes any Standard Bearers, add 1 to the Bravery of its models. Add 2 their Bravery instead if the unit is in cover.

## HORNBLOWER
Models in this unit may be Hornblowers. You can re-roll the dice when determining how far this unit can run if it includes any Hornblowers.

## ABILITIES
**Guardians of the Kindreds:** The Wildwood Rangers have had cause to master the art of hunting monstrous creatures that roam the wildwoods. Rangers' Draichs inflict D3 Damage on **MONSTERS** instead of 1.

**KEYWORDS** | ORDER, AELF, WANDERER, WILDWOOD RANGERS

# ETERNAL GUARD

| MELEE WEAPONS | Range | Attacks | To Hit | To Wound | Rend | Damage |
|---|---|---|---|---|---|---|
| Spear-stave | 2" | 1 | 4+ | 4+ | - | 1 |

## DESCRIPTION
A unit of Eternal Guard has 10 or more models. They fight with long and elegant Spear-staves. Some units of Eternal Guard also carry Glade Shields.

## ETERNAL WARDEN
The leader of this unit is the Eternal Warden. An Eternal Warden makes 2 attacks rather than 1.

## STANDARD BEARER
Models in this unit may be Standard Bearers. If the unit includes any Standard Bearers, add 1 to the Bravery of its models. Add 2 their Bravery instead if the unit is in cover.

## HORNBLOWER
Models in this unit may be Hornblowers. You can re-roll the dice when determining how far this unit can run if it includes any Hornblowers.

## ABILITIES
**Fortress of Boughs:** In your hero phase, this unit can form a fortress of boughs. If it does so, it cannot move until your next hero phase, but until then you can add 1 to all hit rolls, wound rolls and save rolls made for models in this unit.

**Glade Shields:** You can re-roll failed save rolls of 1 for a unit with Glade Shields. You can re-roll failed save rolls of 1 or 2 instead if a unit with Glade Shields is in cover.

| KEYWORDS | ORDER, AELF, WANDERER, ETERNAL GUARD |
|---|---|

# SISTERS OF THE THORN

| MISSILE WEAPONS | Range | Attacks | To Hit | To Wound | Rend | Damage |
|---|---|---|---|---|---|---|
| Blackbriar Javelin | 9" | 2 | 4+ | 4+ | -1 | 1 |
| MELEE WEAPONS | Range | Attacks | To Hit | To Wound | Rend | Damage |
| Deepwood Coven Staff | 2" | 1 | 4+ | 4+ | - | 1 |
| Steeds' Antlers and Thrashing Hooves | 1" | 2 | 4+ | 4+ | - | 1 |

**MOVE** 12"
**WOUNDS** 2
**SAVE** 5+
**BRAVERY** 7

## DESCRIPTION
A unit of Sisters of the Thorn has 5 or more models. They carry Deepwood Coven Staffs and hurl Blackbriar Javelins from the backs of their Fey Steeds. These graceful creatures lash out with their Antlers and Thrashing Hooves.

## HANDMAIDEN OF THE THORN
The leader of this unit is the Handmaiden of the Thorn. A Handmaiden of the Thorn makes 2 attacks with her Deepwood Coven Staff rather than 1.

## HORNBLOWER
Models in this unit may be Hornblowers. You can re-roll the dice when determining how far this unit can run if it includes any Hornblowers.

## STANDARD BEARER
Models in this unit may be Standard Bearers. If the unit includes any Standard Bearers, add 1 to the Bravery of its models. Add 2 their Bravery instead if the unit is in cover.

## MAGIC
A unit of Sisters of the Thorn can attempt to cast one spell in each of your hero phases, and attempt to unbind one spell in each enemy hero phase. You can add 1 to any casting or unbinding rolls made for this unit if it includes 10 or more models. Sisters of the Thorn know the Arcane Bolt, Mystic Shield and Shield of Thorns spells.

## SHIELD OF THORNS
The Sisters cause crawling brambles to burst from the ground and form a living barrier around their allies. Shield of Thorns has a casting value of 6. If successfully cast, pick a unit within 18". You can re-roll failed save rolls for that unit until your next hero phase. In addition, each time you make a successful save roll of a 6 or more for that unit in the combat phase, the attacking unit suffers a mortal wound after all its attacks have been made.

**KEYWORDS** ORDER, AELF, WANDERER, WIZARD, SISTERS OF THE THORN

# SISTERS OF THE WATCH

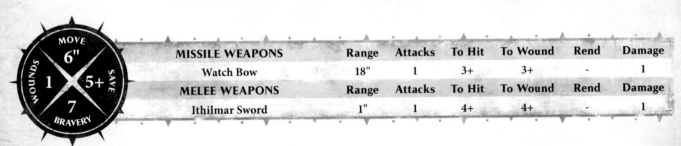

**MOVE** 6"
**WOUNDS** 1
**SAVE** 5+
**BRAVERY** 7

| MISSILE WEAPONS | Range | Attacks | To Hit | To Wound | Rend | Damage |
|---|---|---|---|---|---|---|
| Watch Bow | 18" | 1 | 3+ | 3+ | - | 1 |
| MELEE WEAPONS | Range | Attacks | To Hit | To Wound | Rend | Damage |
| Ithilmar Sword | 1" | 1 | 4+ | 4+ | - | 1 |

## DESCRIPTION

A unit of Sisters of the Watch has 5 or more models. They carry Watch Bows which fire enchanted arrows that burn with a magical flame. Sisters of the Watch also wield Ithilmar Swords.

## HIGH SISTER

The leader of this unit is a High Sister. A High Sister makes 2 attacks rather than 1 with her Watch Bow.

## ABILITIES

**Eldritch Arrows:** Creatures of Chaos cannot abide the magical flames of these enchanted arrows. You can add 1 to any wound roll made when a Sister of the Watch targets a **Chaos** unit with her Watch Bow.

**Quicksilver Shot:** A unit of Sisters of the Watch can attack twice in their shooting phase if they did not move in their movement phase.

**Loose Until the Last:** Once per turn, if an enemy unit ends its charge move within ½" of this unit, the Sisters of the Watch can immediately shoot their Watch Bows against the charging unit.

| KEYWORDS | ORDER, AELF, WANDERER, SISTERS OF THE WATCH |
|---|---|

# WILD RIDERS

MOVE **12"**
WOUNDS **2**
SAVE **5+**
BRAVERY **8**

| MELEE WEAPONS | Range | Attacks | To Hit | To Wound | Rend | Damage |
|---|---|---|---|---|---|---|
| Hunting Spear | 2" | 2 | 3+ | 4+ | - | 1 |
| Steed's Horns and Hooves | 1" | 2 | 4+ | 4+ | - | 1 |

## DESCRIPTION
A unit of Wild Riders has 5 or more models. Wild Riders ride down their foes with Hunting Spears. They ride mystical Steeds that lash out with their Horns and Hooves.

## WILD HUNTER
The leader of this unit is a Wild Hunter. A Wild Hunter makes 3 attacks rather than 2 with his Hunting Spear.

## STANDARD BEARER
Models in this unit may be Standard Bearers. If the unit includes any Standard Bearers, add 1 to the Bravery of its models. Add 2 their Bravery instead if the unit is in cover.

## HORNBLOWER
Models in this unit may be Hornblowers. You can re-roll the dice when determining how far this unit can run if it includes any Hornblowers.

## ABILITIES
**Unbound Fury:** Wild Riders can run and charge in the same turn. You can add 1 to any wound roll made for a Wild Rider's Hunting Spear if it charged during the same turn.

**KEYWORDS** ORDER, AELF, WANDERER, WILD RIDERS

# THE RULES

*Warhammer Age of Sigmar* puts you in command of a force of mighty warriors, monsters and war engines. This rules sheet contains everything you need to know in order to do battle amid strange and sorcerous realms, to unleash powerful magic, darken the skies with arrows, and crush your enemies in bloody combat!

## THE ARMIES
*Before the conflict begins, rival warlords gather their most powerful warriors.*

In order to play, you must first muster your army from the miniatures in your collection. Armies can be as big as you like, and you can use as many models from your collection as you wish. The more units you decide to use, the longer the game will last and the more exciting it will be! Typically, a game with around a hundred miniatures per side will last for about an evening.

## WARSCROLLS & UNITS
All models are described by warscrolls, which provide all of the rules for using them in the game. You will need warscrolls for the models you want to use.

Models fight in units. A unit can have one or more models, but cannot include models that use different warscrolls. A unit must be set up and finish any sort of move as a single group of models, with all models within 1" of at least one other model from their unit. If anything causes a unit to become split up during a battle, it must reform the next time that it moves.

## TOOLS OF WAR
In order to fight a battle you will require a tape measure and some dice.

Distances in *Warhammer Age of Sigmar* are measured in inches ("), between the closest points of the models or units you're measuring to and from. You can measure distances whenever you wish. A model's base isn't considered part of the model – it's just there to help the model stand up – so don't include it when measuring distances.

*Warhammer Age of Sigmar* uses six-sided dice (sometimes abbreviated to D6). If a rule requires you to roll a D3, roll a dice and halve the total, rounding fractions up. Some rules allow you to re-roll a dice roll, which means you get to roll some or all of the dice again. You can never re-roll a dice more than once, and re-rolls happen before modifiers to the roll (if any) are applied.

## THE BATTLEFIELD
*Be they pillars of flame, altars of brass or haunted ruins, the realms are filled with strange sights and deadly obstacles.*

Battles in *Warhammer Age of Sigmar* are fought across an infinite variety of exciting landscapes in the Mortal Realms, from desolate volcanic plains and treacherous sky temples, to lush jungles and cyclopean ruins. The dominion of Chaos is all-pervading, and no land is left untouched by the blight of war. These wildly fantastical landscapes are recreated whenever you play a game of *Warhammer Age of Sigmar*.

The table and scenery you use constitute your battlefield. A battlefield can be any flat surface upon which the models can stand – for example a dining table or the floor – and can be any size or shape provided it's bigger than 3 feet square.

First you should decide in which of the seven Mortal Realms the battle will take place. For example, you might decide that your battle will take place in the Realm of Fire. Sometimes you'll need to know this in order to use certain abilities. If you can't agree on the realm, roll a dice, and whoever rolls highest decides.

The best battles are fought over lavishly designed and constructed landscapes, but whether you have a lot of scenery or only a small number of features doesn't matter! A good guide is at least 1 feature for every 2 foot square, but less is okay and more can make for a really interesting battle.

To help you decide the placement of your scenery, you can choose to roll two dice and add them together for each 2 foot square area of your battlefield and consult the following table:

| Roll | Terrain Features |
|---|---|
| 2-3 | No terrain features. |
| 4-5 | 2 terrain features. |
| 6-8 | 1 terrain feature. |
| 9-10 | 2 terrain features. |
| 11-12 | Choose from 0 to 3 terrain features. |

## MYSTERIOUS LANDSCAPES
The landscapes of the Mortal Realms can both aid and hinder your warriors. Unless stated otherwise, a model can be moved across scenery but not through it (so you can't move through a solid wall, or pass through a tree, but can choose to have a model climb up or over them). In addition, once you have set up all your scenery, either roll a dice on the following table or pick a rule from it for each terrain feature:

### THE SCENERY TABLE
**Roll  Scenery**
1 **Damned:** If any of your units are within 3" of this terrain feature in your hero phase, you can declare that one is making a sacrifice. If you do so, the unit suffers D3 mortal wounds, but you can add 1 to all hit rolls for the unit until your next hero phase.
2 **Arcane:** Add 1 to the result of any casting or unbinding rolls made for a wizard within 3" of this terrain feature.
3 **Inspiring:** Add 1 to the Bravery of all units within 3" of this terrain feature.
4 **Deadly:** Roll a dice for any model that makes a run or charge move across, or finishing on, this terrain feature. On a roll of 1 the model is slain.
5 **Mystical:** Roll a dice in your hero phase for each of your units within 3" of this terrain feature. On a roll of 1 the unit is befuddled and can't be selected to cast spells, move or attack until your next hero phase. On a roll of 2-6 the unit is ensorcelled, and you can re-roll failed wound rolls for the unit until your next hero phase.
6 **Sinister:** Any of your units that are within 3" of this terrain feature in your hero phase cause fear until your next hero phase. Subtract 1 from the Bravery of any enemy units that are within 3" of one or more units that cause fear.

# THE BATTLE BEGINS

*Thunder rumbles high above as the armies take to the battlefield.*

You are now ready for the battle to begin, but before it does you must set up your armies for the coming conflict.

## SET-UP

Before setting up their armies, both players roll a dice, rolling again in the case of a tie. The player that rolls higher must divide the battlefield into two equal-sized halves; their opponent then picks one half to be their territory. Some examples of this are shown below.

*Your Territory*

*Enemy Territory*

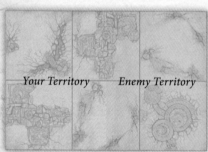

*Your Territory*     *Enemy Territory*

*Your Territory*

*Enemy Territory*

The players then alternate setting up units, one at a time, starting with the player that won the earlier dice roll. Models must be set up in their own territory, more than 12" from enemy territory.

You can continue setting up units until you have set up all the units you want to fight in this battle, or have run out of space. This is your army. Count the number of models in your army – this may come in useful later. Any remaining units are held in reserve, playing no part unless fate lends a hand.

The opposing player can continue to set up units. When they have finished, set-up is complete. The player that finishes setting up first always chooses who takes the first turn in the first battle round.

## THE GENERAL

Once you have finished setting up all of your units, nominate one of the models you set up as your general. Your general has a command ability, as described in the rules for the hero phase on the next page.

## GLORIOUS VICTORY

In the Mortal Realms battles are brutal and uncompromising – they are fought to the bitter end, with one side able to claim victory because it has destroyed its foe or there are no enemy models left on the field of battle. The victor can immediately claim a **major victory** and the honours and triumphs that are due to them, while the defeated must repair to their lair to lick their wounds and bear the shame of failure.

If it has not been possible to fight a battle to its conclusion or the outcome is not obvious, then a result of sorts can be calculated by comparing the number of models removed from play with the number of models originally set up for the battle for each army. Expressing these as percentages provides a simple way to determine the winner. Such a victory can only be claimed as a **minor victory**. For example, if one player lost 75% of their starting models, and the other player lost 50%, then the player that only lost 50% of their models could claim a minor victory.

Models added to your army during the game (for example, through summoning, reinforcements, reincarnation and so on) do not count towards the number of models in the army, but must be counted among the casualties an army suffers.

## SUDDEN DEATH VICTORIES

Sometimes a player may attempt to achieve a sudden death victory. If one army has a third more models than the other, the outnumbered player can choose one objective from the sudden death table after generals are nominated. A **major victory** can be claimed immediately when the objective is achieved by the outnumbered player.

## TRIUMPHS

After any sudden death objectives have been chosen, if your army won a major victory in its previous battle, roll a dice and look up the result on the triumph table to the right.

## THE SUDDEN DEATH TABLE

**Assassinate:** The enemy player picks a unit with the **Hero**, **Wizard**, **Priest** or **Monster** keyword in their army. Slay the unit that they pick.

**Blunt:** The enemy player picks a unit with five or more models in their army. Slay the unit that they pick.

**Endure:** Have at least one model which started the battle on the battlefield still in play at the end of the sixth battle round.

**Seize Ground:** Pick one terrain feature in enemy territory. Have at least one friendly model within 3" of that feature at the end of the fourth battle round.

## THE TRIUMPH TABLE

| Roll | Triumph |
|---|---|
| 1-2 | **Blessed:** You can change the result of a single dice to the result of your choosing once during the battle. |
| 3-4 | **Inspired:** You can re-roll all of the failed hit rolls for one unit in your army in one combat phase. |
| 5-6 | **Empowered:** Add 1 to your general's Wounds characteristic. |

## BATTLE ROUNDS

*Mighty armies crash together amid the spray of blood and the crackle of magic.*

*Warhammer Age of Sigmar* is played in a series of battle rounds, each of which is split into two turns – one for each player. At the start of each battle round, both players roll a dice, rolling again in the case of a tie. The player that rolls highest decides who takes the first turn in that battle round. Each turn consists of the following phases:

1. *Hero Phase*
   *Cast spells and use heroic abilities.*
2. *Movement Phase*
   *Move units across the battlefield.*
3. *Shooting Phase*
   *Attack with missile weapons.*
4. *Charge Phase*
   *Charge units into combat.*
5. *Combat Phase*
   *Pile in and attack with melee weapons.*
6. *Battleshock Phase*
   *Test the bravery of depleted units.*

Once the first player has finished their turn, the second player takes theirs. Once the second player has also finished, the battle round is over and a new one begins.

## PRE-BATTLE ABILITIES

Some warscrolls allow you to use an ability 'after set-up is complete'. These abilities are used before the first battle round. If both armies have abilities like this, both players roll a dice, re-rolling in the case of a tie. The player that rolls highest gets to use their abilities first, followed by their opponent.

## HERO PHASE

*As the armies close in, their leaders use sorcerous abilities, make sacrifices to the gods, or give strident commands.*

In your hero phase you can use the wizards in your army to cast spells (see the rules for wizards on the last page of these rules).

In addition, other units in your army may have abilities on their warscrolls that can be used in the hero phase. Generally, these can only be used in your own hero phase. However, if an ability says it can be used in every hero phase, then it can be used in your opponent's hero phase as well as your own. If both players can use abilities in a hero phase, the player whose turn it is gets to use all of theirs first.

## COMMAND ABILITY

In your hero phase, your general can use one command ability. All generals have the Inspiring Presence command ability, and some may have more on their warscroll.

**Inspiring Presence:** Pick a unit from your army that is within 12" of your general. The unit that you pick does not have to take battleshock tests until your next hero phase.

## MOVEMENT PHASE

*The ground shakes to the tread of marching feet as armies vie for position.*

Start your movement phase by picking one of your units and moving each model in that unit until you've moved all the models you want to. You can then pick another unit to move, until you have moved as many of your units as you wish. No model can be moved more than once in each movement phase.

## MOVING

A model can be moved in any direction, to a distance in inches equal to or less than the Move characteristic on its warscroll. It can be moved vertically in order to climb or cross scenery, but cannot be moved across other models. No part of the model may move further than the model's Move characteristic.

## ENEMY MODELS

When you move a model in the movement phase, you may not move within 3" of any enemy models. Models from your army are friendly models, and models from the opposing army are enemy models.

Units starting the movement phase within 3" of an enemy unit can either remain stationary or retreat. If you choose to retreat, the unit must end its move more than 3" away from all enemy units. If a unit retreats, then it can't shoot or charge later that turn (see below).

## RUNNING

When you pick a unit to move in the movement phase, you can declare that it will run. Roll a dice and add the result to the Move characteristic of all models in the unit for the movement phase. A unit that runs can't shoot or charge later that turn.

## FLYING

If the warscroll for a model says that the model can fly, it can pass across models and scenery as if they were not there. It still may not finish the move within 3" of an enemy in the movement phase, and if it is already within 3" of an enemy it can only retreat or remain stationary.

## SHOOTING PHASE

*A storm of death breaks over the battle as arrows fall like rain and war machines hurl their deadly payloads.*

In your shooting phase you can shoot with models armed with missile weapons.

Pick one of your units. You may not pick a unit that ran or retreated this turn. Each model in the unit attacks with all of the missile weapons it is armed with (see Attacking). After all of the models in the unit have shot, you can choose another unit to shoot with, until all units that can shoot have done so.

## CHARGE PHASE

*Howling bloodcurdling war cries, warriors hurl themselves into battle to slay with blade, hammer and claw.*

Any of your units within 12" of the enemy in your charge phase can make a charge move. Pick an eligible unit and roll two dice. Each model in the unit can move this number in inches. You may not pick a unit that ran or retreated this turn, nor one that is within 3" of the enemy.

The first model you move must finish within ½" of an enemy model. If that's impossible, the charge has failed and no models in the charging unit can move in this phase. Once you've moved all the models in the unit, you can pick another eligible unit to make a charge, until all units that can charge have done so.

## COMBAT PHASE

*Carnage engulfs the battlefield as the warring armies tear each other apart.*

Any unit that has charged or has models within 3" of an enemy unit can attack with its melee weapons in the combat phase.

The player whose turn it is picks a unit to attack with, then the opposing player must attack with a unit, and so on until all eligible units on both sides have attacked once each. If one side completes all its attacks first, then the other side completes all of its remaining attacks, one unit after another. No unit can be selected to attack more than once in each combat phase. An attack is split into two steps: first the unit piles in, and then you make attacks with the models in the unit.

Step 1: When you pile in, you may move each model in the unit up to 3" towards the closest enemy model. This will allow the models in the unit to get closer to the enemy in order to attack them.

Step 2: Each model in the unit attacks with all of the melee weapons it is armed with (see Attacking).

## BATTLESHOCK PHASE

*Even the bravest heart may quail when the horrors of battle take their toll.*

In the battleshock phase, both players must take battleshock tests for units from their army that have had models slain during the turn. The player whose turn it is tests first.

To make a battleshock test, roll a dice and add the number of models from the unit that have been slain this turn. For each point by which the total exceeds the highest Bravery characteristic in the unit, one model in that unit must flee and is removed from play. Add 1 to the Bravery characteristic being used for every 10 models that are in the unit when the test is taken.

You must choose which models flee from the units you command.

## ATTACKING

*Blows hammer down upon the foe, inflicting bloody wounds.*

When a unit attacks, you must first pick the target units for the attacks that the models in the unit will make, then make all of the attacks, and finally inflict any resulting damage on the target units.

The number of attacks a model can make is determined by the weapons that it is armed with. The weapon options a model has are listed in its description on its warscroll. Missile weapons can be used in the shooting phase, and melee weapons can be used in the combat phase. The number of attacks a model can make is equal to the Attacks characteristic for the weapons it can use.

## PICKING TARGETS

First, you must pick the target units for the attacks. In order to attack an enemy unit, an enemy model from that unit must be in range of the attacking weapon (i.e. within the maximum distance, in inches, of the Range listed for the weapon making the attack), and visible to the attacker (if unsure, stoop down and get a look from behind the attacking model to see if the target is visible). For the purposes of determining visibility, an attacking model can see through other models in its unit.

If a model has more than one attack, you can split them between potential target units as you wish. If a model splits its attacks between two or more enemy units, resolve all of the attacks against one unit before moving onto the next one.

## MAKING ATTACKS

Attacks can be made one at a time, or, in some cases, you can roll the dice for attacks together. The following attack sequence is used to make attacks one at a time:

**1. Hit Roll:** Roll a dice. If the roll equals or beats the attacking weapon's To Hit characteristic, then it scores a hit and you must make a wound roll. If not, the attack fails and the attack sequence ends.

**2. Wound Roll:** Roll a dice. If the roll equals or beats the attacking weapon's To Wound characteristic, then it causes damage and the opposing player must make a save roll. If not, the attack fails and the attack sequence ends.

**3. Save Roll:** The opposing player rolls a dice, modifying the roll by the attacking weapon's Rend characteristic. For example,

if a weapon has a -1 Rend characteristic, then 1 is subtracted from the save roll. If the result equals or beats the Save characteristic of the models in the target unit, the wound is saved and the attack sequence ends. If not, the attack is successful, and you must determine damage on the target unit.

**4. Determine Damage:** Once all of the attacks made by a unit have been carried out, each successful attack inflicts a number of wounds equal to the Damage characteristic of the weapon. Most weapons have a Damage characteristic of 1, but some can inflict 2 or more wounds, allowing them to cause grievous injuries to even the mightiest foe, or to cleave through more than one opponent with but a single blow!

In order to make several attacks at once, all of the attacks must have the same To Hit, To Wound, Rend and Damage characteristics, and must be directed at the same enemy unit. If this is the case, make all of the hit rolls at the same time, then all of the wound rolls, and finally all of the save rolls; then add up the total number of wounds caused.

## INFLICTING DAMAGE

After all of the attacks made by a unit have been carried out, the player commanding the target unit allocates any wounds that are inflicted to models from the unit as they see fit (the models do not have to be within range or visible to an attacking unit). When inflicting damage, if you allocate a wound to a model, you must keep on allocating wounds to that model until either it is slain, or no more wounds remain to be allocated.

Once the number of wounds suffered by a model during the battle equals its Wounds characteristic, the model is slain. Place the slain model to one side – it is removed from play. Some warscrolls include abilities that allow wounds to be healed. A healed wound no longer has any effect. You can't heal wounds on a model that has been slain.

## MORTAL WOUNDS

Some attacks inflict mortal wounds. Do not make hit, wound or save rolls for a mortal wound – just allocate the wounds to models from the target unit as described above.

## COVER

If all models in a unit are within or on a terrain feature, you can add 1 to all save rolls for that unit to represent the cover they receive from the terrain. This modifier does not apply in the combat phase if the unit you are making saves for made a charge move in the same turn.

## WIZARDS

*The realms are saturated with magic, a seething source of power for those with the wit to wield it.*

Some models are noted as being a wizard on their warscroll. You can use a wizard to cast spells in your hero phase, and can also use them to unbind spells in your opponent's hero phase. The number of spells a wizard can attempt to cast or unbind each turn is detailed on its warscroll.

## CASTING SPELLS

All wizards can use the spells described below, as well as any spells listed on their warscroll. A wizard can only attempt to cast each spell once per turn.

To cast a spell, roll two dice. If the total is equal to or greater than the casting value of the spell, the spell is successfully cast.

If a spell is cast, the opposing player can choose any one of their wizards that is within 18" of the caster, and that can see them, and attempt to unbind the spell before its effects are applied. To unbind a spell, roll two dice. If the roll beats the roll used to cast the spell, then the spell's effects are negated. Only one attempt can be made to unbind a spell.

## ARCANE BOLT

Arcane Bolt has a casting value of 5. If successfully cast, pick an enemy unit within 18" of the caster and which is visible to them. The unit you pick suffers D3 mortal wounds.

## MYSTIC SHIELD

Mystic Shield has a casting value of 6. If successfully cast, pick the caster, or a friendly unit within 18" of the caster and which is visible to them. You can add 1 to all save rolls for the unit you pick until the start of your next hero phase.

## THE MOST IMPORTANT RULE

In a game as detailed and wide-ranging as *Warhammer Age of Sigmar*, there may be times when you are not sure exactly how to resolve a situation that has come up during play. When this happens, have a quick chat with your opponent, and apply the solution that makes the most sense to you both (or seems the most fun!). If no single solution presents itself, both of you should roll a dice, and whoever rolls higher gets to choose what happens. Then you can get on with the fighting!